The National Idea in Eastern Europe

The Politics of Ethnic and Civic Community

Edited and with an introduction by
Gerasimos Augustinos
University of South Carolina

D. C. HEATH AND COMPANY
Lexington, Massachusetts   Toronto

Address editorial correspondence to:

D. C. Heath and Company
125 Spring Street
Lexington, MA 02173

Acquisitions: James Miller
Development: David Light, Laurie Johnson
Editorial Production: Julie Lane, Rosemary Jaffe
Design: Alwyn Velasquez
Photo Research: Linda Finigan
Production Coordination: Michael O'Dea
Permissions: Margaret Roll

Cover photograph: M. Sutton/FPG International

Published simultaneously in Canada.

Printed in the United States of America.

International Standard Book Number: 0-669-39626-5

Library of Congress Catalog Number: 95-79603

10   9   8   7   6   5   4   3   2   1

Preface

The Problems in European Civilization series encompasses works focusing on critical events in the history of Europe. Each volume brings together selections of representative scholarship from expert commentators and key statements by the makers of history.

The national idea as a problem in European civilization or elsewhere in the world is as significant today as it was at the beginning of the twentieth century, as events in Eastern Europe since 1989 confirm. A historical perspective is particularly appropriate because there is vigorous disagreement over whether the national idea stems from "primordial" forces or is a response to the upheavals of modern society. Those who support the former view often see nationalism as a destructive force emanating from the entropic ethnic identity embedded in a people's culture. Others believe that the national idea is a rather recent manifestation embodying new and revolutionary ways of thinking about political community based on the cultural ties of social community.

This volume looks at the national idea as a fairly recent development that has dramatically affected relations between states and peoples during the last two centuries. It has played out as a dynamic tension between the politics of ethnic and civic community in the demands of intellectuals, social groups, and mass movements that have espoused national causes.

To present the problem in its historical context, I have chosen readings as much as possible from contemporary accounts of the time. Many selections are documents evidencing a specific historical era. In some instances, the readings present a scholarly analysis of some pertinent aspects of the problem.

In choosing the chapter topics, I have kept in mind three fundamental factors that have shaped the political development of the societies in Eastern Europe: ethnic complexity, underdevelopment, and a strategic location that has made the area a zone of contention between great powers. These realities underlie the dramatic upheavals of two world wars and the longer era of communist rule and the Cold War. Under the impress of these basic factors, the peoples of Eastern Europe have confronted the challenge of fashioning states that embody the national idea, yet meet the responsibilities of civic community and the need to accommodate ethnic diversity. In editing the readings, I have sought to retain as much of the text as possible, eliminating only material that is not essential.

With the historic ending of the Cold War era, Europe is no longer divided. As a result, the meaning of the term "Eastern Europe" has become a semantic and cultural point of contention. Here the term "Eastern Europe" refers primarily to the territories and the peoples that were once part of the Habsburg and Ottoman empires. Today this area would best be described as east central and southeastern Europe.

I would like to thank the following readers who reviewed the contents: Seymour Becker, Rutgers University; John Bell, University of Maryland-Baltimore; Gary Cohen, University of Oklahoma; Keith Hitchins, University of Illinois; Richard Lewis, St. Cloud State University; Harry Ritter, Western Washington University; Dennison Rusinow, University of Pittsburgh; Gale Stokes, Rice University; and Sharon Wolchik; George Washington University. I would also like to thank James Miller, Senior Acquisitions Editor at D. C. Heath, for his interest in the project and for his encouragement and support.

G. A.

Contents

V The Collapse of Communism and the Return of Nations 127

VI The National Idea and Civic Community: The Past in the Future of Eastern Europe 155

Chronology
of Events

1804		Austrian Empire's proclamation to maintain Habsburg authority due to imminent dissolution of the Holy Roman Empire Serbs revolt against local overlords
1815		Congress of Vienna Serbia recognized as autonomous
1821		Greek revolt against Ottoman rule
1830		Greece declared independent state Poles revolt against Russian rule
1848		Revolutions in Austrian Empire
1849	April	Kossuth declares Hungary independent of Austrian (Habsburg) Empire
	August	Hungarian revolt crushed
1867		Agreement between Emperor Francis Joseph and Hungarians creating Austria-Hungary
1875		Revolt in Bosnia-Herzegovina; Ottoman sultan promises reforms
1877		War between Russian and Ottoman empires

1878	March	Treaty of San Stefano between Russian and Ottoman empires providing for large Bulgarian state
	July	Treaty of Berlin establishes small autonomous Bulgarian state; Serbia, Romania, and Montenegro declared independent
1897		Habsburg government grants Czech language equality with German in Bohemia; repealed in 1899
1908	July	Young Turk revolt
	October	Bulgaria proclaimed independent Bosnia annexed by Austria-Hungary
1914	June 28	Assassination of Archduke Francis Ferdinand
	July 28	Austria declares war on Serbia
1918	November	Breakup of Austria-Hungary from within
	November	Independent Polish Republic proclaimed
	December	Kingdom of Serbs, Croats, and Slovenes (Yugoslavia) declared
1919		Paris Peace Conference creates "New Europe" of independent nation-states in Eastern Europe
1920	February	Czechoslovak constitution adopted
	March	Admiral Horthy named regent of Hungary
	June	Hungary signs Treaty of Trianon, loses two-thirds of territory
1921	January	New constitution for Kingdom of Serbs, Croats, and Slovenes creates

		centralized government dominated by Serbs
1926	May	Coup d'état led by General Piłsudski against Polish government
1929	January	King Alexander proclaims dictatorship of Yugoslavia (name formally changed in October)
1934	October	King Alexander of Yugoslavia assassinated by terrorist with ties to Macedonian and Croatian nationalist groups
1935	May	General Piłsudski dies; government run by his close supporters
	December	President Masaryk resigns; succeeded by Edvard Beneš
1938	February	King Carol of Romania proclaims personal dictatorship
	March	Austria taken over by Hitler
	September 29	Agreement in Munich cedes Czechoslovak territory to Nazi Germany
	October 5	Slovak nationalists' demand for autonomy granted
	November 2	Hungary takes territory inhabited by Hungarians from Czechoslovakia
1939	March	Bohemia and Moravia declared protectorates
	August 23	Nazi Germany and Soviet Union sign a nonaggression pact
	September 1	Germany attacks Poland; World War II begins
1941	April	Germany attacks Yugoslavia
	June	Germany attacks the Soviet Union

	December	Japan attacks the United States at Pearl Harbor
1944	August	Polish Home Army rises against Nazis; crushed by Germans; receives no aid from Soviet Union
1945	February	Yalta Conference
	March	Tito establishes government in Yugoslavia
	May	World War II in Europe ends
	June	President Beneš announces that German and Hungarian minorities must be expelled from Czechoslovakia
1946–1947		Communists take control of governments in Eastern Europe
1948	February	Communists form government in Czechoslovakia
	June 28	Yugoslavia expelled from Cominform
1949	January	Soviet Union with five East European countries establishes Comecon—economic coordinating organization
	April	NATO established
1951	May	Radio Free Europe and Radio Liberty begin broadcasting to Eastern Europe
1953	March	Stalin dies; Nikita Khrushchev becomes first secretary of Communist party
1955	May 14	Warsaw Pact established institutionalizing Soviet control of Eastern Europe
	May 26	Soviet leaders visit Yugoslavia; Tito gains recognition of Yugoslav right

		to independent path of development
1956	February	Twentieth Congress of Soviet Communist party; Khrushchev approves of "separate roads to socialism" and peaceful coexistence
	June 28	Workers demonstrate in Poznan, Poland
	October 19	Polish Communists adopt liberal policies; Władysław Gomułka elected first secretary of the party
	October 23	Revolution breaks out in Hungary; people demand end of communist monopoly on power and creation of a multiparty system
	November 4	Soviets intervene in Hungary and suppress the revolution; Imre Nagy tried and executed in 1958
1957	March 25	European Economic Community created
1958	May	Soviet troops leave Romania and lower troop levels in Hungary
1961	August 13	Berlin Wall erected
1964	October	Khrushchev ousted from power; Leonid Brezhnev becomes first secretary of the Soviet Communist party
1965	March	Nicolae Ceaușescu becomes leader of Romanian Communist party
1968	January	Hungary introduces New Economic Mechanism—a set of economic reforms
	April	Reform program created in Czechoslovakia; Alexander Dubček, a Slovak, heads the party

	June 27	"Two Thousand Words" manifesto by Ludvík Vaculík published in Czechoslovak newspapers; intellectuals criticize the party
	August 20	Warsaw Pact forces, led by Soviet Union, invade Czechoslovakia and suppress the Prague Spring
	October 30	A two-state federation of the Czech lands and Slovakia is created
	November 12	Brezhnev Doctrine enunciated; maintenance of socialist unity is prime concern
1969	April	Alexander Dubček replaced by Gustav Husák as head of the Czechoslovak Communist party
1970	December 6	West German Chancellor Willy Brandt visits Poland and signs agreement recognizing Oder-Neisse as western border of Poland
	December 16	Workers riot in Gdansk shipyards to protest price increases; Gomułka replaced by Edward Gierek as head of Polish Communist party
1972	May	United States and Soviet Union sign Strategic Arms Limitation Treaty (SALT)
	December	West Germany and East Germany sign agreement establishing formal relations
1973	December	Chancellor Brandt visits Czechoslovakia, signs treaty normalizing relations
1975	July 30	Helsinki Accords signed at first meeting of Conference on Security and Cooperation in Europe;

		human rights guaranteed and borders of signatory states finalized
1977	January 7	Charter 77 issued by Czechoslovak intellectuals demanding observance of human rights
1978	January	United States returns Crown of St. Stephen to Hungary
	October	Cardinal Karol Wojtyła becomes pope, takes the name of John Paul II
1979	June	John Paul II visits Poland for first time after election as pope
1980	May 4	Tito dies; collective leadership established in Yugoslavia
	August 14	Strikes in Gdansk shipyards over price increases; Lech Wałesa begins organizing Solidarity trade union
	October 24	Polish government officially recognizes Solidarity as independent trade union
1981	February	General Wojciech Jaruzelski becomes prime minister of Poland
	September	Solidarity holds first national congress
	December 13	General Jaruzelski, now head of the Polish Communist party, establishes martial law
1982	October	Jaruzelski dissolves all trade unions, including Solidarity
	November 10	Leonid Brezhnev dies, replaced by Yuri Andropov, former KGB head
	November 13	Lech Wałesa released from detention
	December 30	Martial law suspended in Poland

1983	October	Lech Wałesa awarded Nobel Peace Prize
1985	March 11	Mikhail Gorbachev becomes first secretary of the Soviet Communist party
1986	March	Gorbachev calls for reforms in the Soviet Union, including *glasnost* (openness) and *perestroika* (restructuring)
1988	May 20	János Kádár replaced as first secretary of the party in Hungary; reformers take over
	June	Gorbachev calls for new type of Soviet presidency elected by a Congress of People's Deputies and popularly elected republican legislatures to carry out reform
	November 23	Serb authorities move against Albanians in Kosovo who have been protesting reduction in constitutional status of the autonomous province
1989	February 8	Talks begin between Polish government and Solidarity
	February 24	Thousands of Romanian refugees allowed to enter Hungary
	February 28	Hungarian government announces that frontier security system along Austrian border to be dismantled
	May 17	Václav Havel released from prison after serving sentence for dissident activities
	June 6	Solidarity wins overwhelming victory in elections for parliament
	June 7	Thousands of Turks expelled from Bulgaria

June 16	Imre Nagy reburied—mass memorial in Budapest for martyr of 1956 uprising
October 9	A massive prodemocracy demonstration in Leipzig, East Germany
November 9	East Germany opens borders to West Germany and Berlin Wall to West Berlin
November 17	Communist regime collapses in Czechoslovakia
December	Václav Havel elected president of Czechoslovakia
December 21	Overthrow of Ceauşescu regime in Romania

1990

January 5	Hungarian parliament calls for withdrawal of Soviet troops from country
January 10	Soviet bloc trading organization, Comecon, agrees to free-market approach
January 12	Under popular pressure, Romanian government outlaws the Communist party
January 18	Todor Zhivkov, Bulgarian communist leader, under house arrest
January 22	Yugoslav League of Communists votes to end monopoly of political power
January 29	Polish United Workers party (communist) reformed as the Social Democratic party
February 4	Slovenian League of Communists declares independence from Yugoslav Communist party
March 21	Ethnic violence in Romanian city of

	Tîrgu Mureş after local Hungarians celebrate a Hungarian national day
March 29	New name for Czechoslovakia adopted: the Czech and Slovak Federative Republic
April 11	Polish parliament abolishes censorship
April 21	Lech Wałesa overwhelmingly re-elected chairman of Solidarity
May 4–8	Latvia and Estonia declare themselves independent republics
May 20	Romania holds first free elections in fifty-three years; National Salvation Front wins two-thirds of parliamentary seats
May 23	A coalition government led by center-right Democratic Forum formed in Hungary
May 29	Boris Yeltsin elected president of Russian Federation
June 8	In first free elections in Czechoslovakia since 1946, Civic Forum and Slovak sister party, Public Against Violence, triumph
June 13	In Romania, antigovernment protests against National Salvation Front as party of neocommunists are harshly repressed
June 17	Bulgarian Socialist party (former Communist party) wins majority in parliament
June 28	Conference on Security and Cooperation in Europe (CSCE) issues declaration supporting rights of citizens and committing governments to multiparty democracy
July 3	Slovenian parliament declares that its laws take precedence over

	those of the Yugoslav federal government
July 5	Serbia dissolves government and parliament of autonomous province of Kosovo
July 8	Thousands of Albanian refugees sheltered in Western embassies while antigovernment protests mount
July 12	Boris Yeltsin and other reformers resign from Communist party
July 31	"Pentagonale" meeting of Austria, Hungary, Italy, Yugoslavia, and Czechoslovakia declare support for regional cooperation and safeguarding of human rights
September 28	Serbian parliament adopts new constitution; strips Kosovo of autonomy
October 3	East Germany and West Germany reunified after forty-five years of division
November 14	Treaty between Poland and Germany confirms Oder-Neisse as frontier between the two states
November 19	Charter of Paris for a New Europe signed at CSCE meeting to mark end of Cold War and affirm supremacy of democratic process
December 9	Former Solidarity leader Wałesa elected president of Poland
December 9	Slobodan Milošević, leader of Serbian Socialist party (renamed communists), elected president of the Serbian Republic
December 11	Unrest mounts in Albania; Communist party says opposition parties to be allowed

	December 23	Slovenia holds plebiscite on independence
1991	March	Milošević resigns from collective Yugoslav presidency, will not recognize its decisions
	June 25	Slovenia and Croatia declare independence from Yugoslavia
	July	Warsaw pact organization formally ends
	July	Slovene and Yugoslav federal government leaders agree to peace after brief conflict
	July	Attempted coup in U.S.S.R. against Gorbachev
	September 7	EC sponsors peace conference on Yugoslavia; fighting continues in Croatia
	September 19	Croatia and Serbia reject EC peace efforts
	October	Croatian president calls for mobilization of men to defend country
	October 27	Poland holds first free elections since World War II
	November	Poland becomes member of Council of Europe
1992	January 15	Slovenia and Croatia recognized by European Union (EU), marking end of Yugoslav Federation
	January 19	Zhelyu Zhelev re-elected president of Bulgaria in first popular presidential election
	February 29	Bosnia-Herzegovina votes for independence from Yugoslavia; Bosnian Serbs boycott the referendum
	March 1	Montenegro votes overwhelmingly to remain part of Yugoslavia

	March 22	Democratic party wins majority in Albanian parliamentary elections, ending almost fifty years of communist rule
	April 6	EU countries and United States recognize independence of Bosnia-Herzegovina
	April 21	Fighting in Sarajevo as Bosnian Serbs fire on the city
	April 27	Serbia and Montenegro proclaim new Yugoslav state
	May 18	UN reports more than one million refugees created by collapse of Yugoslavia
	June 21	Czech and Slovak delegations agree to end Czechoslovak Federation
	July 20	Václav Havel resigns as president of Czechoslovakia after Slovakia declares sovereignty
	August 2	First elections in Croatia since independence; Croatian Democratic party of president Franjo Tudjman wins
1993	January 1	Slovakia becomes independent state
	January 2	Bosnian peace talks resume; Vance-Owen plan discussed
	February 2	Václav Havel sworn in as first president of Czech Republic
	March 25	Bosnian government signs Vance-Owen plan; Bosnian Serbs reject it
	April 7	UN Security Council recommends admission of Former Yugoslav Republic of Macedonia to the UN
	May 6	UN Security Council adopts Resolution 824 on "safe areas" in Bosnia

	May 15	In referendum, Bosnian Serbs reject Vance-Owen peace plan
	June 14	Muslim troops attack Croat villages in central Bosnia; Bosnian Croats flee
	June 16	Serb and Croat leaders meet in Geneva, propose dividing up Bosnia into three mini-states
	September 1	Peace talks on Bosnia collapse; factions fail to agree on plan to divide up country
1994	January 8	Representatives of Hungarian community in Slovakia assemble to discuss minority rights but stop short of demanding autonomy
	January 23	Milan Martić wins election to presidency of separatist Serbian Republic of Krajina, made up of Serbs in Croatia
	February 2	Romanian Senate overwhelmingly passes bill to punish anyone defaming the country or nation in public
	February 3, 9	Russia and United States recognize Former Yugoslav Republic of Macedonia
	March 8	Hungarian parliament approves legislation to screen high-ranking officials to determine whether they participated in suppression of 1956 uprising
	March 14	Vladimír Mečiár, nationalist Slovak leader, resigns as prime minister following no-confidence vote
	March 18	Representatives of Bosnia and Croatia sign agreement to create a federation of Bosnian Muslims and Croats and link the new federation to Croatia in a loose confederation

March 30	Croatia agrees to ceasefire with self-declared Republic of Serbian Krajina
April 22	Muslim enclave of Gorazde, a safe area in Bosnia, taken by Serb forces; NATO threatens air strikes
April 26	Contact Group (France, Russia, Britain, and United States) formed to address Bosnian crisis
April 28	Serbian Chetnik Movement, paramilitary wing of Serbian Radical Party, abolished; had been accused of war crimes in fighting in Croatia in 1991–1992
May	Hungarian Socialist party, former communists, wins majority in parliamentary elections
May 8	Martić, president of self-declared Republic of Serbian Krajina, reiterates right to self-determination and need to defend links with Serb lands
May 20	Albanian government charges six ethnic Greeks who promoted interests of Greek minority in Albania with fomenting separatism
May 27	Slovak National Council passes law allowing ethnic Hungarians in Slovakia to register their names officially in their original form; Slovak National party had voted to permit only ethnic Slovaks to join the party
June	Croatian President Franjo Tudjman speaks against separatist tendencies in Istrian peninsula
June 27	Ten ethnic Albanians convicted of plotting to organize an "All-Albanian Army" in Macedonia

June 28	Bulgaria launches mass privatization program based on Czech model
July	Ethnic Albanians in Macedonia boycott a census, claiming results would be falsified to undermine Albanian claims for autonomy
July 7	Slovak legislature passes law providing for bilingual road signs in areas where minority population is at least twenty percent
July 8	Ethnic confrontation averted in Cluj, Romania. Romanian nationalist mayor had approved archaeological excavation around a monument to a Hungarian king; Hungarian minority feared destruction of statue
July 14	Gyula Horn, leader of Hungarian Socialist party and prime minister, offers to renounce all territorial claims in Romania and Slovakia in return for guarantees of rights of ethnic Hungarians living there
July 18–19	Assembly of Bosnia-Hercegovina accepts Contact Group's map delimiting ethnic zones; rejected by Bosnian Serbs
August 4	Serbian government closes border with Serb-held Bosnia-Herzegovina, supporting Contact Group proposal for peace
August 9	Leader of Hungarian Democratic Union of Romania calls for special status for ethnic Hungarians in Romania
August 28	In referendum, Bosnian Serbs reject Contact Group peace plan
September 15	Romanian president Ion Iliescu,

	addressing conference on ethnic minorities, calls demand for autonomy by Hungarian minority in Romania unacceptable
November 9	Romanian legislature passes amendments to criminal code specifying prison sentences for flying the national flag or playing the national anthem of other states
November 21–30	Bosnian Serb forces attack town of Bihać, a Muslim safe area
December	In wake of Bosnian Serb attacks, Western allies rethink peace plans, propose making concessions to Bosnian Serbs on the ethnic partition of Bosnia
December 10	European Union members outline plan for eventual entry into EU of several former communist East European states, including Poland, the Czech Republic, Slovakia, Romania, Hungary, and Bulgaria
December 20	Former U.S. president Jimmy Carter helps to work out a ceasefire between the opposing parties in the Bosnian conflict

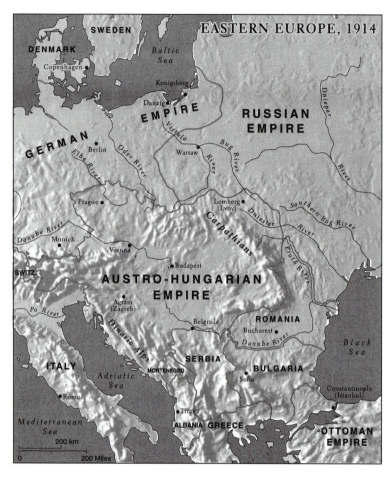

Maps of Eastern Europe from Thomas W. Simons, *Eastern Europe in the Postwar World*, 2nd ed., 1993. Copyright © Thomas W. Simons, reprinted with permission of St. Martin's Press, Incorporated.

Territories gained by Romania
after World War I

EASTERN EUROPE, 1995

*Name is not universally recognized.

Variety of
Opinion

The arrival in [Eastern Europe] of the originally Western European concept of the nation . . . as the only just basis for the organization of a secular modern state, and the awakening to its revolutionary potential by individuals and classes who were or felt themselves to be aggrieved, created a serious "national question" in each of the multinational empires that then dominated the region.

Dennison Rusinow (1992)

Looking back today we can say that the imperial governments were faced with the decision whether to stick to the old principles of legitimacy, or to try to create a secular ideology of state to replace the diminishing loyalty to a divinely sanctioned monarch. The Habsburg Emperors . . . and the Ottoman Sultans . . . made no such attempt. Loyalty to the dynasty remained until the end the only claim, and the only non-material bond holding diverse subjects together.

Hugh Seton-Watson (1964)

One of the powerful democratic forces is the national movement: the striving of subject nations for political independence and their striving for the recognition of their nationality as a higher and more valuable principle than the state.

Thomas Masaryk (1918)

It would be superficial cynicism to maintain that the diplomats at Paris [in 1919] were moved by none but self-interested motives, and that no guiding principles inspired their work. . . . They had certain ideals which they perhaps unconsciously put in the place of self-determination; these were—a belief in small states as a justifiable part of the international order, a belief in the equality of states, . . . and a belief in the right of absolute national sovereignty.

Alfred Cobban (1945)

Instead of mitigating the strains and stresses between the nations and their minorities, the disastrous political frontier-making after World War I only proved that the nation-state principle could not be introduced into Eastern Europe without creating in some cases even more glaring injustices and almost everywhere new hotbeds of nationalist friction.

Paul Lendvai (1971)

The composite character of the population, the impossibility of devising "ethnic" frontiers, and the dismal record of attempts at forced assimilation in the past should be conclusive reasons for abandoning further efforts to carve out national states of cultural uniformity in the war-breeding zone of east-central Europe.

Oscar Janowsky (1945)

One of the duties of Stalin's puppet in Budapest . . . was to eliminate the ideology of nationalism. In its place he attempted to shape a new communist . . . subservient to the whim of Stalin's great Russian chauvinism. Instead of nationalism, the Hungarians were to embrace socialist patriotism. The new patriot was to count out the nation which, according to Stalin, was a historic unit doomed to disappear in the Socialist stage of history.

Peter Pastor (1977)

Years of trying to build up a state resting on a teleology of progressive change and an ideology of internationalism . . . had ended in the realization that the state could adequately con-

struct itself only in terms of what it had at first denied: a teleology of national continuity and an ideology of national values, premised on internal uniformity.

Katherine Verdery (1991)

The identity of a people and of a civilization is reflected and concentrated in what has been created by the mind—in what is known as "culture." If this identity is threatened with extinction, cultural life . . . becomes the living value around which all people rally. That is why in . . . Central Europe the collective cultural memory . . . assumed roles so great . . . .

Milan Kundera (1984)

The desire to renew and emphasize one's identity . . . is also behind the emergence of many new countries. Nations that have never had states of their own feel an understandable need to experience independence. It is no fault of theirs that the opportunity has come up decades or even centuries after it came to other nations.

Václav Havel (1993)

Nationalism is not the struggle for one's own national rights, but a disregard for someone else's right to national and human dignity. Nationalism is the last word of communism. A final attempt to find a social basis for dictatorship.

Adam Michnik (1991)

Nationalism is distinguished from social movements that arise among other aggrieved groups by the powerful emotions associated with it. Nationalist movements, however, cannot be understood as solely "primordial" in nature. They are most often . . . vehicles for the articulation of arguments over rights, goods, status, power, and other material and political issues.

Steven Burg (1993)

That people identify with a particular national group . . . is reality. But that this identity ought to define the institutions and principles of the state that governs the territory considered "home" to this national group, is an understanding of the

> *politics of national identity that is incompatible with democracy. . . .*
>
> Julie Mostov (1994)

> *The reconciliation of these profoundly conflicting trends—the political and nationalist trends affirming state sovereignty, the economic trends forcing their wider association and the ethnically driven fragmentation trends threatening their unity—is a central task for modern statecraft.*
>
> Gidon Gottlieb (1994)

Introduction

The Long View

The vicissitudes of the national idea in Eastern Europe must first of all be seen against the backdrop of the demographic features, social and state structures, and historical events that shaped the development of the area over many centuries. However, the nationalist and ethnic conflicts that have arisen during the twentieth century are also bound up with the major historical forces that have affected the entire world in the last two centuries. These include the development of revolutionary political ideas, the state rivalry within the European great-power system, and the universal imperative to create modern societies.

From the long historical view, many peoples filtered into Eastern Europe both as conquerors and as peaceful settlers, going back to at least the fifth and sixth centuries of the Christian era. Some nations claim an even earlier heritage. This diversity created a complex pattern of coexistent but distinct cultures in the region. Elites from some of these societies, which organized themselves along traditional social lines, with a landed nobility controlling the peasant masses and a small urban element, built states complete with political institutions and defined territorial frontiers. But those frontiers shifted as new conquerors came along. Indeed, Eastern Europe remained a frontier zone of competing peoples, cultures, and faiths until fairly recently. Between the sixteenth century and the end of the eighteenth century three large empires—the Habsburg, Ottoman, and Russian—vied for control of the region and for primacy among themselves.

These empires were multiethnic polities, formed through conquest with little concern for territorial and ethnic congruity. The dynasties, which served as the focus of authority and legitimacy, attained and maintained cohesiveness. With societies organized into estates along simplified horizontal social lines, the rulers embodied the identity of the state. Ethnic identity was linked to faith and local community customs, thus allowing for diversity and accommodation of various cultures within an overarching and nonnational system of political power.

The empires presumed an arrangement of dominant/subordinate relationships between ruler and ruled as well as among different peoples depending on the historical development of their societies. But as Dennison Rusinow points out, by the end of the eighteenth century the development of the national idea introduced a revolutionary factor into the equation of imperial authority. All the empires had to confront this challenge to their legitimacy during the nineteenth century.

In the case of the Habsburg Monarchy, the emperor adopted more than one ad hoc policy to grapple with what quickly became the national question. With the Hungarians, one of several nationalities in the Habsburg Monarchy, the emperor agreed to the forming of a dual state. This new political structure allowed the Hungarians to control their affairs within their own territory. They in turn attempted to build a Hungarian nation by trying, through pressure, to assimilate the non-Hungarian peoples in their land. As yet another tactic employed in the Austrian lands of the Habsburg Monarchy, the emperor allowed the different peoples to compete for imperial favor and encouraged them to make arrangements among themselves that would satisfy competing, ethnically-based political claims. All of these efforts to address the national idea ultimately failed, for behind them lay the demand to link ethnicity to territory in the form of the nation-state.

In the Ottoman realm in southeastern Europe, this demand spurred dramatic changes. Revolts against local authority had erupted well before the nineteenth century, but it was the uprising among the sultan's Greek subjects in 1821 that initiated a series of nationally defined struggles during the nineteenth century. These conflicts in turn led to the elimination of Ottoman power over the Balkans and the creation of several small but nominally independent states in its place.

As for the Russian Empire, in the early nineteenth century the state did not intervene in the affairs of the subject nationalities as long as they remained loyal. However, the government forcibly repressed overt nationalist manifestations like the revolt of the Poles in 1830. In response to that uprising, the Russian government developed a policy of official nationalism. By the end of the nineteenth century, this policy meant the active Russification of the subject peoples. The administrative servants of the tsar sought to inculcate a Russian identity through the use of the Russian language in schools, the support of the Russian Orthodox church, and by the promotion of a national ideology. Despite the willingness of some to assimilate, the multinational character of the empire remained.

The Idea of the Nation

The idea of the nation presupposed a broadened sense of a community differentiated from others by some distinctive feature. As Hugh Seton-Watson notes, in Western Europe the extension of state authority combined with the spread and acceptance of a common culture among peoples to produce the sense of a nation. In Eastern Europe, the joining of state power and territory to a common, distinctive culture did not exist in most instances, nor was it easily established. This link, however, was envisaged and heralded by individuals who sought to challenge the ruling authority in the name of their people, whom they identified through language, faith, and history. These individuals, members of the intelligentsia, came mostly from the urban middle class. Possessing the power of knowledge but rarely that of the gun or the ballot, these middle-class citizens imagined their world reshaped so that their people might possess political power and territorial contiguity.

Although the national idea eventually triumphed in the turmoil and upheaval of the First World War, European governments in the nineteenth century opposed the notion that peoples had a natural right to a separate country encompassing their nation. Also, many who voiced political demands in the Habsburg Monarchy before the Great War desired autonomy, a moderate goal, rather than complete independence, which implied the breakup of the empire.

It was only in the depths of the Great War that the leaders of

the major allied powers—Britain, France, and the United States—
began to consider the principle of national self-determination as
the basis for reorganizing Europe once the fighting stopped.
Moreover, by 1917 a number of east European political leaders,
such as Thomas Masaryk, had emerged as spokesmen for their nations. Determined to see a "new Europe" of nation-states, these
leaders formed "national councils" in the western European capi-
tals to pursue their cause.

Their dream received a lift when President Woodrow Wilson issued the Fourteen Points in January 1918 and then lent his considerable prestige to the idea of national self-determination at the
peace conference in Paris. As the expression of the popular will and
the identity of peoples, national self-determination won acceptance as the legitimating criterion in the breakup of the empires
into smaller states. Defining states primarily along national lines,
however, catalyzed tensions over the demarcation of territorial
frontiers, the nature and purpose of civic institutions in public life,
and the status of peoples not identified with the major nationality.

The "New Europe"

The "new Europe" that emerged out of the ashes of the empires
comprised newly created countries like Poland, Czechoslovakia,
and Yugoslavia; other considerably enlarged nation-states such as
Romania; and still others from among the defeated states such as
Hungary and Bulgaria. In all cases, these countries' leaders were
determined to secure their nations' interests. Competing national
claims complicated the process of drawing up the peace treaties
and defining the frontiers of the new states. The area's political
and economic turmoil, the divergent interests of the Allied leaders, and *faits accomplis* carried out by nationalist groups only
worsened matters.

In the end, as Alfred Cobban indicates, the Allied leaders had
to compromise on a number of issues, and the frontiers that were
drawn up were determined as much by the claims of national
leaders as by the popular will of the peoples affected by the
changes. Seeking above all to establish a stable order, the statesmen in Paris accepted the principle of the nation-state system as

the foundation for managing the problems of postwar Europe. Thus they agreed to the establishment of a number of national states in Eastern Europe to replace the defunct imperial powers.

Recognizing that the new states were far from perfect expressions of the alignment of nationality and territory, the Paris participants established the League of Nations to deal with problems arising from the treaties, to help stabilize the new European state map, and to protect the rights of millions of people who were made minorities and refugees by the changes. This protection took the form of provisions in the treaties that the defeated powers signed and minority treaties that the new or enlarged states endorsed with the Allies.

The states of the "new Europe" received no respite from pressing problems once the treaties were signed. The economic toll of the war, postwar inflationary pressures, the flood of refugees, heightened discontent among an agrarian population hungry for land, and demands for better work and living conditions by urban laborers combined to strain the administrative and financial resources of even the established states, let alone the newly created countries.

In addition, governments had to cope with peoples' fears and even hatred generated by the war's social and political dislocations. Under all these concerns lay two broad issues that went to the heart of the postwar development of these countries. First was the question of the nature of the state. How its role was perceived shaped the administrative relations between the government and citizenry. In new countries like Poland, Czechoslovakia, and Yugoslavia, the differing views came to define political life in the state. Some believed that the nation could develop only through a centralized government. An opposing view held that the country could realize its potential only by recognizing the varied and distinct groups that made up the population and accommodating this diversity through administrative autonomy or even the implementation of a federal system.

The second and potentially more troubling issue centered on the nature of the nation. Here again, strongly divergent views buffeted political life and the lives of citizens. No country in Eastern Europe was ethnically homogeneous. Indeed, in Poland and Romania, minorities amounted to almost 30 percent of the population. Czechoslovakia and Yugoslavia could best be described as nationality states. Ethnic diversity, therefore, became a political powderkeg.

At stake was the fundamental question of power among different peoples. Some groups sought government recognition of their distinct ethnic identity, and perhaps protection through cultural autonomy, and even a loose political configuration. To others, however, such policies entailed negating the very idea of what constituted the nation, along with everything for which they had fought. In these people's view, the state was the guarantor, if not the instrument, of the national will. Even a leader like Thomas Masaryk saw his country as forging a new national unity even as it recognized the existence of minorities.

As Jerzy Tomasezewski indicates, relations between the state and its peoples were not simple. Governments generally carried out assimilation campaigns, but in some instances they also sought to differentiate peoples as part of their nationalist strategy. Rulers had to consider social and economic factors as well in the development of the national question. Moreover, the growth of a national consciousness did not go in one direction only. In some instances, promoting a unified national society served to crystallize the national identity of others within the country. Jews experienced particular difficulty as governments seeking to use them to improve the position of the dominant nationality pulled them in different directions.

As the political tide during the interwar era swelled with demands for national unity, the various ethnic groups found little consolation in being in the boat of a national minority. The states in Eastern Europe had obligated themselves to implement a dual policy: not to discriminate against individuals because they were different in language, religion, or race and, at the same time, to help minority groups maintain their identity. Further removed, the League of Nations was charged with protecting minorities' rights. Thus the minorities had to work within a system that recognized the sovereign interests of their national states and the international organization's role in maintaining peace among those states. By 1934, when the Polish government declared that it would no longer cooperate with the League on minority protection, the system had foundered.

The Separation of Peoples and the Role of the Communists

As Oscar Jászi observed, the Great Depression and the rise of fascist movements worsened social divisions in Eastern Europe and heightened fears both within and outside the region. Demands for national unity now combined with right radical ideas about the organization of society. Fascist movements like the Iron Guard in Romania and the Arrow Cross in Hungary turned the national idea into a weapon for attacking civil society and for excluding entire groups from what the fascists defined as the "integral" and "corporate" national body.

The Second World War began in Eastern Europe with Hitler's attack on Poland in 1939. In the ensuing six years, the region suffered vast physical and human destruction, some of it done in the name of the nation. The damage included the taking of territory, the extermination of peoples, conflict between peoples, and the forced movement of still others. Hungary, Bulgaria, Poland, and the Soviet Union all seized territory from neighbors, claiming historical or ethnic justification. Jews and Gypsies were treated as enemies of the nation. In Yugoslavia, Serbs and Croats fought each other and the communist Partisans in a bloody ethnic civil war as the country struggled under foreign occupation.

In the end, the forces of nazism and fascism fell to defeat, and the national states survived the onslaught. But as a consequence of the war, two great changes profoundly altered the states and societies, and in turn the dynamics, of the national idea in Eastern Europe. The first was demographic and territorial. While concerned individuals like Oscar Janowsky sought ways to accommodate ethnic complexity with proposals for restructuring the state system, national leaders demanded the separation of peoples as the only solution. Millions of Germans were expelled from the region and thousands of Hungarians left Czechoslovakia for Hungary. Moreover, territorial adjustments to the Soviet Union's western frontier created waves of refugees and pulled large areas into a new political and social orbit.

The second major change—the establishment of communist regimes throughout the area over the next few years—did not alter the nominal sovereignty of the national states in Eastern Europe. However, it marked the onset of a political and social revolution within the states and the inauguration of what might be described as a new imperial system. It posed both an implicit and explicit challenge to the national idea. Not only was communism theoretically at odds with the notion of the primacy of unique political units centered on the nation, but the new rulers were determined to eliminate what they considered a politically deleterious and now outmoded concept that they believed would hinder the socialist development of the region.

The communists shouldered a triple burden. To begin with, in most instances they had come to power with the help of the Soviet Union and, except for Czechoslovakia and Yugoslavia, they had little popular domestic support. They also had to cope with resistance to change from traditionalist segments of society and expectations for better social and living conditions from others. Finally, rebuilding and further developing their countries after the war took place under the shadow of Soviet demands for materials and increasing controls.

It was Yugoslavia, as Vladimir Dedijer affirmed, that responded most dramatically to all three challenges. In a tense confrontation with Stalin in 1948, the Yugoslav communist leader, Tito, asserted the right to create a socialist society that acknowledged the particular conditions in his country. Having built a powerful resistance movement during World War II, the Yugoslav communists claimed to have carried out a revolution and to have brought the peoples of Yugoslavia into a new era. Over the next two decades, they went on to redefine the role of the party, the mechanisms for developing the economy, and the relations between the various nations and nationalities in Yugoslavia. "Titoism" became synonymous with national communism, or the possibility of diverse paths to modernity.

But the radical economic and social transformation of states under the thumb of a single controlling party was fraught with danger. From the outset in countries like Poland, Romania, and Hungary, the people expressed little liking initially for the communists. Relations between the party and the people grew even more strained as the Soviet Union harshly imposed its model of development, featuring a drive to build heavy industry and the collectivization of agriculture in the late 1940s and the 1950s.

Though the U.S.S.R. relaxed its grip somewhat on the people of Eastern Europe after Stalin's death in 1953, this easing only exacerbated tensions between the people and the Communist party in some instances, and in 1956 popular unrest shook Poland and Hungary. Political protest in Hungary exploded into a national revolt against a despised regime. Soviet armor brutally suppressed the uprising.

Soon some communist leaders realized that they needed to build support within their country. While tinkering with their economies and speaking of reforming the party, they also cultivated a close sense of identity with their people by selectively promoting the national culture. Although seeking out the nation's past had its limits, as Peter Pastor shows, it made sense to tap into the strong national sentiment of the people. The Romanian communist leader Nicolae Ceauşescu, who took over as party leader in 1965, cultivated these ties of legitimacy between the party and the people through the nation with special enthusiasm. As Katherine Verdery demonstrates, a weak regime in a small state sought to build strength at home while putting on an independent face internationally by appealing to the nation.

The national idea, though suppressed at some times, and nurtured at others, was not eliminated in Eastern Europe during more than four decades of communist rule. On the contrary, it became entwined with the politics of socialism, shaped by it and in turn shaping its discourse. During the 1960s, those who continued to believe in the future of socialism in Czechoslovakia and Yugoslavia argued for political and economic reforms while hoping for a new national identity that would unify their peoples. Yet as George Klein argues, ethnicity became a key issue in the politics of those states. Indeed, it proved a major factor in the political crisis that developed in Yugoslavia in the late 1960s and a concern for those who crafted the reforms in Czechoslovakia during the spring of 1968.

"Living in Truth" and the Surge to Nationhood

In the succeeding years, many lost all hope in the system. Some, like Czech writer Milan Kundera, rejected politics and economics and placed their hope in the nation's culture as a bulwark against "them," those who controlled their country backed by the power of a foreign imperial state.

Nevertheless, constituent elements of civil society emerged in some east European countries in the 1970s. People who decided to "live in truth," like the Czech intellectual Václav Havel, adopted the politics of moral suasion. That the people could act as a civil society found dramatic confirmation in the birth of the first nongovernment-authorized trade union in Poland. In 1980 Solidarity became a national labor movement among urban and rural workers, and the communist government was forced to recognize it as a legitimate organization. Though the regime counterattacked and tried to destroy the Solidarity movement, it eventually had to face the instrument of popular will.

With a reforming communist at the helm in the Kremlin by the mid-1980s, the east European regimes had lost their external support. Mikhail Gorbachev, promoting openness and the restructuring of the Soviet Union, expected the governments of the neighboring communist states to follow suit. With no backing without and mostly hangers-on within, the party-governments during 1989 negotiated their way out of power (Poland and Hungary), abdicated in the face of popular protest (Czechoslovakia and Albania), or were removed (Romania and Bulgaria).

Eastern Europe had lived with decades of one-party rule and noncompetitive, inefficient, and technologically deficient economic development, so the opening of the postcommunist era sent shock waves through the peoples and successor governments of the region. Seeking an anchor in the economic storms that their societies have weathered in steering towards a market system, many turned to the collective reassurance of nationalist appeals. Given the opportunity once more to express themselves freely prompted others to search out their ethnic past and to make long-desired but unfulfilled nationalist political demands.

While empathizing with such responses, Václav Havel urged the peoples of Eastern Europe to create understanding by developing the common outlook found in all civil societies, rather than allowing narrower visions of national security to divide them. To Adam Michnik, on the other hand, expressions of nationalism provided the last haven for communists seeking a new way to empower themselves. In political leaders' playing on peoples' fears and turning them against one another, he discerns the destructive side of the national idea that seemed to have roared to life once more. But as Steven Burg points out, although the ethnically driven political turmoil that resurfaced in Eastern Europe after the collapse of communism has a basis in the perceived ethnic wrongs from the not-too-distant past, other issues merit consideration as well. Ethnic movements, whether emerging from within a people or promoted by political leaders, provide the platform for expressing grievances over status, rights, and access to power. However, the emotional strength of nationalism too often can block political opportunities intended to ease tensions through negotiation.

The case in point is Yugoslavia, where the first military conflict in Europe since the end of World War II has wrought tremendous human and physical destruction. Society remained segmented along ethnic lines from the very inception of the country after the First World War. Believing that they had learned the lessons of history in the failure of the first Yugoslavia, the communists under Tito attempted to resolve the national question by introducing a historically grounded federal framework, by fostering a balance of power among the various nationalities, and by constructing a new identity myth of revolutionary struggle while suppressing historical questioning. Over time, numbers of people came to view themselves as "Yugoslavs." But the political decentralization and the redistributing of federal wealth among the various regions, carried out by the party with Tito's approval in the name of local involvement and self-management, only led to a politically fractionalized society and widespread economic grievances. By the late 1980s, as Lenard Cohen makes clear, political leaders in the various constituent republics were projecting those grievances in ethnic terms and mobilizing local support. Individuals' use of nationalist appeals to build personal power and an unwillingness to accommodate the concerns of other groups led to open conflict in 1991.

The undoing of imperial systems and their accompanying mentalities in favor of the national idea has continued throughout the twentieth century. As ethnic identity has been attached to territory, a number of new states fulfilling national aspirations have emerged. The surge to nationhood is symbolically exemplified in these countries' flags, which blaze with a recovered or invented heritage. Vividly colored cloth cannot, however, obscure the patent reality of the diversity, ethnic and otherwise, that still characterizes these states. In the legal manifestations of these polities—their constitutions—one can see the various formulations for combining civil and ethnic belonging.

In the postcommunist era, all the states in Eastern Europe, both the older and those recently established, have declared their adherence to democratic principles of government. Yet as Julie Mostov explains, it is the balance between individual and collective rights that holds the key to the development of open, pluralist governments. Civic participation is possible only if all people are treated equally as citizens. In contrast, rights defined by national criteria burden some while benefiting others.

Whatever the promise of democratic society, the fact remains that areas of Eastern Europe as well as other parts of the world present human mosaics of ethnic diversity that do not conform to state frontiers. Can these different groups be legitimately accommodated by invoking the principle of national self-determination proclaimed early in the twentieth century? The question continues to have relevance, especially in light of the outbreak of ethnic conflict in a number of areas. Some scholars like Gidon Gottlieb argue against employing the national principle as the "hard" basis for defining state borders. Echoing ideas that stretch back to the time of the Second World War, these writers believe that the link between ethnic communities and the state needs to be more flexible.

During the twentieth century, the national idea has not only persisted but prevailed in Eastern Europe, as states have organized themselves around communities of culture. This pattern has prompted social exclusivity rather than inclusiveness. Moreover, in times of stress the nation has been used as the defining bulwark against "outsiders," whether within the country, in the region, or beyond. Securing the ethnic community in political and cultural life has come at the expense of the individual in civil and state institutions. This trade-off continues to trouble political life in the region. But ethnic and civic community are not mutually exclusive. Participatory politics and civic education are the bridges between the two communities, and they must be rebuilt.

As much by the length of his reign (1848–1916) as by his indomitable will, Francis Joseph I embodied the idea and the institution of the supranational monarch. The emperor of Austria-Hungary poses here at the celebration of the fiftieth year of his reign. (Bilderdienst Suddeutscher Verlag)

From Empire to Nation: The National Idea Triumphant

Dennison Rusinow

Empires and Ethnic Politics

By the nineteenth century, all of the multiethnic states in Eastern Europe, including the Russian and Ottoman empires and the Habsburg Monarchy, confronted what became known as the national question. States that for many centuries had controlled a complex mosaic of peoples and cultures through traditional authority were now challenged by the revolutionary idea that governments ought to reflect the sovereign will of the people whose distinctive character was embodied in the nation. Dennison Rusinow, a historian who has observed and written about the development of the Yugoslav peoples for many years, examines the strategies undertaken in the Habsburg Monarchy—which detractors dubbed the "ramshackle empire"—to solve this pressing issue.

Nowhere else in the world has as much political and scholarly attention been paid to ethnonational diversity and fragmentation, and to their consequences in "the age of nationalism," as in East-Central Europe. Historically the region provided the first important testing ground for the diffusion of the Western European concept of the nation-state, intimately identified with nineteenth-century Western European definitions of "nation." . . . In the process East-Central Europe, and especially the lands of the Habsburg Empire and its successor states, became the world's oldest laboratory for conscious efforts to solve "the national question" in an ethnic shatterbelt, either by remaking the boundaries or the population of existing states to conform to the doctrine or by finding an alternative to it. . . .

The ethnic map of East-Central Europe, especially in those lands that comprised the Habsburg Empire and Ottoman Europe at the beginning of the nineteenth century, is a patchwork in which the fragments are bewilderingly mixed, frequently minute, and often changeable, leading geographers to apply the graphic label "ethnic shatterbelt" to the region. Both the ethnic patchwork and the region's failure to produce enduring, stable, centralizing local states (of the kind that were forging the French, English, and some other Western European nations out of also diverse peoples since the later Middle Ages) were notoriously the consequences of its tortured history as Europe's southeastern marches, a buffer zone absorbing invasions and migrations that alternately depopulated and repopulated its plains and valleys in accordance with the whims and needs of foreign dynasties and tribes. Its peoples usually lived under the rule of aliens, in peripheries of multinational empires or ephemeral buffer states between them.

The arrival in this region of the originally Western European concept of the nation (usually defined as an ethnolinguistic group) as the only just basis for the organization of a secular modern state, and the awakening to its revolutionary potential by individuals and classes who were or felt themselves to be politically, economically, and/or socially aggrieved, equally notoriously created a serious "national question" in each of the multinational empires that then dominated the region. The national question was particularly acute for the Habsburg Monarchy, in which no one nation accounted for a majority or even a numerical predominance, and where the Habsburg Emperor and his ministers were the only rulers in Europe (unless one also counts the Ottoman Empire as European) who could not shift their claim to legitimacy from divine right or the dynastic principle to the will or consent of a national community. The latter-day history of the Habsburg Empire is therefore dominated by the national question and by experiments in the search for an alternative foundation for a modern state. The search was cut short by one of its incidental consequences, World War I.

One aspect of this familiar story that merits recapitulation here, despite its familiarity, concerns the social content of the national struggle in the Empire's last century. In addition to its centrality in explaining the nature of the question and why it became so vital, this factor also provides an important basis for comparison and contrast with the national question in the . . . Ottoman Empire and for an understanding of the post-Habsburg fortunes and misfortunes of the Empire's peoples.

In the Habsburg Empire in the early nineteenth century, and in many provinces as late as the early twentieth century, there was a rough but significant correlation between nationality and social status. There were urban nations and peasant nations (partly but not completely corresponding to what were also described as "historic" and "unhistoric" nations). Later there were middle-class nations and proletarian nations.

It is worth recalling that until the rapid growth of cities, usually only after 1850 and only sometimes associated with industrialization, the towns of the Empire were almost all German in language, culture, and (where such existed) national consciousness. The only significant exceptions were in Galicia and in the

Habsburg possessions in northern Italy and Dalmatia, where ancient and distinguished Polish or Italian communes had not been created or repopulated by German merchant colonists in earlier centuries. The populations of these towns were not necessarily or predominantly ethnic Germans (or Poles or Italians) in origin, however. Their ancestors had usually come from the natural source for urban recruitment for each urban center, its surrounding countryside, which was usually Slav or Magyar [Hungarian] or Romanian. But they had become townspeople in towns founded or restored by German-speaking merchants and artisans and in a German-ruled empire for which German was the language of government and commerce. So they had "become" German (or Polish or Italian) as a part of the process of their urbanization, "forgetting" their ethnic origin in a generation or two. To be urban was to be German or Polish or Italian.

The "national revival" of the peasant nations combined with the accelerated growth of towns characteristic of the nineteenth century, the beginnings of industrialization, and the spread of classic liberalism among the urban middle classes of the Monarchy to challenge this comfortable division. The process began after 1815 in Bohemia, soon to become the industrial center of the Empire, and reached even the still-traditional market towns of remote provinces like the Istrian hinterland and Bukovina by the end of the century. The transition to urban life-styles was made easier if the newcomers, in any case now far more numerous, listened to the teaching of poets and intellectuals of the romantic generation, who had already "rediscovered" their own identities in the peasant nations from which they had sprung, sung of their ancient glories, and preached the equality of their cultures and values with those of the "historic" nations. One could come to Prague or Brno and remain Czech, to Ljubljana or Trieste and remain Slovene, to Bratislava as a Slovak or to Cluj as a Romanian. The peasant became urban without losing his (peasant) national identity, and the German (or Italian or Polish) islands in a Slav or Romanian sea were overwhelmed one by one.

The acute phase of the national question in the Habsburg Empire, marked by growing competition and eventually bitter mutual hatred and incomprehension, was born of this phenomenon. It began as a reactive nationalism among the Germans of the threatened towns, who sought to defend jobs in the bureaucracy or monopolies in local business or the professions against pushy newcomers of alien tongue. The newcomers, inspired by their poets and intellectuals, those romantic generals who had at last found an army, responded with counteroffensive organizations of their own. The struggle was characterized, significantly, by the use of rival cultural institutions, which founded and financed ethnic schools, libraries, banks, marching bands, voluntary fire brigades, and alpine and youth clubs. The style was that of military warfare adapted to the cultural front, and at organizational headquarters "battle" maps were sometimes employed, on which front lines (language borders and ethnically besieged towns) and the disposition of "enemy" institutions were displayed as a basis for strategy. Political clubs and ethnic political parties followed, as the partial triumph of liberalism broadened the franchise enough to make them meaningful.

In many provinces ethnic groups could be identified with social classes on the land as well, with feudatories and large landowners belonging to one nation and peasants to another. German landowners were predominant in Slovene Carniola and Czech Bohemia, Magyars in Slovakia and much of Croatia, Italians in Istria and parts of Dalmatia, Poles in Ukrainian Eastern Galicia, and so on. With the spread of literacy from the towns into the countryside in the last decades before World War I, the new nationalism at last flowed back toward its source among the peasantry of the peasant nations. The latter, learning to read and write in their native dialect, "discovered" their heretofore latent nationality and began, like their urban cousins, to identify social grievances with national grievances. The same phenomenon was repeated in the towns, where the new urban proletariat was usually of different nationality from the older, established capitalists. Demands for land reform, for a wider franchise, or for trade unions consequently became another battleground for ethnic conflict.

Thus the national question masked both a crisis of access and class warfare. In both cases tensions were increased by clashes between differing life-styles and value systems of the participant ethnic groups, formerly segregated by language borders or in separate villages but now rubbing shoulders uncomfortably in city streets and in the proliferating institutions of an industrializing, urbanizing society.

Frustrated desires for personal social mobility, an entrepreneur's, lawyer's, or bureaucrat's fear of competition for business or jobs, a capitalist's fear of organized labor and labor's resentment of the boss's power and prerogatives, the peasant's hatred of the great landowner and the landowner's fear of the peasantry, value clashes between old and newly urbanized, between secularist and clericalist and among Catholic, Protestant, and Orthodox worldviews — all were projected as clashes among nationalities, largely because in any locality the role players in each category could usually be identified with a particular ethnic group. Such a situation was not uniquely East-Central European: almost every society has its Ireland or its excluded minority. But the Habsburg Monarchy was unique in being totally composed of "Irelands" and ethnic minorities.

To understand fully the frustrating subjective difficulties encountered by every later attempted solution of minorities questions in East-Central Europe, one must understand the intensity of emotion that came to surround the question of nationality when every grievance, and perceived injustice, was projected as a national issue. Characteristic of the resultant atmosphere in many parts of the Monarchy is the following description of one ethnically disputed corner of the Empire on the eve of World War I, the city of Trieste and the towns of Istria (Venezia Giulia), which urbanization was then in the process of converting from Italian into Slovene or Croat centers:

> *From this, in the years preceding the other world war, a growing disquiet in the Italian bourgeoisie of Venezia Giulia, an irritability and almost pathological hypertension of national sentiment, which even more than in the preceding decades became a daily atmosphere, almost obsessive in its fixation, in which the Italian of this region lived and to which all value judgments, all measures of merit were referred as to a single motive; the degree of national temperature displayed by each person became the criterion by which his honor and human dignity were judged; the Italian in his particularity took precedence over man in his universality. This hypertrophy of national passion was felt in everything, in social and personal relations, in taste, in judgments concerning the most ordinary mat-*

ters, to which elsewhere no one would think of applying a national criterion of evaluation; this was reflected above all in the cultural climate, impregnated with national passion to the saturation point. . . . [H]ere it is the exasperation of wills which have chosen a single road, a single culture exalted and transfigured into a myth. . . .

Thus the Habsburg national question entered its critical phase.

One of the less-disputed clichés in Habsburg historiography identified four "master nations" in the polyglot Empire's later history: the Germans and Magyars, undoubtedly, and the Poles and Italians, whom some demote to quasi-master nations. These nations are also widely held to have been more deeply infected with the nationalist virus by 1848, meaning that more of their members (or more members of their elites) had caught it, than the Empire's other nationalities. In the revolutions of 1848, or in their Galician rehearsal in 1846, the Magyars and Austria's Poles and Italians attempted to secede. The secession of most of the Monarchy's Italians, to join a new Italian nation-state that would soon be seeking to redeem the *Italiani irredenti* of Trento and Trieste, was consummated with the help of French and Prussian armies in 1859 and 1866. The Magyars' political class, largely synonymous with their large gentry class, exploited the second of these military defeats, which also ended Habsburg pretensions to primacy in Germany, to strike a deal with the Emperor for an autonomy that was tantamount to confederation. The Polish ruling class consolidated its de facto autonomous control of Galicia. Except in Galicia the Monarchy's other "newly awakened" nationalities would henceforth confront two "master nations": the Germans and the Magyars. . . .

A proliferation of proposals for the resolution of the Monarchy's national question accompanied its growing intensity, urgency, and extension to include nationalities . . . and social classes . . . that were latecomers to national consciousness. Most of these schemes never became more than blueprints or the stuff for later myths about what might have been. . . . Three basic strategies, of which two were imposed by the Magyar political class and one by expediency, can be discerned in what actually happened. . . .

[E]ach of the three . . . represented an attempt, in Berthold Sutter's words, "to solve the problem, which after as well as before [1860] consisted in finding a compromise between a strong central power, essential for the maintenance of Austria's Great Power status, and the desire for national development of the individual peoples." . . .

The first derived from the constitutional nature and consequences of the Compromise of 1867 [*Ausgleich*] between the Emperor and the Magyars, whose demands for less than total secession he could not ignore after (and in the hope of avenging) Prussia's victory at Königgrätz. The result was de facto a loose confederation between the Kingdom of Hungary (including Croatia, Transylvania, and all other "historic" lands of the Holy Crown of Saint Stephen) and the Emperor's other possessions. . . .

After 1867 Hungary was in effect an independent state in all except foreign policy, defense, and some limits to its economic sovereignty. . . . Even in these areas the rulers of Hungary enjoyed equality with the Dual Monarchy's [Austria-Hungary] other half, and in practice often more than equality, through the system of delegations mandated by the Compromise.

The *Ausgleich* was an answer to the Magyar question that left other pieces of the Empire's national question (including even the German one) unanswered and in fact harder to resolve. Later attempts to extend this kind of solution to other nations or clusters of nations — as in the idea of "Trialism" in place of Dualism to accommodate the South Slavs — foundered on Magyar opposition and the difficulty of accommodating both South Slavs and Czechs either together or separately. For the Crown and the Magyars, however, the *Ausgleich* they had negotiated was a promising and on balance satisfactory "compromise between [the minimum of] a strong central power essential for the maintenance of Austria's Great Power status," which the leading faction in the Magyars' ruling class had now joined Franz Joseph in desiring, and at least the Magyars' "desire for national development." It was thus a formula that both the Crown . . . and the Magyars could live with, although neither was entirely satisfied, and that others . . . would consider worthy of adaptation to other parts (or indeed the whole) of the Monarchy.

The problem, of course, was that the Kingdom of Hungary

was not a Magyar nation-state and that other potential candidates for equivalent status in a territorial confederation under Habsburg rule were also not national units. This was a problem because the idea of confederation, as a solution to the national question, carried an implicit assumption that the political boundaries of the confederated states would correspond, at least *in grosso modo*, to national boundaries. Everyone knew that this was not the case in Hungary or in most of the Monarchy's other "historic" units. This awareness led some to devise schemes for nonterritorial national autonomy, a secular and national Habsburg version of the Ottoman millet system.[1] Others played with the map, vainly seeking to redesign the boundaries of historic units to correspond to national ones. In the context of a Dualism that could not be generalized into a Habsburg Confederation, these and the rest of the arsenal of hypothetical solutions to multinationalism—coercive or modernization-driven assimilation to a regionally dominant nation, cultural autonomy, legislated minority rights, or some combination of these—would now be considered, and sometimes attempted, within the parameters imposed by Dualism. The spotlight passes to the separate strategies, the Hungarian and Austrian. . . .

The Hungarian strategy was straightforward and basically simple, despite complications imposed by the Nationalities Law of 1868, designed to protect non-Magyar cultures and participation. . . . The rulers of Hungary after the *Ausgleich* sought to create a nation-state on the Western European model—a state for the Magyar (Hungarian) nation, which comprised less than half of the Kingdom's population. . . . National community building, for the rulers of this state, could only be conceived through national assimilation of the non-Magyars (their Magyarization) and the exclusion from effective citizenship of those who resisted. The means they used to achieve this combination of assimilation and exclusion, although some were primarily or equally aimed at more efficient administration or communications through use of a single language, are well known. Hungarian became the exclusive

---

[1]The non-Muslim subject peoples of the Ottoman Empire were organized into confessional communities headed by their religious leaders.—Ed.

state language, despite provisions in the Nationalities Law of 1868 guaranteeing cultural (including linguistic) autonomy to minority districts. The use of local languages and customs in public life was gradually but ruthlessly suppressed. Local autonomy in Transylvania, with its Romanian majority, was finally liquidated. . . . The "historic state's right" of dependent Croatia was eroded, albeit with more difficulty, and major crises in relations with the Croats at the beginning of the twentieth century arose from the extension of the Hungarian language for official use into Croatia as well. The school system was Magyarized almost everywhere, and even the local German majority . . . attended Magyar schools. The prospects of the Slovaks for survival as a nation were particularly bleak: they lacked the cultural and psychological support of fellow nationals organized in a nation-state of their own beyond Hungary's borders, such as the Romanians and Serbs enjoyed; they had no legal and traditional autonomy to defend them, as the Croats did; and their own "national awakening" was among the newest and consequently most traditionless in Central Europe.

Hungarian ethnic policy . . . which was to define the effective community as the Magyar nation and exclude all others, was not, however, racist. "Magyar" was defined culturally (or, as some have suggested, as a class concept), not genetically. Any Jew, German, Slovak, Romanian, Serb, or Croat could "become" a Magyar and so gain admittance to the community defined as nation, with as much social mobility and other perquisites of full citizenship as any lineal descendant of the Magyar horsemen of the tenth century.

This strategy was not without some apparent success. . . . [B]etween 2.5 and three million non-Magyars were assimilated ("became Magyars") between 1780 and 1914, about two million of them in the period between the censuses of 1850 and 1910. The 1780–1914 figure includes one million Germans, over 700,000 Jews, and 500,000 Slovaks. . . .

However, . . . assimilation was an almost exclusively urban phenomenon. The countryside was barely touched by it. Moreover, an identical process and similar magnitudes of urban assimilation to local majority nations (German in Vienna, Czech in Prague, Slovene in Ljubljana, etc.) were being recorded in most other, non-Hungarian parts of the Monarchy. How much of this process in Hungary can therefore be attributed to the Magyars' nationality policies? How much should instead be traced to the imperatives of "modernization," which require learning the language and adapting to the culture that do or may provide access to jobs and opportunity (upward mobility) in modern sectors and a modernizing society? In Hungary these went hand in hand and were mutually supportive, but similar results in [Austria] strongly suggest that state-mandated pressures to assimilate were contributory and facilitative (the latter because they ensured that education, where provided, would be in the language and culture of access rather than a language that inhibited mobility) rather than primary.

The same argument helps to explain the greater millions of non-Magyars, especially those who were also non-Jewish and non-German and usually nonurban, who did not avail themselves of the opportunity or succumb to the pressure to become Magyars. These were mostly of two kinds. The first, which included millions of Magyar as well as non-Magyar peasants, consisted of those who were content, or at least willing, to stay where they were— on the land and in villages and in the social status and categories these places offered. (The reasons might include lack of ambition, fear of change, pessimism about one's prospects or abilities, love of hearth, field, and traditional values, or all of these and more.) The second kind consisted of those whose frustrated hopes and ambitions, focused on the cultural barriers raised by the regime's policies and the Kingdom's alien, "chauvinistic" cities, led them to seek an alternative "at home" in their own culture and land—autonomous, independent, or joined to a nation-state of their own kind beyond the Monarchy's borders. . . . Both rejected assimilation and thus the extension of the Magyar nation to fill and fulfill the Magyar nation-state—although most of Hungary's rulers, content with less if they could continue to rule the whole, did not seem to mind and were very likely relieved. But the second category, growing in number and building the cultural and cooperative infrastructure of their own nationhoods and autonomist, separatist, or irredentist nationalisms, magnified Hungary's national question rather than diminishing it. As a net result the Hungarian countryside, measured in terms of communes gained and lost by the Magyars, became less rather than more Magyar between 1867 and 1918.

The Hungarian strategy of deliberate nation building through a combination of domination, assimilation, and exclusion was simply not feasible, and was never attempted, in the other half of the Dual Monarchy. The Emperor was German-speaking, as was much of the aristocracy. German was the language of the bureaucracy and army, and some of the Germans of the Austrian half of the monarchy sometimes dreamed of Germanizing the land on the Hungarian pattern; but for demographic, historic, and political reasons this was never possible. With its Czechs, Poles, Ukrainians, Slovenes, and Dalmatians, the Austrian half actually had a Slavic majority, but with interests and geographic distribution too diverse to permit effective cooperation or opposition to the Germanic tradition of the court.

With such an ethnic stalemate, the Austrian half of the Empire inevitably remained stubbornly non-national in an age of nationalism. It was ruled, as the historians' clichés have it, by playing the nationalities off against one another to preserve the power of the Crown and its ministers, who did their best to maintain a more-or-less balanced and equitable distribution of dissatisfaction among the more important nationalities.

For most of the participants in this game, it was always clear that this was a nonsolution and a temporary expedient. Surprisingly few of even the most fervent nationalists, however, favored a formal dissolution of their joint community into its ethnic components, until the course of World War I induced them to espouse such a policy. Instead, they devised ingenious schemes, most of them involving a federal solution, for restructuring and "democratizing" the Empire in a way that would grant effective local autonomy to some or all of the nationalities. In acting in this way they were motivated in part by a consciousness of the advantages of belonging to a larger state (and the disadvantages of a "Balkanization" of Central Europe), in part by the practical and political difficulties that would come with any attempt to draw ethnic frontiers in an ethnic patchwork, and in part by a kind of psychological rigidity or traditionalism: the dynastic conglomerate ruled by the Habsburgs had been around so long that a Central Europe without it was almost literally unthinkable.

The failure of every plan to federalize the Austrian half of the Empire, and the key role of the Hungarians in frustrating the more hopeful of them, are well-known. In ethnically mixed provinces, meanwhile, a generally agreed compromise, setting forth the rights of the ethnic communities and mutually satisfactory rules for their public interaction and cooperation, could sometimes be achieved, as was done in Moravia in the 1890s. More frequently, however, agreement was frustrated by an irreducible conflict between the "ethnic" and the "historic" principles, with a province's majority nationality insisting on its "right" to treat the "historic" province as its own national territory. The Czech majority used this argument against the German minority in "historic" Bohemia, and the German majority used it against the Slovene minority in "historic" Styria, with the minority in each case demanding administrative partition or national equality.

The failure to achieve an agreeable solution in places like Bohemia and Styria was further proof of the blind alley in which nineteenth-century European thinking about community definition found itself when the nation-state was generally accepted as the only legitimate focus of loyalty. Even when there was agreement to live together in a larger, multinational state, on the basis of administrative ethnic autonomy, the administrative units could only be thought of as sub-nation-states, within which a national definition of community must be applied. Given the ethnic map, such a conception could only reproduce in miniature, in almost every multinational province, the crisis of the multinational empire.

However, the Austrian strategy of improvisation and ad hoc "fire-fighting" responses to crises on the nationality front is no longer so widely regarded as the rarely mitigated and fateful failure portrayed by most first-generation, post-1918 historians, a failure that combined with Czech and South Slav nationalisms and separatists to make the disintegration of the Empire inevitable. Probably most historians now agree that the inevitability-of-disintegration thesis was usually based . . . at best on a selective and often nationally prejudiced reading of the evidence. It is therefore arguable (and has been argued by those willing to indulge in might-have-been historiography) that the Austrians' supposed penchant for "muddling through," and thereby sometimes

purposefully maintaining a balanced distribution of national grievances and tensions among the Empire's peoples, was not only a
logical nonsolution for an unsolvable national question but
enough to have assured the indefinite survival of the Habsburg's
multinational state — if it had not been destroyed by the dynamics
and outcome of World War I. This thesis also begs many questions, including the war as itself a product of the Monarchy's and
the South Slavs' national questions. However, by calling into
question the inevitability of the Monarchy's disintegration in the
face of its multiple, conflicting nationalisms, it leaves open the
question of whether "the Austrian strategy" could someday and
somewhere . . . provide a sufficient, if never satisfactory, answer.

Hugh Seton-Watson

Nations Against Empires

A new political principle was elaborated in Western Europe during
the eighteenth century. According to this view, the state was based
on the sovereign will of the nation whose members possessed civil
rights. By the nineteenth century this concept had found fertile
ground among educated individuals who were subjects of the empires in Eastern Europe. It was the interaction between this concept
and particular social and political conditions, however, that determined the character of the national movements that developed during the nineteenth century. Hugh Seton-Watson was for many years
a leading historian of Russia and Eastern Europe. Here he discusses
the various ways in which the national idea unfolded in Eastern Europe. The evolution of nationalism depended on the particular social
structure of a people, whether there were traditional elites such as an
aristocracy or new ones that developed from within urban society.
Seton-Watson stresses the role of intellectuals and culture in the
growth of the national movements.

From Hugh Seton-Watson *Nationalism and Communism*, Praeger, 1964, pp. 3–8,
11–20. Reprinted with permission from Reed Consumer Books Ltd.

There have been many great empires in human history, and the subjects of many of these have included people of different religion, language and social customs. But the expression 'multinational empire' can only be used of the period since the birth of the modern concept of secular nationalism. . . .

Nationalism and Legitimacy

In the traditional empires of the past, subjects were expected loyally to obey and serve their ruler, whose position was believed to be sanctioned by divine law. The monarch was the ruler appointed by God, and responsible only to God. He in turn accepted the devotion of his subjects, and had the duty to protect them. This did not, however, imply equality among his subjects. Not only were there social privileges and hierarchies, rich and poor, but whole categories of persons might be regarded as second-class subjects. This was notably the case in Christian and Moslem empires. Here the division was one of religion. . . . This does not necessarily mean that they were persecuted for their religious beliefs, though this did happen from time to time in all these cases. . . .

The principle of nationalism emerged gradually in Western Europe, and was theoretically formulated in revolutionary France. Nationalism is essentially secular and essentially democratic. It gradually replaces (though it does not necessarily completely eliminate) loyalty to the religious community and loyalty to the ruler by loyalty to the nation. . . .

Nationalism, as a political movement, dates from the Revolution of 1789. Thenceforth, it was increasingly claimed that the interests of whole nations (interpreted of course by those who claimed to represent their will) should have first priority in political life, both domestic and international. Nationalism, in fact, provides a new principle of *legitimacy* for government, an alternative to the traditional legitimacy of monarch and religion.

However, the problem then arose, how was one to define the nation. Nationalisms have become an effective force only where there has been national consciousness among at least an important section of the people concerned. The growth of national consciousness always precedes the birth of nationalism. Historically this growth has had different origins in different countries.

The Growth of National Consciousness

In the oldest nations, national consciousness was *the product of the State and the monarchy*. England and France are the obvious examples. The English monarchy arose from the union of a number of Saxon kingdoms, and was later strengthened by the Norman conquest. The French monarchy resulted from the extension of the power of the Capetian kings from their original small territorial base in the Ile de France. In both cases the monarch had to struggle against powerful regional forces as well as independent-minded social *élites*. In both cases the subjects of the monarch included people of several languages. . . .

National consciousness can also be preserved by the memory of a State. Poland is the obvious case. Throughout 150 years of partition, the Polish educated classes (nobility, priests, and secular intellectuals) kept alive the tradition of Polish patriotism. The same is true of Hungary from 1526 to 1867: the period of foreign rule was longer, but the foreign rulers made less determined efforts to destroy the patriotism than in the case of the Poles. . . .

Natural consciousness has been *derived from religion* in the case of peoples ruled by foreigners whose religion is different from their own. . . . The subject peoples of the Ottoman Empire in the Balkans always regarded themselves as distinct from their rulers: they were Christians, and the rulers were Moslems. For a long time 'Christian' was more or less identified with 'Greek', since the great Christian State of the Balkans, the Byzantine Empire, had been a Greek State, and the Orthodox hierarchy was in Greek hands. The medieval Serbian State had been independent of Constantinople until the Turkish conquest, and after the conquest many Serbs found refuge under Austrian rule. Thus the Serbs were never so subject to Greek influence as the other Balkan Orthodox. It was not until the mid-nineteenth century that the Roumanians and Bulgarians acquired a national consciousness, in relation to the Greeks, comparable to the religious consciousness which they had always had in relation to the Turks. . . .

The last category on which national consciousness has been based, and in modern times by far the most important, is *language*. In the old nations of Europe, national consciousness grew from other roots, despite diversity of language, but the national language was forged in the process, and became the expression of a nationality which was already there. Thus, the English, French, Spanish, and Russian languages have become the expression of nationality and patriotism. . . . In more modern national movements, which began on the basis of a sense of distinction from the rulers, based on religion, further differentiation has taken place on the basis of language. This process has clearly been connected with cultural and social secularization, with the declining influence of religion on society. There have even been some cases of nationalities artificially created on the basis of languages, not only by nationalist intellectuals or politicians but even by imperial governments seeking to disrupt nationalist movements directed against themselves.

In the Ottoman Empire, the Roumanians and Bulgarians became aware, during the nineteenth century, that they were different from the Greeks, because they spoke different languages. The struggle against Greek supremacy was conducted in the economic field and within the ecclesiastical hierarchy. . . . Linguistic distinction was the main basis of nationalism, but it was buttressed by claims based on romantic interpretations of history. . . .

The relative importance, in the development of the national consciousness of each nation, of these different factors — monarchy, state machine, historical memory, religion and language — largely determined the relative importance of different social classes in the leadership of each nationalist movement. Monarchs and aristocracies played a leading part in England and France. In cases where historical memory was preserved unbroken under foreign rule, such as Poland [and] Hungary, . . . surviving social *élites* — landowners [and] Catholic priests . . . were decisive. . . . In countries where national consciousness has been derived from some combination of the religious and linguistic factors — and these form the great majority of cases in the last hundred years — the dominant social group has been the intellectual *élite*. One must here stress the vital distinction between the traditional *élite*, which in nearly all such cases has been the priesthood, and the modern *élite*, which is derived from a secular system of education introduced from Western Europe. . . . Both the traditional and the modern *élite* have been concerned with the religious factor, but whereas the traditionalists have usually been content with negative and sterile opposition to the foreign rulers, the modern *élites* have sought to modernize religious institutions and even religious thought, in order to strengthen the people's capacity to resist the foreigner. . . .

Language was, however, the principal instrument of the modern *élite* in the East European empires and the Middle East. In these countries the development of linguistic nationalism steadily strengthened the importance of the modern *élite* — or intelligentsia — within the nationalist movements. . . .

It is a general characteristic of all those nationalist movements of the last hundred years which have arisen within an 'underdeveloped' social and economic framework, that they have been led by a modern secular *élite* or intelligentsia. It is necessary here to say something of this social group, and to give some historical examples of its leadership.

The Intelligentsia

Intelligentsia is a Russian word, and it is in nineteenth-century Russia that the phenomenon first appeared. . . . But the intelligentsia is not a specifically Russian phenomenon. It is something which is to be found in all societies which have been forced at a late stage into the processes of modernization. . . . The intelligentsia is a modern secular intellectual *élite* which, unlike those of the Western nations, has not grown up organically with its society — as happened in the West between the sixteenth and nineteenth centuries — but has been deliberately created by rulers who have set themselves the political task of bringing their countries at forced speed into the modern world. Inevitably this small new modern *élite* finds itself isolated from the great mass of its compatriots. Where the political system is autocratic or oligarchical, as in Imperial Russia or the Ottoman Empire, the contrast between the political ideas which the intelligentsia has learnt as part of its modern education, and the brutal political reality, still further increases the frustration caused by the social and cultural isolation. . . .

Whether recruited from landed nobility, free professions, the army, or even from merchant families, the intelligentsia form the distinct social group, which has had a distinct political role to play. The issue is only confused if one speaks, as has become fashionable for example in recent years in regard to Latin America, of a 'middle class'. The point about societies in process of forced modernization is that they do not possess *a* middle class, or a bourgeoisie, but several middle classes, distinct in outlook and origin from each other, and not united, as the West European bourgeoisie became united between the end of the Middle Ages and the Industrial Revolution, by a common ethos. The politically significant and operative group is the intelligentsia, and it is this group which has provided the leadership of social and national revolutionary movements.

The Intelligentsia in Nationalist Movements

In the Habsburg Monarchy in the nineteenth century the Czech and Hungarian nationalist movements do not fit this pattern. The Czechs were the only nation of the Monarchy, apart from the Germans, who had a more or less homogeneous bourgeoisie of the Western type, uniting all the middle classes with a common bourgeois ethos. It was this bourgeoisie which led the Czech national movement. . . . The Hungarian nationalist movement, however, up to 1867 was led by the nobility. Its leaders included persons of noble origin who were employed in an intellectual profession: Louis Kossuth himself is an example.[1] But essentially the strength of the movement lay in the landowning class rather than the intellectual *élite* as such. Among the Croats and the Galician Poles, both intelligentsia and landed nobility had a part to play. The Croats of Dalmatia also possessed a bourgeoisie in the Western sense, formed by centuries of overseas trade under Venetian rule. Among the remaining national movements within

---

[1]Louis Kossuth (1802–1894) was a defender of Hungarian national rights and a leading figure in the revolutionary events of 1848–1849 — Ed.

the Monarchy—the Slovenes, Slovaks, Roumanians, and Serbs—the role of the intelligentsia was overwhelming. The leaders were lawyers, journalists, school-teachers, priests, and pastors. It should also be noted that, as methods of government in the Monarchy were much more liberal than in Russia, and as the differences between the ruling Germans and Hungarians and the subject nationalities were much less sharp, . . . the distinction between intelligentsia and intellectuals, discussed above, has less validity. Rather, perhaps, one should say that the leaders of these nationalist movements came from the intellectual professions. . . .

In the Ottoman Empire, the role of the intelligentsia was more important in the later than the earlier movements. The leaders of the Serbian risings of 1804 and 1815 were local notables, prosperous farmers with little former education. At this time there hardly existed a Serbian intelligentsia in Ottoman Serbia, unless the Orthodox priesthood be so considered, but among the Serbs of the Monarchy, across the rivers Sava and Danube, the number of persons with a modern education was considerable. The leaders of the Greek struggle for independence included merchants, aristocrats, intellectuals, and local notables of the same type as in Serbia. In the preparation of the movement, which was much longer and more systematic than in the Serbian case, the Greek intelligentsia played a predominant role. In Roumania the intelligentsia played a decisive part in the revival of national consciousness, connected with the development and purification of the Roumanian language. But Roumanian independence was achieved not by a national struggle against the Turks but by the intervention of the European Powers. Insofar as Roumanians played a part in these events, the most important social group was the landowning aristocracy. Bulgarian independence too was achieved by external action, by the Russian army. But in Bulgaria there was also a national rising, heroic but pitifully ineffective. This rising was prepared and led by conspirators who provide a classic example of a revolutionary intelligentsia. They were indeed in contact with the Russian revolutionary intelligentsia of the 1870s. The last revolutionary nationalist movements among the Christians of the Ottoman Empire took place in Macedonia at the end of the century. These were led by elements of the intelligentsia, largely village school teachers or priests or children of priests. The Macedonian movements can, however, hardly be regarded as 'pure' nationalist movements, since they were largely controlled by the Governments of the neighbouring states of Bulgaria, Serbia, and Greece, each of which was pursuing territorial aims hostile not only to the Ottoman Empire but also to the other states. Nationalist movements, based on language, arose much later among the Moslem peoples of the Ottoman Empire. The Albanians were led by tribal chiefs or landowning *beys*. . . .

. . . In Russian Poland the intelligentsia was the most active element. Its importance was increased by the fact that after the rebellions of 1830 and 1863 many Polish landowners lost their properties, and Poles of noble birth, being excluded from public service as they were not considered reliable by the Russians, and scorning business as an unworthy occupation for noblemen, had no other opportunity open to them but the intellectual professions. It was this Polish intelligentsia, largely though not wholly of noble origin, which provided the political leadership of the Russian Poles. Even the socialist movement which developed from the 1890s had among its leaders such noblemen as Joseph Piłsudski.[2] . . .

The role of the intelligentsia does not cease with the attainment of national independence. The experience of the Balkan states is here of interest. The revolutionary intelligentsia which had played a heroic part in the struggle for Bulgarian freedom in 1876 provided many of the rulers of the new state. This generation became rich and self-satisfied, and began to rule with methods not so different from those of the Turkish pashas whom they had replaced. The next generation revolted against the *embourgeoisement* of their elders, and turned to the ideas of social revolution. The social injustices and political repression, the gulf between the upper layer and the masses and the contrast between modern democratic principles and the reality of their country . . .

[2] Józef Piłsudski (1867–1935) was a Polish soldier and statesman. He led Polish forces against the Bolsheviks in 1919–1920. His dislike of political instability led him to stage a military coup in 1926. Piłsudski remained minister of war until his death and was the power behind the political scene. —Ed.

operated for many decades in the liberated Balkan states. At the same time, however, the Balkan intellectual youth were held back from subversive action against their governments by the nationalist issue. Every one of the new Balkan states had an *irridenta*, had claims for territory against the Habsburg or Russian Empire or against the remnant of the Ottoman Empire. In the face of the national enemy, even the revolutionaries — or at least a very large part of them — could be persuaded in a crisis to rally round the Government. This state of affairs even continued after the First World War. In these years the social and political problems still remained unsolved. The gap between rulers and masses had still not been closed, political freedom still not achieved. The intellectual youth thus continued to be radical or revolutionary, to denounce the régimes in power. Yet every one of the East European states either had an *irridenta* or was concerned to maintain its swollen frontiers against its neighbours' claims. . . .

Official Nationalism as the New Legitimacy

We have noted that the growth of nationalism in nineteenth-century Europe undermined the traditional basis of legitimacy. Looking back today we can say that the imperial governments were faced with the decision whether to stick to the old principles of legitimacy, or to try to create a secular ideology of state to replace the diminishing loyalty to a divinely sanctioned monarch. The Habsburg Emperors, in the 'Austrian' part of their dominions and the Ottoman Sultans in Europe and Asia, made no such attempt. Loyalty to the dynasty remained until the end the only claim, and the only non-material bond holding the diverse subjects together. It must be admitted that this bond remained effective until a remarkably late date. Many Ottoman Christians remained loyal to the Sultan until late in the nineteenth century, and *Kaisertreue* was a real factor even among many Czechs, South Slavs, and Roumanians until 1918. . . .

The traditional principles of legitimacy did not, however, save the Habsburg [or] Ottoman . . . empires. When the opportunity came to achieve independence, the nationalist leaders seized it and their compatriots followed them. The Ottoman Sultans were defeated in a series of wars, and on more than one occasion were compelled by the European Powers to surrender territory even when they had not been defeated. The Habsburgs lost their empire through defeat in one world war. . . .

Instrumental in the creation of Czechoslovakia, Thomas Masaryk
attempted to forge a nation of Czechs and Slovaks. The multinational
state's first president, shown here in 1930, Masaryk looked to the West and
actively promoted tolerance and social justice in the country, which
remained the only democracy in Eastern Europe in the 1930s.
(UPI/Bettmann Newsphotos)

II

The New Europe: Civic Ideal and Nationalist Imperatives

Thomas Masaryk

The Principle of Nationality

In the aftermath of the Great War, the Habsburg and Ottoman empires disappeared. They were replaced by entirely new successor states such as Czechoslovakia and Yugoslavia or, like Romania and Bulgaria, by countries that had come into existence just a few decades before. To Thomas Masaryk — a professor at the University in Prague, a member of the Austrian parliament before World War I, and ultimately a leader of Czechoslovak independence and unity — this development represented the fulfillment of the national ideal.

From Thomas Masaryk, *The New Europe*, 2nd ed., Bucknell University Press, 1972, pp. 55, 59–65, 77–81, 83–86. Reprinted by permission of Associated University Presses.

Peoples who had once been the subjects of foreign and authoritarian rulers could now look to a future of progress and development as citizens of sovereign national states.

Masaryk, who became the first president of the Czechoslovak Republic, embodied the ideals of enlightened and tolerant self-rule in Europe. He well knew the problems inherent in joining nations into new states that were bound to include minorities. Yet he struck an optimistic note for the future when he expressed his views on the principle of nationality in the fall of 1918.

The demand of the Allies for a proper consideration for the small nations as well as for the great, resulted from the recognition of the principle of nationality. In order to have a proper understanding of the war and to have a just basis for the conclusion of a lasting peace, it is very important that the principle of nationality should be made clear. . . .

The principle of nationality is a distinctive and very powerful feeling; it is the love for the mother tongue and for the group of men speaking the same or very closely related language, and for the soil on which this group lives, and for the manner in which it lives. But this love is not only the feeling arising out of the natural habitual life, but it is also an idea of conscious love; nations have their own cultural and political program growing out of a common history and in its turn directing this history; it is modern patriotism in this wide and complicated sense, different from the old patriotism of loyalty to the dynasty and ruling classes. There is a real principle of nationality, the ideal of nations and not merely national feeling or instinct. . . .

It is very important for the understanding and appreciation of the principle of nationality to determine more exactly the relation of the nation to the state. . . . It is my opinion that nation and nationality should be held to be the aim of social effort, while the state should be the means; *de facto*, every self-conscious nation tries to have its own state.

The principle of nationality is comparatively new and unsettled, whereas the state is a very old institution and so universal that many for that very reason look upon it as the most necessary and most valuable achievement of human society.

There are 27 states in Europe (the German states, 26 in number, are not counted here, and Austria-Hungary is counted as one state), but there are more than twice that many nations in Europe. . . . This contrast between the boundaries of states and nations, and the fact that the nations in the mixed states are striving for independence, indicate that the states arose by conquest. . . . Thus arose the modern absolutist states; but in opposition to them and within them, democracy gained strength. So at the present stage of political development, monarchical theocracies and the beginnings of democracy stand opposed to each other. . . .

One of the powerful democratic forces is the national movement: the striving of subject nations for political independence and their striving for the recognition of their nationality as a higher and more valuable principle than the state. In Prussia, Austria, Russia, Turkey, the national movements naturally fought against absolutism, and absolutism was the enemy of nationalism.

The difference between the Allies and the Central Powers is the difference between democracy and theocratic monarchies. . . . The Allies declare for the rights of nations and self-determination, the state thus being made subordinate to nationality; the Central Powers are nonnational and even anti-national.

Nationality might have become political power merely as a historical fact, but the Allies recognize the *right* to self-determination of nations. President Wilson declared that no nation shall be forced to have a government which is not its own nor for its own interests. . . .

According to the program of the Allies, the small nations and states shall be treated with the same respect politically and socially as the great nations and states. A small nation, an enlightened and culturally progressing nation, is just as much a full-fledged unit and cultural individual as a great nation. The problem of small nations and states is the same as the problem of the so-called small man; what matters is that the value of the man, the individuality of the man, is recognized without regard to his material means. This is the proper sense and kernel of the great humanitarian movement which characterizes modern times, as manifested in socialism, democracy, and nationalism. The modern humanit[arian]ism recognizes the right of the weak. . . . Every-

where the weak, oppressed, and exploited unite themselves—
association is the watchword of our era: federation, the free federation of small nations and states will be the consummation
of this principle securing the final organization of the whole
of mankind. . . .

That the smaller and small nations should become independent is
not contrary to the tendency of the development which makes interstate and international relations ever closer and closer; individuals and nations, it is true, have a direct need for union with others, and history aims at the organization of all mankind.

This historical development is a double process: together with
the individualization of all departments the organization of individuals is taking place. Politically expressed, there is going on the
development of autonomy and self-government of individuals,
classes, nations; and at the same time individuals, classes, and nations are uniting closer, are being organized and centralized. This
process goes on within the nations themselves, but also between
one nation and another—interstatism and internationalism become more intimate. Europe emphatically tends toward a conti-
nental organization.

The principle of nationality stands alongside the international
(interstate) principle. The European nations, while becoming indi-
vidualized, tend to draw closer together economically and with respect to communication (railroads, and so forth) and their entire
technical culture; but individualization and centralization are
deepened also spiritually by a growing interchange of ideas and of
all culture (knowledge of foreign languages, translation, and the
like). Europe and humanity are becoming more unified.

Between nationality and internationality there is no antagonism, but on the contrary, agreement: nations are the natural organs of humanity. Humanity is not supernational, it is the organization of individual nations. If, therefore, individual nations
struggle for their independence and attempt to break up states of
which they have heretofore been parts, that is not a fight against
internationality and humanity, but a fight against aggressors, who
misuse states for the purposes of leveling them and enforcing political uniformity. . . .

Political independence is for an enlightened, civilized nation a vital need — politically dependent nations have even in the most civilized states been oppressed and exploited economically and socially. The more thoughtful and energetic the nation, the more it feels its subjection. . . .

Europe has been organized by states and churches and has been organized in days when the principle of nationality was not accorded the recognition that it obtains in modern times, and for that reason, as was already pointed out, nearly all the states are nationally mixed, and are now disturbed by the problem of nationality.

Many statesmen of a conservative turn of mind, while admitting the justice of the principle of nationality, advocate a nonradical solution of national problems; and they agree to the formation of certain new national states, but favor the maintenance, as far as possible, of the political *status quo* by proposing to solve the national problems to the largest possible extent by national and language autonomy.

. . . It is true that some nations, smaller and less highly developed, would be satisfied with autonomy, at least for the time being; it is true that there are several nations that have no national and political aspirations at all. . . . But it is not a question of nations like these, but rather of nations who will not be satisfied with autonomy in a foreign state and who demand political independence.

If Europe is to be truly democratic, and if we are to have a permanent peace, a more radical solution of national problems is necessary. Nevertheless, as things are, it is to be expected that even in the reconstructed Europe there will be national minorities, and therefore mixed states. The problem is to make these minorities as small as possible. But when two nations (Belgium) or three (Switzerland), themselves decide to maintain their mixed state, the will of such national parts will surely be respected.

National difficulties and struggles are to a large extent questions of national minorities. . . . Very important is the problem of minorities scattered here and there on territory of another nation, as in cities or industrial centers. Such minorities will remain even in the reconstructed states. The rule for reconstruction must be to have the minorities as small as practicable, and to have them protected in their civic rights. It would therefore be desirable that the Peace Congress should adopt an international agreement for the protection of national minorities; perhaps there could be erected an international arbitration tribunal for national questions. . . .

The delimitation of ethnographic frontiers will be governed by the parliamentary and democratic principle. For example, in restored Poland and Bohemia there will be German minorities; in Bohemia these minorities will be considerable; but the number of German population in free Poland and free Bohemia will be far smaller than the number of Poles and Czechs in Polish and Czech territories at present under German and Austrian rule. Poles and Czechs are equal to the Germans in rights and worth; the Germans are not superior to them, and it is therefore more equitable than the present condition that there should be in Poland and Bohemia German minorities that will be smaller than the present Slav bodies oppressed by the Germans. . . .

The settlement of ethnographic boundaries after the storm of war will possibly be provisional in some cases; as soon as the nations quiet down and accept the principle of self-determination, a rectification of ethnographic boundaries and minorities will be carried out without excitement and with due consideration of all questions involved.

The Minorities Treaty for Poland

As part of the Paris peace settlement at the end of the Great War, the Allied powers negotiated agreements with the governments of Poland, Czechoslovakia, Yugoslavia, Romania, and Greece that aimed to protect the rights of minorities. Some of the same provi-

From H.W.V. Temperley (ed.), *A History of the Peace Conference of Paris*, Hodder and Stoughton, 1921, V. 5, pp. 437–442.

sions were introduced in the peace treaties with Austria, Hungary, Bulgaria, and the Ottoman Empire. By these agreements, the Allied leaders hoped to ensure just treatment for the millions of people who now lived in states in which they were not members of the major nationality. They were classified as racial, linguistic, or religious minorities, and their rights were to be guaranteed by the newly established League of Nations. The treaty with the new state of Poland was signed on June 28, 1919.

The United States of America, the British Empire, France, Italy and Japan, on the one hand, confirming their recognition of the Polish State, constituted within the said limits as a sovereign and independent member of the Family of Nations, and being anxious to ensure the execution of the provisions of Article 93 of the said Treaty of Peace with Germany;

Poland, on the other hand, desiring to conform her institutions to the principles of liberty and justice, and to give a sure guarantee to the inhabitants of the territory over which she has assumed sovereignty. . . .

After having exchanged their full powers, found in good and due form, have agreed as follows:

Chapter I

Article 1.

Poland undertakes that the stipulations contained in Articles 2 to 8 of this Chapter shall be recognized as fundamental laws, and that no law, regulation or official action shall conflict or interfere with these stipulations, nor shall any law, regulation or official action prevail over them.

Article 2.

Poland undertakes to assure full and complete protection of life and liberty to all inhabitants of Poland without distinction of birth, nationality, language, race or religion.

All inhabitants of Poland shall be entitled to the free exercise, whether public or private, of any creed, religion or belief, whose practices are not inconsistent with public order or public morals.

Article 3.

Poland admits and declares to be Polish nationals *ipso facto* and without the requirement of any formality German, Austrian, Hungarian or Russian nationals habitually resident at the date of the coming into force of the present Treaty in territory which is or may be recognised as forming part of Poland, but subject to any provisions in the Treaties of Peace with Germany or Austria respectively relating to persons who became residents in such territory after a specified date.

Nevertheless, the persons referred to above who are over eighteen years of age will be entitled under the conditions contained in the said Treaties to opt for any other nationality which may be open to them. Option by a husband will cover his wife and option by parents will cover their children under eighteen years of age.

Persons who have exercised the above right to opt must, except where it is otherwise provided in the Treaty of Peace with Germany, transfer within the succeeding twelve months their place of residence to the State for which they have opted. They will be entitled to retain their immovable property in Polish territory. They may carry with them their movable property of every description. No export duties may be imposed upon them in connection with the removal of such property.

Article 4.

Poland admits and declares to be Polish nationals *ipso facto* and without the requirement of any formality persons of German, Austrian, Hungarian or Russian nationality who were born in the said territory of parents habitually resident there, even if at the date of the coming into force of the present Treaty they are not themselves habitually resident there.

Nevertheless, within two years after the coming into force of the present Treaty, these persons may make a declaration before the competent Polish authorities in the country in which they are resident, stating that they abandon Polish nationality, and they will then cease to be considered as Polish nationals. In this connection a declaration by a husband will cover his wife, and a declaration by parents will cover their children under eighteen years of age.

Article 5.

Poland undertakes to put no hindrance in the way of the exercise of the right which the persons concerned have, under the Treaties concluded or to be concluded by the Allied and Associated Powers with Germany, Austria, Hungary or Russia, to choose whether or not they will acquire Polish nationality.

Article 6.

All persons born in Polish territory who are not born nationals of another State shall *ipso facto* become Polish nationals.

Article 7.

All Polish nationals shall be equal before the law and shall enjoy the same civil and political rights without distinction as to race, language or religion.

Differences of religion, creed or confession shall not prejudice any Polish national in matters relating to the enjoyment of civil or political rights, as for instance admission to public employments, functions and honours, or the exercise of professions and industries.

No restriction shall be imposed on the free use by any Polish national of any language in private intercourse, in commerce, in religion, in the press or in publications of any kind, or at public meetings.

Notwithstanding any establishment by the Polish Government of an official language, adequate facilities shall be given to Polish nationals of non-Polish speech for the use of their language, either orally or in writing, before the courts.

Article 8.

Polish nationals who belong to racial, religious or linguistic minorities shall enjoy the same treatment and security in law and in fact as the other Polish nationals. In particular they shall have an equal right to establish, manage, and control at their own expense charitable, religious and social institutions, schools and other educational establishments, with the right to use their own language and to exercise their religion freely therein.

Article 9.

Poland will provide in the public educational system in towns and districts in which a considerable proportion of Polish nationals of other than Polish speech are residents adequate facilities for ensuring that in the primary schools the instruction shall be given to the children of such Polish nationals through the medium of their own language. This provision shall not prevent the Polish Government from making the teaching of the Polish language obligatory in the said schools.

In towns and districts where there is a considerable proportion of Polish nationals belonging to racial, religious or linguistic minorities, these minorities shall be assured an equitable share in the enjoyment and application of the sums which may be provided out of public funds under the State, municipal or other budget, for educational, religious or charitable purposes.

The provisions of this Article shall apply to Polish citizens of German speech only in that part of Poland which was German territory on August 1, 1914.

Article 10.

Educational Committees appointed locally by the Jewish communities of Poland will, subject to the general control of the State, provide for the distribution of the proportional share of public funds allocated to Jewish schools in accordance with Article 9, and for the organisation and management of these schools.

The provisions of Article 9 concerning the use of languages in schools shall apply to these schools.

Article 11.

Jews shall not be compelled to perform any act which constitutes a violation of their Sabbath, nor shall they be placed under any disability by reason of their refusal to attend courts of law or to perform any legal business on their Sabbath. This provision however shall not exempt Jews from such obligations as shall be imposed upon all other Polish citizens for the necessary purposes of military service, national defence or the preservation of public order.

Poland declares her intention to refrain from ordering or permitting elections, whether general or local, to be held on a Saturday, nor will registration for electoral or other purposes be compelled to be performed on a Saturday.

Article 12.

Poland agrees that the stipulations in the foregoing Articles, so far as they affect persons belonging to racial, religious or linguistic minorities, constitute obligations of international concern and shall be placed under the guarantee of the League of Nations. They shall not be modified without the assent of a majority of the Council of the League of Nations. The United States, the British Empire, France, Italy and Japan hereby agree not to withhold their assent from any modification in these Articles which is in due form assented to by a majority of the Council of the League of Nations.

Poland agrees that any Member of the Council of the League of Nations shall have the right to bring to the attention of the Council any infraction, or any danger of infraction, of any of these obligations, and that the Council may thereupon take such action and give such direction as it may deem proper and effective in the circumstances.

Poland further agrees that any difference of opinion as to questions of law or fact arising out of these Articles between the Polish Government and any one of the Principal Allied and Associated Powers or any other Power, a Member of the Council of the League of Nations, shall be held to be a dispute of an international character under Article 14 of the Covenant of the League of Nations. The Polish Government hereby consents that any such dispute shall, if the other party thereto demands, be referred to the Permanent Court of International Justice. The decision of

the Permanent Court shall be final and shall have the same force
and effect as an award under Article 13 of the Covenant.

Alfred Cobban

National Self-Determination and the Peace Treaties of 1919

In his Fourteen Points, President Woodrow Wilson proclaimed that a
just and lasting postwar settlement needed to be based on the principle of national self-determination. When the Allied leaders and their
advisers gathered in Paris to draw up the peace treaties signed in 1919
and 1920, they had to take a host of other considerations into account
as well.

As World War II ended, Professor Alfred Cobban, a leading
British historian of modern France at the time, examined the problem of implementing the principle of national self-determination in
creating new and often small nation-states. Cobban believed that the
"New Europe" that had emerged from the peace conference was not
the realization of the ideal of national self-determination. Rather, it
was the result of the interaction between a few basic principles held
by the Allied leaders and problems of the time, such as competing territorial claims by the leaders of national groups and the difficulty of
determining the popular will of peoples.

From *The Nation State and National Self-Determination* by Alfred Cobban, Apollo
Editions, 1945, rev. 1969, pp. 57–58, 63, 65–71, 73–84. Copyright © in this revised
edition 1969 by Muriel Cobban. Reprinted by permission of HarperCollins Publishers, Inc.

Allied Policy and the Principle
of Self-Determination

When the Peace Conference opened in 1919, its leading principle, or so the world thought, was to be self-determination for all nations. . . . To the tribes of man, sickened by four years of carnage, the product of a generation of imperialism and centuries of power politics, it appeared as the light of salvation, beaconing humanity onwards to a happier future. . . .

. . . It is true that there were demands in the Fourteen Points which were hardly reconcilable in practice with self-determination, and that the Americans and British . . . did not contemplate its application to colonial populations. It is also true that the difficulties involved in a consistent working-out of the principle were not entirely ignored in all quarters before the Peace Conference. But the important fact is that world opinion certainly thought that the victorious Allies were committed to the principle of self-determination in its most absolute form, and expected it to be clearly and unequivocally put into practice. . . . The statesmen who assembled in Paris had fewer illusions. They had used the appeal to self-determination as an instrument of war, not necessarily hypocritically; but not many were anxious to apply it where it conflicted with the interests of their own states in drawing up the terms of peace. . . . The key to the understanding of Wilson's conception of self-determination is the fact that for him it was entirely a corollary of democratic theory. . . . Self-determination was to Wilson almost another word for popular sovereignty. In this he followed the French and the American, rather than the British, political tradition. . . .

It was because he was firmly convinced of the goodness of the people's will that he believed in the possibility of building up a new and better international order on the basis of national sovereignty, in which he assumed the democratic will of the people to be embodied. . . .

The fundamental weakness of Wilson's ideas was his failure to realise how indeterminate a criterion nationality might be, and how little assistance it might sometimes give in deciding actual frontiers. Although he had spoken of self-determination as though it were an absolute principle of international right, from the very beginning he perforce allowed competing principles to influence his decisions and derogate from its claims. Even in the Fourteen Points he had introduced reservations in favour of historically established allegiances in the Balkans and in Poland, and had promised to both Poland and Serbia free access to the sea, as something justifiable in itself, without specific reference to the wishes of the populations affected. . . .

Practical Difficulties in the Application of Self-Determination

. . . Turning from theory to practice, even if it had been desired to adopt a strict policy of self-determination all round in 1919, we may argue that it would not have been possible. We shall be looking at the question in the wrong perspective if we imagine the Allies sitting down with a blank map of Europe, a list of principles, and a free hand in drawing up the new frontiers. In many cases the claims had already been staked out and occupied and only military action on a large scale could have ousted the new possessors.

Another difficulty was that the great powers in making their decisions, although in a few instances they sent commissions of inquiry to ascertain as far as possible the actual sentiments and composition of the populations concerned, inevitably took in most cases one or another group of national leaders as representative of the wishes of each nationality. The assumption that the point of view of the nationalist leaders was identical with that of the whole nationality was in some cases a grave injustice. While peoples such as the Czechs, Serbs, and Poles were well organised and adequately represented, some of the lesser nations, or subnations, which were only just beginning to emerge into political consciousness, had views attributed to them which may possibly have represented the ideas of only a small section. . . .

Three other major obstacles emerged to the practical application of the principle of self-determination. In the first place, as has been said, the Allies had no intention of applying self-determination at the expense of their own empires. Secondly, it proved impossible, in altering frontiers or setting up new states, to avoid creating new minorities. These two weaknesses in the settlement were only fully appreciated in the years that followed the Peace Conference. Thirdly, and this was a point of immediate importance, there was the difficulty of discovering a generally valid definition of the conditions a nation should satisfy before it could legitimately claim a right of self-determination.

In this last difficulty was implicit the basic problem of the whole policy of self-determination: to what kind of community should it apply? . . . The leaders of the nations that were to form the successor states of Austria-Hungary took the . . . view . . . that when President Wilson spoke of the self-determination of nations 'his thoughts never went as far as the small communities.' . . . In practice, it is true, the disintegrating process of self-determination had to be stopped at some point or other. But on what principle could that point be fixed? The advocates of the new states were hard put to it to discover an answer to this question.

Closely allied with this problem was that of discovering some means of deciding when a number of affiliated communities constituted a nation, and could therefore properly be grouped together in a single state. There was a general tendency to believe that language was an adequate test of nationality. . . . Unfortunately the exceptions were extensive enough to rob the language criterion of much of its practical value. Nor was it universally accepted by the nations claiming self-determination. Each nation clung to the language test where its effect was favourable, and rejected it where it worked against the national interest. . . .

The Use of Plebiscites

If language was not a safe guide, there was certainly no other objective test of nationality on which the conference could fall back. Logically, therefore, if it wished to apply the principle of self-determination, it should have taken a popular vote wherever the issue was in doubt. . . .

The number of plebiscites that were in fact held was many fewer than might have been expected. . . . [T]he connexion between the principle of self-determination and the plebiscitary device is so close that the causes of the failure to employ it more extensively should be examined. . . . In general the opposition to the plebiscitary mode of determining the future of communities came from the victorious Allies, especially from the lesser states, while the demand for plebiscites was a defensive weapon employed by the defeated powers. . . .

The simplest explanation of these changes of policy would be that each side was prepared to appeal to the principle when it assisted in the defence of national interests, and to discard it when its influence was no longer favourable. But it is also true that, however carelessly leading politicians may have spoken, even those who most sincerely accepted the principle of self-determination at Versailles did not expect it to be applied with no regard to other considerations. Even where plebiscites were held they were not regarded as the only factor to be considered in the construction of frontier lines. . . .

The new states that were constituted by the Peace settlement, as might have been expected from all that has been said, were far from embodying the strict principle of self-determination. The union of Slovaks with Czechs represented an aspiration towards national identity, rather than an existent fact. In the same state the Ruthenes were treated practically as a colonial population, and there was only a pretence at consulting their wishes; while the Bohemian Germans were also included willy-nilly in the new state. Similarly in Poland a large Ukrainian and White Russian population was annexed, regardless of its wishes or natural affiliations, though it is true that the parts east of the Curzon line were taken by the Poles on their own responsibility and not by a decision of the Peace Conference. The new Roumania included millions of Magyars and a large body of Saxon Germans, as well as other non-Roumanian elements. The wishes of the partners in the Triune Kingdom [Yugoslavia] were more adequately represented, but even here it is doubtful if the Croats would have accepted the union if it had not been for fear of Italian aggression. . . .

The Substitute for Self-Determination

It remains to ask how it has come about, if the settlement was not founded on self-determination, that it was believed to be so founded, perhaps even by many of those who drew it up, who were presumably not unaware of the wide divergences from the ideal. The answer to this question is to be found in the hardly noticed substitution in the peace negotiations of an allied but different set of ideals for that of self-determination. It would be superficial cynicism to maintain that the diplomats at Paris were moved by none but self-interested motives, and that no guiding principles inspired their work, apart from those represented in the establishment of the League of Nations. . . . They had certain ideals which they perhaps unconsciously put in the place of self-determination; these were—a belief in small states as a justifiable part of the international order, a belief in the equality of states, great or small, and a belief in the right of absolute national sovereignty.

1. Belief in Small States

It is not difficult to account for the dominance of this idea over the policy of the Allies. Great Britain had a long tradition of friendship with the smaller states and nations of Europe—Portugal, Greece, Belgium, Piedmont, Denmark could provide illustrations of positive aid, or at least sympathy. . . . President Wilson, shortly before the United States also entered the war, had started his view of the essential basis of world peace in terms of the rights of small nations. . . . France, for her part, had a tradition of reliance on the support of a group of client states against any strong rival on the other side of the Rhine. Thus when the war ended in the disintegration of three great empires, and the military collapse of a fourth, it was not unnatural that European peace arrangements should be envisaged in terms of free and independent small states.

2. Equality of States

In the second place we find the principle of the equality of all states. The influence of the idea of equal sovereignty was particularly strong in the American delegation. . . .

The crucial struggle came over the drafting of the League Covenant. What was to be the position of the small states in relation to the Council of the League? Colonel House, in sending his suggestions for a League of Nations to Wilson in July, 1918, proposed to confine it to the great powers. 'If the smaller nations are taken in,' he wrote, 'the question of equal voting power is an almost insurmountable obstacle.' . . . The British point of view, expressed by Lord Robert Cecil, was that 'the great powers must run the League and that it was just as well to recognize it flatly as not.' . . .

. . . The great powers for various reasons were not united in the determination to assert their authority in the League Council. On behalf of France, M. Bourgeois virtuously expressed the view that if too much power were given to the great powers they might seek for peace rather than for peace founded on justice. French sympathy for the smaller states even went as far as a proposal to add Monaco to the list of states invited to accede to the League Covenant. Italy added her support of the smaller states to that of France. When the neutral states were brought into consultation by the drafting Committee, the cry for recognition of the equality of all states and the demand for increased representation of the small states was redoubled, and in face of this opposition Great Britain and the United States had to accept the principle that the lesser states should be represented on the Council. . . .

The reasons for the successful establishment of their claims by the smaller states in 1919 are not very obscure. Two great powers, Germany and Russia, were temporarily excluded from effective intervention in world affairs. The remaining four great powers had divergent interests and views. France was hoping to create a system of client states in Europe, and the prospect of the support of some of these on the Council of the League was not unwelcome to her. Great Britain could not, out of deference to the susceptibilities of the Dominions, too strenuously resist the claims of the small states. President Wilson's personal sympathies were with them. Finally, progressive opinion was generally on the side of the small states.

3. National Sovereignty

Along with the general belief in the virtue of small states, and in the juridical equality of all states, great or small, there went, in third place, a firm conviction of the rights of national sovereignty.

The French delegation was practically alone in its willingness to abandon the principle of complete, independent national sovereignty in the interests of a new international order. . . . The French wished to convert the League into a great military alliance in which independent sovereignty should to an appreciable extent be sacrificed in the interests of military security. . . . President Wilson seems to have refused to acknowledge, even to himself, that there could be any conflict between the organisation of a peace system in the form of the League of Nations and the principle of national sovereignty. . . .

. . . The peacemakers of 1919 were . . . generous in their attitude to the smaller states, but they hardly realised how impermanent would be the guarantees they had provided for the survival of these states in the event of a recurrence of the threat represented by the defeated power, or the difficulty of reconciling their belief in national sovereignty with the conception of a new international order embodied in the League of Nations. . . . The attempt to combine a faith in small states, equality of states, and absolute national sovereignty, with the construction of an international system of security, may indeed be considered the greatest theoretical weakness in the peace settlement.

It may well be asked how it came about that the potential danger involved in this contradiction was not more clearly apprehended, especially by the British and American delegations, which were the keenest on the new League organisation. The answer to this question brings us back to the principle with the discussion of which we are primarily concerned. Self-determination for various reasons did not have as decisive an influence over the territorial settlements as might have been expected, but public opinion was far from realising this fact. Many of the limitations on self-determination in the peace treaties were undoubtedly forced on the Conference by circumstances. Millions of Poles, Czechs, South Slavs and others had been freed from alien rule, and it was natural in 1919 that this should seem the dominating fact. However important the numerous cases in which self-determination had not been followed came to seem later, in 1919 it still retained its ideological predominance. The emancipation of the nations by self-determination was the point on which attention was concentrated. . . . Consciously or unconsciously, by wrapping up national sovereignty in the idealistic language of self-determination the peacemakers concealed from themselves the flaw in the system they had created. . . .

In the last analysis we are bound to conclude that the force of self-determination had achieved its real triumphs before the Armistice, in a series of national revolts for which the conditions of the war had provided the opportunity. At the Peace Conference it had passed from the offensive to the defensive. The right of self-determination invariably made its appearance in the discussions before every territorial settlement, and wherever it was patently overridden the Conference was ill at ease. . . .

The more we study the work of the Peace Conference, the less it seems to have been under the control of the principle of self-determination. This conclusion, of course, cuts both ways. If self-determination was applied with so many limitations, and was neglected in so many cases, this was doubtless because circumstances prohibited a more complete application. Politicians should have realised, as some of them undoubtedly did, and as the experts proved, that it was only one principle among many and could not claim an overriding authority. . . .

Jerzy Tomaszewski

The Imperative of National Integration

The leaders of the "New Europe" saw their states as the fulfillment of the national idea. But Poland and other new states in Eastern Europe faced daunting social and economic problems. In confronting these problems, political leaders naturally emphasized the need for national

Jerzy Tomaszewski, "The National Question in Poland in the Twentieth Century," in *The National Question in Europe in Historical Context*, ed. by Mikulas Teich and Roy Porter, 1993, pp. 305–315. Reprinted with the permission of the author and Cambridge University Press.

unity. Yet about a third of Poland's people were members of minorities, including Ukrainians, Belorussians, Jews, Lithuanians, and Germans. They proved large enough to make their interests known and to play a role in determining the country's public policies. Professor Jerzy Tomaszewski, who is on the faculty of the Institute of Political Sciences at the University of Warsaw and on the Council of the Jewish Historical Institute in Poland, examines the economic and social concerns of the nationalities and the response of the Polish state to them. Conflict arose as the minorities' interests clashed with the government's emphasis on national state unity.

The Polish state came into being as a result of the disaster that befell the great powers of central Europe and as a result of the revolution that overtook the whole of central and eastern Europe towards the end of the First World War. The Polish national movement, aiming at the creation of an independent state, was part of that revolution, as were the national movements of other societies of that part of Europe: the Belorussian, Czech, Lithuanian, Slovak, Ukrainian, and others. The Polish Republic was a fruit of that movement; it came into being as a state created by the Polish nation, but extended over an area inhabited also by other national groups. This gave rise to fundamental conflicts. Almost all Polish political parties greeted the creation of the Republic as the realization of Polish national aspirations. The Polish nation regained its lost sovereignty; it freed itself from foreign domination and could decide its own fate, in its own democratic state. In 1931, however, national minorities constituted over a third of the inhabitants of this state. Furthermore, in some regions these minorities were in the majority; this applied particularly to the Belorussians and the Ukrainians in the eastern provinces; and in some northern areas to the Lithuanians also. Of course, the Jews were not in a majority in any one area (with the exception of a few small towns in the east), but they made up around 10 per cent of the population, and so an extremely high proportion. The percentage of Germans was very small and quickly decreased at the beginning of the 1920s due to emigration to Germany. In sum, the young state's national minorities appeared to be sufficiently large for them to aspire to participation in the formation of policies—if the democratic programmes of the majority of Polish political parties are to be taken seriously.

Estimates of the national make-up of the Polish population have one essential defect: they assume clear and unambiguous divisions between nationalities. However . . . reality was rather more complicated. To date, we do not have the means to calculate how many people belonged to groups of intermediate or incipient national consciousness. One should also take into consideration that this consciousness proceeded to develop during the interwar period alongside processes of assimilation. . . .

Aspirations to create a Polish nation-state prompted disparate attitudes among Polish society. Right-wing groups—headed by the National Democracy—rejected the notion that in a *Polish* state representatives of *non-Polish* minorities could participate in decisions over the most important questions of state. In Parliament clear political alliances arose naturally on more than one occasion between politicians representing national minorities and Polish left-wing groups, who acknowledged the principle of civic equality more or less consistently. . . .

The national question in interwar Poland had a political aspect—linked with the conflict between a variety of aspirations and programmes—as well as a social, economic and philosophical side. These problems differed slightly in almost every national group.

The greatest similarities can be found in the situation and aspirations of the Belorussians and Ukrainians, and to a certain extent in that of the Lithuanians, although their much smaller numbers and concentration in a relatively small territory meant that the Lithuanian question was of relatively minor importance in Poland. A clear majority of these three societies was made up of peasants, whereas the propertied classes were small in number. There were also relatively few workers; they worked mainly as agricultural labourers or in enterprises connected with the countryside (e.g., in the wood industry, in quarries). The peasants were mainly the owners of smallholdings. . . .

For the peasant national minorities the land question was of the utmost importance. Large-scale properties were to be found mainly in Polish hands, as were political positions. The landed gentry were the mainstay of Polish influence in the eastern borderlands of the state. The peasants demanded agricultural reform, and thus the parcelling and liquidation of estates. In the central provinces this issue was social and economic in character, in the eastern borderlands it also became a key national question. The conflict between the poor village and the wealthy manor most often corresponded to the conflict between the Polish nobleman (often a magnate; there were estates of over 100,000 hectares) and the Belorussian, Ukrainian and Lithuanian peasant; the tradition of antagonism stretched far into the past. Even if some Polish politicians took up the question of agricultural reform, they still proposed to resettle Polish peasants from other provinces in the eastern borderlands, so that only a part of the reapportioned estates would pass into Belorussian or Ukrainian hands. Such resettlement was actually realized aside from any agricultural reform, particularly in the first half of the 1920s. This exacerbated the Polish-Ukrainian and Polish-Belorussian conflicts, since the newcomers were treated as thieves, stealing land which rightly belonged to the local peasants.

The Polish-Ukrainian conflict was the more acute since in the years 1918–19 the West Ukrainian People's Republic existed for a short time in Eastern Galicia (afterwards part of the Polish state) before its defeat in battle with the Polish army. Ukrainian society treated the Polish administrative authorities as an occupying power. Admittedly some Polish politicians perceived the need to find some kind of compromise with moderate Ukrainian circles, but the extremely nationalistic attitudes of Polish circles in Eastern Galicia proved an obstacle to this. A Ukrainian university was never successfully established (with the sole exception of the illegal university in Lwów), the number of schools with Ukrainian as the language of instruction gradually decreased, and the local authorities employed all manner of oppressive measures against people stubbornly using the Ukrainian language (in some circumstances, Polish law permitted the use of Belorussian, Lithuanian or Ukrainian in court or in addressing the authorities).

In 1922–24 armed detachments existed in the provinces inhabited by Belorussians and Ukrainians. They fought the Polish administration and attacked manors and properties belonging to

Poles. They often received help from abroad—from Lithuania and the USSR—and enjoyed the hidden sympathy of the village populace. This movement was successfully crushed, as much by an improvement in the Polish economy after 1925 as by force, although the basic ethnic (national) problems were not solved. After 1929 radical moods grew in conjunction with the great crisis. Nationalist activity increased, particularly among the Ukrainians—the illegal Ukrainian Military Organization whose members perpetrated terrorist acts against the Poles. In response, a number of arrests (from which Ukrainian deputies were not exempt) followed from mid-September to the end of November 1930 on the recommendation of Józef Piłsudski (1867–1935), and repressive measures directed against many villages; during searches and the hunt for hidden arms the police and army destroyed property, and people were often beaten, particularly those who protested. This so-called pacification strained Polish-Ukrainian relations immeasurably and contributed to a growing hatred of Polish government. Despite the obvious facts, despite the growing conflict which reflected the developed awareness of its own national identity on the part of Ukrainian society, the nationalistic Polish right wing treated the Ukrainians (whom they stubbornly referred to as Ruthenians) as an 'ethnographic mass' which was bound to submit to either Polish or Russian influences. In the 1930s, the administrative authorities made efforts to encourage separate awareness of the regional groups of people speaking Ukrainian dialects; a policy analogous to that carried out by the Germans towards the inhabitants of Mazuria, Warmia and Silesia. In statistical data, the Ukrainians were listed separately from the so-called Ruthenians and support was given to those organizations that cut themselves off from the Ukrainian national movement and declared their links with the Russian nation. Despite all this, Ukrainian self-awareness grew stronger with the passing of time.

Similar tendencies dominated among people speaking Belorussian. Schools with Belorussian as the language of instruction were practically non-existent, numerous obstacles were put in the way of Belorussian institutions and organizations, the use of the Belorussian tongue was eliminated in Catholic churches (Russian was the traditionally dominant language in Orthodox churches), attempts were made to influence Belorussian children by taking them on trips designed to introduce them to the greatness and power of the Republic — despite all this Belorussian intellectuals, social and political activists slowly increased in number. Very often Polish schools, whose task was to strengthen the influence of Polish culture, actually helped the development of Belorussian national consciousness. In the memoirs of an outstanding writer a Polish schoolmistress is mentioned who 'knew our literature and folk poetry and during the few hours devoted to Belorussian language revealed to us our very own native glory'. The very teaching of Polish literature and history provided the pupils with models of love of fatherland and work for its liberation and development, awakening national consciousness.

As a result of pressure exercised by the administrative powers, discrimination against those maintaining Belorussian, Lithuanian or Ukrainian traditions, and finally the activities of Polish schools and organizations, the assimilationist processes among the national minorities (which always occur to some degree) began to gain force, but could not threaten the existence of distinct nations. In this sense nationalist politics failed, but led instead to a sharpening of national conflicts and contributed to the strengthening of nationalistic stances — decidedly hostile towards the Poles — among national minorities in the eastern regions of the state whose population reaped the tragic fruits of this process during the Second World War.

The situation in the western provinces developed rather differently in more than one respect. The creation of a Polish state led, above all, to a fundamental change in the position of the German populace. Previously a privileged social group, they had enjoyed various forms of state support, and, moreover, lived in the conviction of their own cultural superiority. After these lands were incorporated in the Republic they suddenly became a minority, and one viewed with hostility at that, as much by the authorities . . . as by their Polish neighbours. Many Germans emigrated, in justified fear of vehement hostile reactions on the part of the hitherto discriminated against Polish populace. . . . Of greater significance was the fact that the Germans ceased to be a privileged group, and a certain section of them saw no prospects for employment in Poland. These were the functionaries of the apparatus of oppression understood in its widest sense — policemen, judges, bureaucrats, and also teachers of whom there appear to have been too many given the needs of what was not after all a very numerous German minority in Poland. Their positions were taken over by Poles. Professional German military personnel also left Poland, and even some landowners sold their estates in order to avoid living in a predominantly Polish (numerically speaking) environment, with authority being exercised by a Polish administration. After 1923 the German Foreign Office (*Auswärtiges Amt*) in Berlin realized that the mass German exodus from Poland was undermining arguments in favour of revising the borders established at Versailles. German consulates in Poland took steps aimed at making emigration more difficult, and before long German organizations began to receive financial help, with the aim of maintaining their strength and influence. . . .

Such a state of affairs had far-reaching consequences. In Silesia it favoured the continuance — mentioned above — of ideologically neutral groups, and contributed to demoralization, sometimes to personal dramas. Throughout the area of the former Prussian partition it strengthened Polish-German national conflicts, and contributed to nationalistic stances on both sides. Financial help from the Third Reich, in conjunction with political activity, made the quick dissemination of National Socialist influences possible. The situation of Germans who rejected nationalism, above all the Social Democrats, turned out to be particularly difficult. They incurred the hostility of the Polish authorities on two counts: as Germans, and as the organizers of a political movement linked with the Polish Left, questioning the social and political status quo. On the German side — particularly after 1933 — they were treated as a group threatening national unity. The German Social Democrats weakened as a force, but they maintained certain influences among German workers in Poland throughout the interwar period. They later took part in the anti-Nazi underground during the occupation. . . .

All the national minorities mentioned so far had one common characteristic: they were members of nations which lived in neighbouring states where they could seek support against the politics of the Polish authorities. Because of this background, conflicts often become particularly acute, especially with Lithuania and Germany. These two states contained Polish minorities within their borders — minorities suffering discrimination in a variety of forms. The Polish government could also justifiably fear that the minorities would become the political instruments of neighbouring states, facilitating the eventual separation from the Republic of its bordering lands. . . .

The situation of the Jews was completely different. First, they were scattered throughout almost the whole state (with the exception of the western provinces, where they constituted an insignificant percentage of the population). Secondly, Poland had no neighbouring Jewish state, which did not in any case exist at that time anywhere in the world, so the Jews could not become a force potentially threatening any part of Polish territory. Thirdly, Jewish organizations had no ambitions to create a separate political organism, and at the most they aimed (though not all of them) to establish autonomous organs of national-cultural self-government. Some Jewish groups declared their absolute loyalty to the Republic, others even took part in its fight for independence. The existence of a Jewish minority within the Polish borders did not therefore create a political threat to the state's interests. It is true that some Jewish organizations declared a programme of social revolution, and even sympathized with Soviet Russia. This was a result of internal political differences within Jewish society. Analogous political movements also existed in Polish society.

On the other hand, the Jewish question did have real social and religious aspects. In some regions of the country tradesmen and craftsmen were almost all Jewish, and economic conflicts between small farmers and merchants began to acquire nationalist and religious elements. The conviction that trade was basically dishonest was often to be found in the villages, and the merchant who profits because he cheats turned into the stereotype of the Jewish trickster, exploiting the Christian peasant. At the same time the belief that Jews bore the responsibility for the death of Christ persisted in Christian tradition. In Catholic papers for 'the people' there were even — though very rarely — statements to the effect that Jews require the blood of Christian children for the

Passover (Pesakh). In the years 1918–21 when the Polish administration and army were still in the process of formation, when local
authorities were often in a state of disorganization and with the
added upheaval of the Polish-Soviet war, pogroms were known to
occur (the bloodiest in Lwów in November 1918) and a variety of
excesses took place.

The years of revolution and creation of the Polish state also
brought with them an accelerated development of Jewish national
consciousness. In traditional orthodox circles, of course, a dis-
tance continued to be maintained from secular affairs, and the
conviction persisted that the Jews constitute only a religious community linked by history, divine laws and the hope for the coming
of the Messiah, but in the new Poland secular groups began to
come to the fore of Jewish life who declared their conviction that
Jews were a nation like any other. They proposed that Jews should
be granted the rights common to national minorities. . . .

The idea of establishing national-cultural autonomy for Polish
Jews had no chance of realization. From the Polish state's political
perspective, this would constitute a precedent which if applied to
other national minorities would have consequences conflicting
with interests of state. It was also rejected by the statesmen of the
states of the victorious Entente; during talks between the heads of
these states held in 1919, David Lloyd George (1863–1945)
stressed that equal rights for Jews in Poland ought to lead to assimilation. Reality proved to be different, however. The assimila-
tory process embraced only some Jewish circles and was opposed
by the majority of Jewish political parties and by Polish nationalists, and Jewish national culture in Poland flourished instead.

The 1930s brought a sharpening of national conflicts in the Polish
state. The perceptive observer will see behind them the growth of
social conflicts linked with the great economic crisis. The sudden
drop in living standards of the rural population strengthened op-
positional stances. The land question — with overpopulation becoming more acute in the villages — became decisive for the future. In the eastern provinces this meant an intensification of
antagonism between the mainly Polish manor and settlers and the
local people who were of a different nationality. At the same time

there was a growth of hostility, and even hatred among these people for the administration, which defended the property of landowners and settlers. Of course, there were other causes of dispute, such as the limitation of education in languages other than Polish and the discrimination against non-Polish organizations and societies. The Ukrainians did not forget the traditions of their own statehood. Without a solution to the land problem one could not speak, however, of any compromise solution in the relations between Poland and these minorities.

The Jewish question also had a social basis. In the villages conflicts intensified between the peasant farmer, who constantly received less for his products, and the merchant who struggled for every penny of his earnings to maintain his family. In the towns there was growing competition between various groups of tradesmen and craftsmen. Furthermore, the number of small entrepreneurs began to grow, as the unemployed — despairing of ever finding work — began to trade on a small scale and to carry out various crafts. The number of people wanting to earn a living in this way grew, and the number of potential clients correspondingly decreased. The nationalistic argument reared its head anew in this competitive battle — aimed against Jewish traders and craftsmen. Even if one accepts that the gradual transformation of the structure of Polish trade and crafts was a natural phenomenon, especially its modernization, for which the majority of people carrying out these trades at that time did not have the means, then the basic question must be raised: what was to be done with the people ousted from these traditional professions, in conditions of acute unemployment, when possibilities of emigration were limited by the policies of every state in the world? One should not underestimate the political and philosophical motives behind a number of nationalistic undertakings. Radical groups (though they were not very influential in Poland) drew inspiration from the racist policies of the Third Reich. But quite apart from this, there was no chance of solving the problem of the Jewish minority in Poland without fundamental economic progress and without elimination of, or at the very least a real decrease in, the huge unemployment in the towns.

The German question also had economic aspects, since the

strengthening of German nationalistic organizations was made easier due to financial means received from Germany. In this way they had the advantage over those forces in German society in Poland which opposed nationalism, as the latter received no help from Berlin, nor could they count on the help of the Polish authorities. The victory of Adolf Hitler in Germany contributed to the consolidation of nationalistic stances among Germans in Poland. Attempts made by the Polish authorities to counteract Nazi tendencies had no greater chance of success in a situation where a significant part of the German minority felt the Versailles Treaty to be unjust, delivering them into the hands of the disdained Poles.

The national minority question in Poland was not solved during the interwar years. There were too many substantive causes in the way. Attempts at appeasement or at removing conflicts would have had to be based on real economic progress and the solving of social questions—and there was no hope of that. This would not in any case have sufficed. After all, conflict and hostility against the background of ethnic (national) differences had persisted for many decades in the consciousness of antagonistic national groups. Some prejudices had religious authority and several centuries of tradition behind them. The elimination of these elements demanded considerably more time than the twenty-one years of existence vouchsafed to independent Poland.

Such a statement does not preclude critical evaluation of the national policies of the Polish state, or the stances of politicians who too rarely perceived and understood the problems of national minorities. Nor does it entail suspending criticism of nationalistic trends appearing among minorities which approached the whole of Polish society as the enemy, regardless of the fact that there existed Polish groups and outstanding political writers who condemned Polish nationalism.

Paul Lendvai

Denying Others in a National Society

Burdened with economic backwardness, bitter social divisions between urban and rural society, cleavages between dominant and minority ethnic communities, and strident ideological movements, political life in much of Eastern Europe grew increasingly authoritarian. Paul Lendvai, a Hungarian-born journalist who became a citizen of Austria, describes what was sometimes a double dilemma for many Jews in the region. Seen as economic competitors and social outsiders by the expanding national urban society in the developing states, they encountered political obstacles as well when they attempted to assimilate into a country's dominant nationality.

A number of states emerged from the ruins of World War I, all of them created under the promising banner of national self-determination, democracy, protection of minority rights, and agrarian reform. The restoration of Poland, the birth of a new Czechoslovak state, and the creation of an immensely enlarged Rumania and Yugoslavia at the expense of truncated Hungary drastically changed the political map of Central and Eastern Europe. The dreams of progress and equality (except for Czechoslovakia and there only for the Czechs) were cruelly disappointed in the interwar period under the dual impact of misrule by intensely nationalistic, inefficient, and irresponsible ruling classes and such crucial external factors as the Great Depression and the rise of Italian Fascism and German Nazism.

Instead of mitigating the strains and stresses between the nations and their minorities, the disastrous political frontier-making

From Paul Lendvai *Anti-Semitism without Jews*, Doubleday, 1971, pp. 40–45.

after World War I only proved that the nation-state principle could not be introduced into Eastern Europe without creating in some cases even more glaring injustices and almost everywhere new hotbeds of nationalist friction. The geographic distribution of ethnic groups and traditional loyalties in these regions is so tangled that no clear-cut and wholly satisfactory demarcations are possible. In addition to such vexed territorial issues as Transylvania, Bessarabia, Kosovo, Eastern Galicia, Carpathian Ruthenia, and countless other contested regions all over the area, Eastern Europe bristled with many-sided minority problems. In 1939, out of a population of 110 million, some 22 million belonged to minorities. In spite of the Minority Treaties, which were signed by all the governments, the rights guaranteed remained almost everywhere dead letters. Czechoslovakia and Yugoslavia faced even more serious problems in the conflicts between majority and minority "state nations," in the first case between Czechs and Slovaks, and in the second Serbs versus Croats and Slovenes.

All Successor States were permeated with the spirit of . . . nationalism with regard to both their respective unreliable minorities and their small-power imperialism against neighboring states.

For a variety of reasons, the Jews became (except in the Czech lands and Bulgaria) the targets of nationalist fury and social protest. Not surprisingly, in the three countries that had the largest Jewish communities, Poland, Rumania, and Hungary, fascist mass parties were born in the 1930s. What came as a shock, however, immediately after the First World War was that the most assimilated and most "nationalized" Jewish community, Hungarian Jewry, became the victim of rampant anti-Semitism and terroristic outrages.

It must be said that Hungary was the great loser in the war, deprived of two thirds of its former territory and population. Neither Germany nor Austria suffered a comparable national catastrophe. Some 3.3 million Hungarians, well over one third of the nation, many of them living in large compact groups just beyond the new frontiers, were incorporated into the new Successor States. It is impossible to examine closely here the roots of the Hungarian tragedy and the political turbulence following the defeat, which led first to the proclamation of the Republic and then, under the combined pressure of Rumanian-Czech attacks and the incredible political blunders of the Allies, to the peaceful takeover by a small group of Communist agitators who proclaimed Hungary a Soviet Republic.

The 133 days of the disastrous Communist experiment in a mutilated and disarmed country surrounded by strong and hostile neighbors shattered what only a few years earlier seemed to have been a Golden Age of security. The strong Jewish element in the leadership of the Communist regime and the pent-up animosity against the prominence of Jews in so many fields made Jews easy targets for the "White Terror" unleashed by the counterrevolutionaries. To make things worse, tens of thousands of Hungarian refugees from the lost territories, mainly bureaucrats who had been the "masters" in Transylvania and Slovakia, now flocked into the towns of the truncated country. There they found the Jews. Inevitably the whole fury of national frustration and emotional reaction was directed against what was now the only alien body in a mutilated but completely homogenous nation-state.

The demagogic reactionary regime of Admiral Horthy,[1] though permeated with the spirit of militant Catholicism, was the first government to anticipate Hitler's highly successful propaganda, the cry of a secret alliance between the Jewish capitalist and the Jewish socialist. The outbursts of savage anti-Jewish terrorism were, however, only a passing phase. . . . In fact the situation of the Hungarian Jews until the late 1930s was almost idyllic in comparison with that in other East European countries and with what followed. There is a peculiar tragedy in the fate of Hungarian Jewry: it survived intact until the middle of 1944 and was then annihilated in less than eight weeks, when even the perpetrators knew that the war was lost.

There has been another unfortunate paradox in the history of Hungarian Jewry. After the Treaty of Trianon in 1920, 51 per cent became citizens of Rumania, Czechoslovakia, and to a lesser extent of Yugoslavia. Those who remained in Hungary, however assimilated and patriotic, were regarded by the middle class and the state bureaucracy as well as by the prevailing clerical-national

---

[1]Miklos Horthy (1868–1957) was regent of the Kingdom of Hungary throughout the interwar era and exercised all the prerogatives of a monarch. He was a staunch conservative who sought to maintain the traditional social order.—Ed.

ideology of the authoritarian regime as a menace to the purity of the Hungarian nation. Those who became Rumanian, Czechoslovak, or Yugoslav citizens were intensely resented by their fellow citizens as Jews who, in addition to being "irretrievably alien," insisted on calling themselves Hungarian. Loyalty to Hungary became an involved personal problem for every individual Jew among the almost half a million incorporated into the neighboring countries. For over two decades they were crushed between Hungarian "revisionism" (meaning here the revision of the Treaty of Trianon) and Rumanian, Slovak, and Serbian nationalism, each accusing them in turn of "treason."

The fate of the Hungarian Jews vividly demonstrated that the degree of cultural assimilation to the ruling nation could not defuse the Jewish problem, and under the new conditions after World War I it even became the source of additional problems. Yet lack of assimilation was usually regarded as constituting not only the main line of division among the Jews but also the perhaps most important reason for the endemic anti-Semitism in Poland and Rumania. As Isaac Deutscher noted: "Polish nationalism, anti-Semitism, and Catholic clericalism on the one hand, and Jewish separatism, orthodoxy, and Zionism on the other, worked against a lasting and a fruitful symbiosis." As the overwhelming majority of Polish Jews lived in ghettos, with 87 per cent giving Yiddish or Hebrew as their mother tongue at the 1931 census, and were at the same time, both in actual numbers and in proportion of the total population, numerically the strongest Jewish community in Europe, their presence constituted an exceptionally difficult problem.

It is not unimportant that the same regimes that thundered against the unassimilable aliens also did their best to retard the assimilation process for very obvious reasons. In view of the shaky balance between "state nations" and national minorities in Czechoslovakia and Rumania, the ruling nations in both countries preferred "Jewish Jews" to "Hungarian Jews" or "German Jews." It was better to record a higher number of "Jewish nationality" at the census than to tolerate the swelling of the ranks of the already large "separatist" minorities such as the Hungarians, Germans, or Ukrainians. Thus it happened that Rumanian census-takers in Transylvania, the most bitterly contested area with mixed population, insisted that Hungarian-speaking Jews should declare Yiddish as their mother tongue, and succeeded in producing at the 1932 census the staggering number of 111,000 Yiddish-speaking citizens out of 192,000 Jews the overwhelming majority of whom had for decades been Hungarian in language and culture. To a lesser extent the same practices were reported from Czechoslovakia and Yugoslavia. For good reasons intensely chauvinistic regimes either tolerated or actually encouraged Hebrew education and the Zionist movement. . . .

Everywhere, however, except in the western regions of Czechoslovakia and in Bulgaria, anti-Semitism was widespread and in the 1930s, under the combined impact of economic crisis and Nazi influence, increasingly virulent. It embodied a variety of motives and moods—national, economic, political, and religious. "Which group of people would turn anti-Semite, in a given country at a given historical moment, depended exclusively on general circumstances . . . But the remarkable similarity of arguments and images which time and again were spontaneously reproduced have an intimate relationship with the truth they distort. We find the Jews always represented as an international trading organization, a world-wide family concern with interests everywhere, a secret force behind the throne which degrades all visible governments into mere façade or into marionettes whose strings are manipulated from behind the scenes."

Whether Jews were hated as representatives of liberal individualism or of cosmopolitan finance capitalism or, worse still, as carriers of international Communism, they were invariably regarded as actual or potential agents of internationalism and universalism.

But nationalism, not internationalism, was the new reality. The "Hungarian-Jews" in Transylvania and Slovakia, the "German-Jews" in Bohemia and Moravia (the Czech regions), Silesia and Croatia, the "Russian-Jews" in Bessarabia and eastern Poland were in a double sense outside the pale of the dominant society and nation. The neurotic nationalism in interwar Eastern Europe saw the Jews as a menace whatever their national origin, social status, or political creed: "a foreign body when cultivating their own identity; a menace to the purity and integrity of the national creative genius when attempting to participate in the spiritual life of the nation." The native brands of romantic nationalism, later increasingly infected by the germs of Nazi racism, provided the single most important and permanent background against which the fortunes of the assimilated, foreign, and "Jewish Jews" must be seen. . . .

Oscar Jászi

Social Upheaval and Nationality Problems

By the mid-1930s, the East European states were coping not only with the impact of the depression on their economies but also with radical ideologies vigorously promoted by more powerful neighboring states like Germany and Italy, bent on challenging the international order. Oscar Jászi (1875–1957) was a Hungarian historian and sociologist who served as minister of nationalities in a short-lived liberal government at the end of the Great War. He later wrote a now-classic account of the "dissolution of the Habsburg Monarchy" that emphasized the role of the national question. Jászi traveled through much of Eastern Europe in the early 1930s and grew alarmed by the social discontent that he believed was contributing to heightened nationalist tensions in the area.

A sojourn of several months in the Danubian Succession States, with which my life has been intimately connected, convinced me that this territory is in a state of continuous preparatory war, of a potential fight, which will assume actuality if the victor States created by the World War: Czechoslovakia, Roumania, and

Oscar Jászi, "Neglected Aspects of the Danubian Drama," from *Slavonic and East European Review*, v. 14 (1935–36), #40, pp. 53, 56–64, 67.

Jugoslavia, together with the vanquished States: Austria and Hungary, remain unable to solve their common fundamental problems.

Travelling in those countries, any more serious observer feels physically, so to say, the growing tension, the increasing insecurity between, and in, different strata of the population. Especially the intellectual middle class, harassed by poverty or unemployment, is in a state of nervous agitation. Something new, violent, and unheard-of must happen in order to save the world, they believe. . . .

What are the reasons of this silent warfare? Before all, it is caused by a radical upset of the social structure. The expropriation of the German and Hungarian ruling classes in Czechoslovakia, Roumania, and Jugoslavia, with their expulsion from public office, has created a new atmosphere, undermining the traditional bulwarks of authority, and intensifying very strongly the feeling of irredentism on the part of the former rulers. In these victorious countries a new middle class arose, mostly sons of peasants, small artisans, and other members of the lower bourgeoisie. This new ruling class is in its social manners, administrative ability, and sometimes even in public honesty, below the former expert Austrian bureaucrats and the feudal *Herrenklasse* of Hungary. Therefore, many foreign observers complain that entire territories have become "Balkanised," that the former urbanity of manners has diminished, that the administration has become more venal and clumsy. All this is true to a certain extent. Yet those aristocratic observers forget to mention that at the same time high schools and universities are crowded with the children of peasants who formerly were the victims of artificial assimilation, that those backward nationality groups are now developing their own national culture. . . .

It is interesting to note that the antagonism in the class structure has become a cause of conflict not only between nations whose racial origins differ, and who fought each other during the War, but also between nations who are closely connected racially, and who are both beneficiaries of the Great War.

This has happened in the case of the Czechs and the Poles. There is a growing tension between Poland and the Czechoslovak Republic which manifests itself in complaints of the Poles on behalf of their national minority in Czechoslovak territory, and in their increasing coolness towards the Little Entente, and ostentatious friendliness towards Hungary and Germany. As the Polish minority in Czechoslovakia is totally insignificant (about 80,000 people), and as the Czechs have no animosity against them, the existence of this problem indicates a deeper and hidden cause of aversion. As a matter of fact, this dislike is motivated by conflicting collective psychologies of the two nations. The Czech democracy of peasants and small bourgeoisie is distasteful to the dictatorship of colonels and feudal aristocrats. Furthermore, the Czechs, ardent supporters of the League of Nations, do not enjoy the high esteem of the Polish Imperialists. But what is of a still greater importance is that the autonomy accorded to Carpathian Ruthenia by the Czechs is felt to be a serious menace to Poland, who suppresses ruthlessly her own Ukrainian (Ruthene) minority. . . .

Needless to say, the economic and political expropriation of the former ruling classes in Czechoslovakia, Roumania, and Jugoslavia creates an unbridgeable gap between the past and the present. This tension is further aggravated by the competition between the middle classes of the ruling nations, and those of the national minorities. This is only partly due to the distrust between the various races; it is caused to a large extent by the general economic crisis. The disastrous effects of economic nationalism and the continuously growing war budget make the future outlook of the middle classes practically desperate. As Madách, the great Hungarian poet, said in his *Tragedy of Man,* "There are too many Eskimos and too few seals." This is exactly the situation of the intellectuals relative to their jobs. One of the most influential men in Roumania told me that he was unable for several years to procure a minor job in the State administration for his private secretary, a brilliant former student of the Sorbonne. In this desperate struggle for existence, the national difficulties offer an appropriate ideology for the elimination of the minority middle class from offices. . . . The struggle for bread has become a highly patriotic affair: "foreigners" should be eliminated, otherwise the existence of the nation will be imperilled.

This state of mind is poisoned by the real dangers of the new

States: there is a very active irredentist propaganda from Budapest, and a Nazi propaganda from Berlin which gives substantial nourishment to nationalistic tendencies. The recent tragic expulsion of Hungarians from Jugoslavia was a symptom of the growing mass hysteria. There is a continuous suppression of foreign newspapers and propaganda material, but these measures give little help to the ruling national group, because they are unable to stop the air waves, and a hostile propaganda is daily going on through the ether. These unhappy Succession States are Siamese Quintuplets shouting in each others' ears the most terrible accusations, and they arm each against the other for the future war which all regard as inevitable.

No wonder if under such conditions one finds in all these States two widespread types of intellectuals, both utterly incapable of understanding surrounding realities. I had a long conversation with one of the most influential journalists of Roumania, a powerful leader of public opinion. His current of ideas may be regarded as typical of the Fascist intellectuals, though his is more brilliant than the average. . . . He gave me a long lecture in his palatial editorial office on the present difficulties of his country: Parliamentarianism is finished, . . . the authoritarian State under the leadership of the new élite is inevitable, but nobody knows from where it should come, and how it will be able to get into power. . . .

This formidable personality conducted a vast inquiry in his paper under the title "What to do with the Foreigners?" For weeks he published violent manifestations against Magyars, Jews and Germans. On the other side of the frontier the most-read Hungarian newspaper announced a prize for the best irredentist poem. The fruit of this literary harvest was published under the title "One Hundred Torches," and described the new rulers of the former Magyar territories as intruders or robbers . . . .

Scarcely more clear-headed is the other Danubian intellectual type: the Bolshevik intellectual. The Marxian ideology destroyed in his mind all the prestige of the West. The Balkans have nothing to learn from England and France, and the other "decadent" countries, as the sun is already shining in the East. All Soviet information is accepted at its face value, and is commented upon as a glorious sign of the approaching world revolution. . . .

Besides these economic, national, and social difficulties, the victorious group of the new States: Czechoslovakia, Roumania, and Jugoslavia, have other troubles, which I would call *regional*. By this I mean radical divergencies in the ranks of the ruling national group due to their different historic traditions and patterns of culture. This is the antagonism between Czechs, Slovaks, and Ruthenes in Czechoslovakia; between the old Regat, and Transylvania, the Banat, and Bessarabia in Roumania,[1] and between Serbs, Croats and Slovenes in Jugoslavia. The Slovaks, who have lived for a thousand years in the feudal and clerical atmosphere of the Magyar domination, have difficulties in accommodating themselves to the highly industrialised, rationalistic Czechs. This antagonism has led to a movement for Slovak autonomy, which was, however, compromised in the eyes of the Czechs by the fact that Slovak autonomy became also a shibboleth of Magyar irredentism, having had underground connections with some of the leaders of the Slovak movement. . . .

In Roumania, regional differences are also a cause of serious trouble. Transylvania, and the Banat, the former Hungarian part, and Bukovina, the former Austrian part, feel themselves superior to the "Regat," the old Roumanian kingdom. They represent a higher standard of culture, and had before the War a better administration. Now these provinces are flooded by Byzantine corruption, the old spirit of the *Phanariots*[2] (the Greek officials of the Porte) who regarded administration only as a tax-gathering business, and for personal gain. And though the younger generation resents very much these atavistic currents, until now it has been unable to check them, especially in a time when living on the State has become almost the only job. . . .

The most acute and dangerous regional problems are those of Jugoslavia. Until now, no real compromise has been found be-

---

[1]The Regat made up the territories of pre–World War I Romania; after the war, Transylvania and the Banat were acquired from Hungary, and Bessarabia was acquired from the Russian Empire. — Ed.

[2]In the Ottoman Empire, the Phanariots were Greek families, originally from Istanbul, who became very influential during the eighteenth century in the administration and trade of the Romanian Principalities, which later formed the Regat, or Old Kingdom. — Ed.

tween the western Croats and Slovenes, and the eastern Serbs. Croatia was successful under the Hungarian rule in building up a kingdom of its own with a strong national culture and tradition. At the same time the Slovenes, under the Habsburg rule, became the most advanced branch of the Southern Slav family, with a wonderful popular culture which exterminated illiteracy completely. These two groups . . . resent the Serb domination in the new State. . . . The extreme centralisation of Belgrade, the so-called Jugoslav Idea, is felt by the western part of the population as simply a compulsory Serbisation. . . . Furthermore, the centralised Belgrade administration is felt by the more advanced, and, therefore, far richer, western provinces as an economic exploitation for the benefit of the Serb warriors and bureaucrats. . . .

These are some undercurrents in the Danubian situation. Small rivulets, hidden from the eyes of the fashionable tourist, or the sentimental peacemaker. Yet these rivulets, if not canalised in their course, will surely develop in a few years into mighty rivers which will influence the history of the Danubian countries . . . decisively.

Sudeten Germans from Czechoslovakia getting off the train at the border on their way to a distribution center in Allied-occupied Germany as part of the population transfer implemented by the Czechoslovak government in 1946. (Ullstein Bilderdienst)

PART

III

The Legacy of
World War II:
National States and
Nationalities in a
Socialist Imperium

Oscar Janowsky

Federation as a Solution
to National Diversity

As World War II ended, two stark realities confronted the East European states and those who sought to lead them after the war. First,
the Soviet Union was undeniably the predominant political power in
the region and was certain to play an influential role in the future of
the area. Second, the war had exacerbated the ethnic and national
problems of the interwar era. Oscar Janowsky, a historian at the City
College of New York at that time, was aware of the first reality and
sought to offer solutions to the second. He considered the future of

From *Nationalities and National Minorities* by Oscar Janowsky, 1945, pp. 135–143,
145–148, 163–164. Published by Macmillan Publishing Co., Inc.

the East European nationalities in the light of past policies. Janowsky argued that the relocation of peoples, whether voluntarily or involuntarily, to achieve ethnic and territorial congruity only produced suffering and dislocation. He believed that the problem could better be addressed when the region's national states instead recognized and secured the ethnic diversity of peoples within their borders and linked themselves politically and economically through federations.

All discussions of the minority problems of east-central Europe begin and end with an unyielding fact; namely, the population lacks national-cultural homogeneity. Numerous nationalities differing in ancestry, language, religion and historical traditions live side by side in compact settlements on the land, or entirely interspersed in the urban centers. Practically every territory which might be designated as a geographic, economic or historical unit will comprise several peoples or segments of peoples, each determined to guard its home as the national homeland. . . .

We have already shown that east-central Europe cannot be reconstructed along the lines of the culturally uniform national states of the West. "Ethnic" frontiers would be the obvious means of eliminating minorities. But such frontiers are impossible both because national enclaves live in the midst of alien majorities, and because the web-like populations of border areas cannot be disentangled.

Is Transfer of Populations the Solution?

The composite character of the population, the impossibility of devising "ethnic" frontiers, and the dismal record of attempts at forced assimilation in the past should be conclusive reasons for abandoning further efforts to carve out national states of cultural uniformity in the war-breeding zone of east-central Europe. Yet so strong is the desire to emulate the homogeneous state of the West that a drastic plan has been proposed as a solution of the problem of national minorities; namely, the exchange or transfer of populations. . . .

Although such a project might strike one as too stupendous to be practicable, it must be examined with the utmost care, for with it has become associated the name of no less distinguished a statesman than Eduard Beneš, President of Czechoslovakia. . . .

Dr. Beneš knows that the compulsory transfer of large masses of people can create injustices, and he does not relish any method which would involve brutality or violence. . . . The present writer is forced to the conclusion that when President Beneš speaks of population transfers he has in mind not a solution of the problem of national minorities, but the elimination of those Germans and Hungarians who as disloyal irredentists plotted the destruction of the Czechoslovak State. He is properly incensed against the cynical exploitation of minority difficulties by the brutal Nazi régime, and no doubt embittered by the false charges of oppression leveled against his country, which was finally dismembered on the pretext of rendering justice to minorities. . . .

. . . Granting the difficulties and inadequacies of the pre-war system of minorities protection, it is still necessary to reiterate that the mass transfer of minority populations cannot be regarded as a solution of the nationalities problem, and to insist that emphasis upon the idea of population transfers can result only in discouraging efforts to find a genuine solution.

The exchange of minorities between Greece and Turkey and between Greece and Bulgaria in the 1920s is often adduced as evidence that large populations can be transferred successfully. . . . Properly speaking, only about 150,000 of the Greeks resident in Turkey were exchanged. The overwhelming majority — almost a million Greeks — had been obliged to flee for their lives after the collapse of the Greek invasion of Asia Minor in 1922, and before provision had been made for an orderly transfer. Some 400,000 Moslems, compelled to leave Greece under international supervision, likewise suffered hardships, and protested vigorously against what was really expulsion from their ancestral homes. And a great many of these people . . . were not a troublesome minority, but loyal to Greece, speaking, as a rule, the Greek language and sharing many of the customs of the majority. The exchange of Greek and Bulgarian minorities was termed "voluntary," but, in fact, pressure was widespread; and even compulsion did not succeed in clearing Greece of Bulgars, a minority of about 80,000 remaining in the country.

If an orderly transfer of populations implies compensation for property left behind, the Greek, Turkish and Bulgarian exchanges were a failure. The Greco-Turkish Mixed Commission failed altogether to indemnify the people affected, and payment in bonds of a large part of the Greco-Bulgar sums resulted in heavy losses through depreciation.

Suffering, too, was widespread and intense. Many thousands perished. The peaceful life of masses of people, rooted in their surroundings for centuries, was shattered. The cost of settling refugees imposed upon the Greek people a heavy burden of indebtedness. And many of the Greek traders and artisans, unable to achieve economic usefulness in their new homes, became an unemployed and pauperized urban proletariat. . . .

This experience gained from the Near Eastern experiments with population transfers should serve as a warning. To remove a minority from its home requires compulsion, for "voluntary" transfers have not been effective, and forced migration means expulsion, at least to the people concerned. . . .

The exchange of minorities may be possible in special areas and on a small scale. For example, where farming communities live interspersed on the frontier, adequate international supervision should find it possible to disentangle a mixed population with a minimum of suffering. Where exchange of land holdings is not possible, the transfer of a farming population would involve uprooting a mass of people and casting them adrift in overcrowded cities. And the transfer of urban minorities presents even greater difficulties. Petty traders or artisans who perform a useful economic function and earn a livelihood in their old homes are likely to be ruined by removal to a new environment. Laborers, too, might not find their skills in demand when transferred to a new country. If urban minorities are shifted, provision must be made for retraining and other economic readjustments.

Even the transfer of relatively small groups of people requires stable, peaceful conditions, with a maximum of international supervision. But, to solve the minorities problem, it would be necessary to shift many millions of people under the least favorable circumstances. . . .

We are forced to the conclusion that the minorities problem will not be solved by the elimination of minorities through forced migration. . . . The dislocations and suffering involved in compulsory, large-scale transfer of populations, or in forced assimilation, are not only painful and harmful, they are unnecessary. The solution of the problem of minorities must be sought not in centralized uniformity, but in the decentralization of the cultural functions of government and in national federalism. . . .

A New Approach: National Federalism and Economic Unity

We have seen that the European national state has assumed two forms, namely, the intolerant state of strict cultural uniformity like the Prussia of Bismarck's time, and the tolerant national state like Great Britain, in which one language and a national culture predominate, but minorities enjoy the freedom to cultivate locally their languages and customs. Since neither variation of the national state is suitable to conditions in east-central Europe, it is here proposed that the region be reorganized on the basis of national federalism. In essence this means that minorities are not to be endowed with special privileges, that their status is not to be an exceptional one involving toleration, but that they be organically incorporated in the structure of the multi-national state.

No state can enjoy domestic tranquillity when some of its minorities entertain hopes of its destruction. During the past quarter century, many of the states of east-central Europe failed to win the loyalty of some of their minorities, and the resulting insecurity vitiated the entire League régime for the protection of minorities. Plans for the future must rest on the foundations of loyalty and cooperation. But the devotion of minorities will not be achieved through injunctions or threats. Nor will toleration suffice, for it implies a measure of exclusion and inferiority. Loyalty is best rooted in a sense of belonging, and minorities will regard the state as their homeland when they, along with their institutions and customs, are fully integrated in the life of the larger community.

National federation can function within the framework of regional federations, thus satisfying at the same time the national requirements of minorities and the economic needs of all. Early in this war steps toward federation were taken by several governments-in-exile. For example, on November 11, 1940, the Polish and Czechoslovak governments declared their determination to enter "into a closer political and economic association," as the nucleus of a larger regional union. These efforts have since been abandoned, apparently because the Soviet Union disapproved for fear of another *cordon sanitaire*. . . .

If reason alone were to govern European reconstruction, we would propose that each regional federation be subdivided into its component national elements; that is, that every nationality inhabiting a given territory become a self-governing unit in the federal union. . . . However, since this is probably unattainable, it would be wiser to build less logically but more securely on the foundations of the present. In other words, the states as constituted before the outbreak of this war could combine into federations, retaining their historic unity but delegating to the central government specific functions. The structure of each state, however, must be changed: the national state in which the majority language and culture predominate should give way to the multi-national state. Each state-unit in the regional confederation would itself become a partnership of the leading nationalities (or linguistic and cultural groups) inhabiting its territory. The multi-national state would constitute national federalism.

Thus Jugoslavia (a member of the Balkan regional confederation) would consist of national territorial subdivisions like Serbia, Croatia, Slovenia, each enjoying full equality, especially with respect to language and culture. In each national subdivision (Croatia, for example) the language of the majority would be official, and this local national unit would have charge of the local administration, especially of cultural affairs, including education.

Regional confederation would help meet the economic needs of east-central Europe, while national federalism (that is, the reorganization of the state-members of the confederation into multi-national units) would eliminate many of the most acute minority problems, because cultural groups like the Sudeten Germans or the Hungarians of Transylvania would cease to be minorities. They would become equal partners in the multi-national state. However, small and scattered minorities would remain in the self-governing territorial subdivisions. For such national fragments, minority rights would be necessary.

The Rights of National Minorities

The actual freedoms which minorities require may be divided into two categories, namely, (1) human rights, and (2) national or cultural rights. The first category embraces the time-honored elementary rights of man—that is, citizenship, the protection of life and liberty, equality before the law, civil and political rights, religious freedom, and freedom from discrimination generally, including equality of economic opportunity. The national or cultural rights of minorities are concerned chiefly with special safeguards against linguistic and educational discrimination which might undermine the national-cultural cohesion of the group.

Precise and emphatic in their provisions for human rights, the Minorities Treaties may serve in part as a guide for the future, except that "freedom from want" will require clear formulation. The cultural safeguards, however, were inadequate, chiefly because minorities were denied recognition as corporate or group entities. The rights of man may be assured to a member of a minority as an individual, but language and culture are essentially *group* factors which depend upon common action for their preservation. . . .

The Critical Character of the Transitional Period

For parts of east-central Europe, the transitional period between war and peace is about to begin: it has indeed already begun. Measures taken during this period, although termed provisional and temporary, may prove of great moment for the future. Therefore, the spokesmen of the United Nations and the local leaders should be mindful of the fact that in east-central Europe they are dealing with a heterogeneous population, each of its segments within a territory differing in language, religion, culture and national feeling. They should be careful not to view conditions through the spectacles of a Western focus.

In the first place, it must be remembered that the Minorities Treaties were never legally terminated. Until a new régime is set up, the provisions of those Treaties should be considered as in force. Equality of status and treatment should be assured to all sections of the population, regardless of differences in race,

language or religion. The indiscriminate expulsion of habitual residents, whatever their national and cultural affiliation, should be
rigidly barred. Care will have to be taken that the technicalities of
repatriation do not operate to the disadvantage of national minorities. Relief agencies, like the UNRRA, should make provision for
the religious and linguistic requirements of all groups. Even the
military administration would gain in effectiveness if it could
learn to [negotiate] with the various nationality groups and take
advantage of their cohesion and internal organization. . . .

Ludvík Němec

The Separation
of Peoples as a
National Solution

Peoples in Eastern Europe, like the Jews and the Roma (Gypsies), suffered destruction during World War II, while bitter ethnic conflict
tore Yugoslavia apart. Expulsions and transfers of populations at the
end of the war determined the fate of other minorities. Czechoslovakia, a nationality state home to a number of minorities during the interwar era, endured partition when the minorities became involved in
the region's power politics in the 1930s. During the war, the
Czechoslovak government-in-exile, headed by Edvard Beneš, judged
a transfer of certain minorities necessary to the reconstruction of the
country once the fighting ended. This idea became the official policy
of the new government in 1945 and was accepted by the great powers
at the Potsdam Conference. The German and Hungarian minorities
were targeted because feelings against them ran high in the country.

From Ludvík Němec, "Solution of the Minorities Problem," from A *History of the
Czechoslovak Republic, 1918–1948,* ed. by Mamatey and Luza, pp. 416–427. Copy-
right © 1973 by Princeton University Press. Reprinted by permission of Princeton
University Press.

Carried out in an orderly fashion in Czechoslovakia, the transfer of populations became the way in which some East European governments affirmed their states' status as national societies.

In East Central Europe numerous historical migrations had resulted in a confluence of various ethnic groups that had little in common except the land they inhabited. Thus, in 1918 and again in 1945, Czechoslovakia inherited ethnic groups that had lived for centuries on its territory. The future of these minorities became an integral part of wartime plans for the reconstruction of the Czechoslovak Republic.

Although in the course of the war the idea of transferring these minorities from Czechoslovakia was accepted in principle by all the Great Powers, it remained to be seen what their reaction would be when they were confronted with a workable plan for its implementation.

At the end of July, 1944, the European Advisory Committee of Britain, Soviet Russia, and the United States, meeting in London, requested the Allied governments to submit their proposals for the capitulation of Germany. In its reply on August 24, 1944, the Czechoslovak government in exile submitted a memorandum proposing a concrete plan for the transfer of its German minority: some 1,600,000 Germans were to be removed to Germany and about 800,000 reliable Germans were to retain their citizenship. . . . The transfer would take about two years, with some compensation assured for the immovable properties of the transferees. This principle was to be inserted as an armistice condition of the Reich's capitulation to make certain that the idea of a transfer was recognized and accepted by the Germans. . . .

The reaction of the Western powers was marked by an attitude of caution. While the British government pondered the plan "with care and sympathy," the United States advised that it be carried out "under international auspices, gradually and in an orderly manner." The Soviet government reaffirmed its support of the plan, to which it had already assented in 1943. Further negotiations with Britain followed.

The Czechoslovak government regarded agreement by the Great Powers as a basic precondition for the plan, because of their responsibility to the great number of people to be affected by the transfer. The Great Powers viewed the transfer as a necessary evil, closely related to the solution of the problems of postwar Europe. They hoped that by carrying out the plan, some measure of balance would be achieved in East Central Europe.

The concept of the transfer became part of the official program of the new Czechoslovak government set up at Košice. It was incorporated into [the] Košice program of April 5, 1945. The program assured those members of the German and Magyar minorities in Czechoslovakia who had *actively* fought against nazism and fascism of full rights as Czechoslovak citizens. As for other members of the German and Magyar minorities, it provided as follows:

> . . . [t]hose Germans and Magyars who will have been prosecuted and condemned for a crime against the Republic and the Czech and Slovak people, [they] will be declared to have forfeited their Czechoslovak citizenship and, unless they are under sentence of death, will be expelled from the Republic forever.

The program was regarded as being relatively moderate, since it offered the right of option and thus handled the minority question cautiously. However, the communists did not yet fully appreciate the radical mood of the country. During the Nazi occupation national feelings had been so aroused that the expulsion of the Germans and Magyars assumed the status of a crusade. It was regarded as a protest against the sufferings of the past rather than as a mere political arrangement. . . .

It is important to note the different moods prevailing in Slovakia and in the Czech lands fully to understand their different reactions to, and acceptance of, the Košice program. The Slovaks were indignant against the Magyars with whom they had had painful experiences during the existence of the Slovak state. They had not forgotten that their compatriots in the southern regions, incorporated within Hungary in 1938, had suffered at the hands of the Magyar authorities. Toward the Germans, the Slovak attitude was pragmatic. . . . The Czechs had more justification for being adamant enemies of the Germans, which explains why the solution to the problem of the German minority took precedence among the Czechs over other minority problems in the period immediately following the war. . . .

President Edvard Beneš exhorted the Czechs and Slovaks to act with reason and patience. He insisted that no final settlement, especially one that involved a transfer, could be reached without the sanction of the Great Powers, and such agreement might be withheld if the people were not more circumspect in their actions.

On July 3, the Prague government requested the three Allied powers to place the question of the transfer on the agenda of the approaching Potsdam conference (July 17–August 2, 1945). On July 22, Prague submitted its completed plan to the Great Powers for the orderly removal of the Germans. On July 25, the question was put on the agenda and a subcommittee was appointed to draw up a draft of the question. After a discussion on July 31, the transfer was approved and it became Article XII of the Potsdam Declaration. . . .

On January 8–9, 1946, a series of meetings were held in Prague between American and Czechoslovak officials to complete plans for the organized transfer. It was agreed that each trainload would include 1,200 persons in 40 heated cars. The Czechoslovak government was to provide sufficient food for the trip and for three additional days. Families were to be kept together, clothing was to be adequate, and every person was to be permitted to take with him personal belongings totaling 30 to 50 kilograms and an allowance of 1,000 Reichsmarks. . . .

The Czechoslovak authorities, mindful of world opinion, made every effort to carry out the transfer according to the principles laid down at Potsdam. Their actions were noted by foreign correspondents, official observers, and diplomatic representatives. . . . One aspect, which perhaps casts a shadow over the transfer procedure, was the expropriation without compensation of all the properties of the transferees except their personal belongings. It must be said in justice, however, that President Beneš had proposed compensation, but his plan was rejected by the Czechoslovak communists and some extremists. . . .

Besides the organized transfer, there were voluntary emigrations of Germans from Czechoslovakia, amounting to about 30,000 persons by June, 1949. . . . Finally, what may be called a philanthropic emigration should be mentioned. On October 26, 1949, the Bonn government applied to the Allied High Commission for the transfer of some 20,000 Germans in order "to reunite these persons with their relatives." By agreement with Prague, a total of 16,832 Germans were removed by April 28, 1951. After all the transfers there still remained in Czechoslovakia about 165,000 registered Germans. This indicates how difficult it is in practice to achieve a truly national state.

One interesting feature of the Potsdam conference was its concentration on the Germans. The handling of their satellites was left to the various states. As a result, the question of the Magyar minority reverted to the Czechoslovak government, which applied the principle of collective responsibility to the Magyars since they had, at the time of the Munich crisis, manifested a desire to be united with the country of their origin and had exploited the weaknesses of the republic toward this end, with the full support of Nazi Germany. The removal of the Hungarian minority was envisaged in the Košice program and reaffirmed by the decision of the political parties of the National Front on April 11, 1946, which established the principle that Czechoslovakia was to be a national state of Czechs and Slovaks only.

. . . The Czechoslovak government was handicapped in its attempt to resolve this problem because Budapest was initially unwilling to accept any removal of Hungarians from Slovakia. The arbitrary expulsion of the Magyars, their deprivation of civil rights, and the confiscation of their property, seemingly justified by the Košice program, so alarmed Budapest that a Hungarian delegation arrived in Prague in the autumn of 1945 to discuss this issue. . . . The Hungarian delegation accepted the idea of an exchange, but categorically refused to approve any expulsion. In their second conference, held on February 27, 1946, at Tatranská Lomnica in Slovakia, the Hungarian delegate agreed that Czechoslovakia could "expatriate as many Hungarians as there were Slovaks in Hungary naturally desirous of returning to establish themselves in Czechoslovakia." In return, Prague pledged to suspend expulsion, halt the confiscation, and make compensation for what had already been taken.

The exchange was to begin in August, 1946. However, the Hungarian government adopted delaying tactics in the hope that the Paris Peace Conference would oblige the Czechoslovak government to grant civil status to the Magyar minority in Czechoslovakia, and that the exchange would then become unnecessary. The Czechoslovak delegation to the Paris Peace Conference held to the plan for the unilateral expulsion of 200,000 Magyars in addition to the exchange previously agreed upon, but did not insist upon the confiscation of their properties. The conference recognized Czechoslovakia's right to insist on the principle of a national state and acknowledged the principle of an exchange of population, but rejected any further unilateral transfer. . . .

To whittle down the Magyar ethnic minority, the Czechoslovak government scattered a part of it over the country, especially in the Sudeten borderland regions. The dispersal was carried out under the provisions of presidential decree No. 88/1945 concerning "The Mobilization of Manpower," which authorized the recruiting of laborers for a limited time to perform urgently needed public works. This action began on November 17, 1947, and was effected with the help and support of the army. It was brought to an end on February 25, 1948.

On the whole, the program was unsuccessful because many Magyars preferred to escape or pass secretly into Hungary. This operation was, of course, designed to camouflage the compulsory internal resettlement, for in some cases family members as well as workers were evacuated from their homes by force and the promise of receiving property as compensation in their new homes. . . . The attempt to liquidate the Magyar minority was unsuccessful. . . . [A]ccording to recent calculations, the Hungarian minority in Czechoslovakia still numbers between 720,000 and 740,000. . . .

The after-effects of these solutions to the problem of ethnic minorities in Czechoslovakia are evident even today. The suffering inflicted upon these peoples and the feelings of resentment that it engendered brought a tragic end to the centuries-old ethnic symbiosis that had been a feature of Central European history. . . .

In Hungary dislike of the communist regime turned into a nationalist rising against Soviet domination in the fall of 1956. Demonstrators insert a Hungarian national flag into the remains of a huge statue of Stalin, which was toppled from its pedestal during the struggle. (UPI/Bettman Newsphotos)

PART

IV

Communism and Nationalism: The Persistence of the National Idea

Vladimir Dedijer

Titoism

After World War II, Soviet military might and political influence helped communists come to power in Eastern Europe. Yugoslavia was an exception. Here the communists, led by Tito, organized a significant resistance movement called the Partisans during the war. The movement succeeded in taking over the multinational country in 1945. Stalin's determination to exercise greater control over the East European states led to a clash with the Yugoslavs, and they were ousted from the communist fold in 1948. The Yugoslav communists defended themselves and rallied the country by arguing that they were building a socialist society congruent with national interests.

From *Tito Speaks* by Vladimir Dedijer, Weidenfeld and Nicolson, 1953, pp. 435–446, 450. Reprinted by permission of Weidenfeld & Nicolson Ltd.

Vladimir Dedijer fought as a Partisan and was a member of the Central Committee of the Yugoslav Communist Party. He later devoted himself to historical writing. In the selection below, he outlines several tenets that became known as "Titoism," or national communism. The Yugoslav communists claimed that they had inspired a national revolution during the war, were building a socialist society, and were creating a "Yugoslav" national identity (Yugoslavism) based on the notion of "brotherhood and unity"—all while staying true to the ideas of Marx and Lenin regarding the role of the state and the party in society.

If we ask ourselves today what Yugoslavia has gained since she came into open conflict with the Soviet Union, we can reply quite definitely that the Yugoslavs, by preventing the subjugation of their country, have defended their right to an unhampered, independent development. They have rejected the Moscow thesis that "imitation of the Russian icon is the only correct and possible road towards socialism."

Accordingly, the international significance of Yugoslav resistance against Soviet expansion does not consist only in the fact that a small country has maintained and successfully defended the principle of equality between States, and in particular equality between large and small countries. Apart from that, Yugoslavia's internal development, especially during the last four years, has shown clearly in practice all the absurdities of the Kremlin contention that its way must be the way of all other countries. Defending the right of each country to move forward freely, in its own specific way, the Yugoslavs rebelled against a monopoly of socialism, even against a monopoly of their own socialism.

The Yugoslavs do not consider their course to be the only possible course. It may perhaps be useful as an experience, but it is not the inevitable course others must follow. In Yugoslavia there is a belief that socialism in the world today is developing in various ways; that the elements of a new society are mingling with elements of the old society, that the elements of the socialist society are emerging in a series of States, although they are not called socialist. In Yugoslavia it is believed that one revolutionary path is not inevitable for all other countries, especially for the economically advanced countries. In principle, the view of the Yugoslav Communists is that no progressive movement should once and for all renounce the philosophy of the revolutionary path. But it is obvious that no one should make a revolution just for the sake of revolution. If the advancement of society, that is to say, the solution of economic, social, and political problems, can be achieved without revolutionary means, so much the better. . . .

There is no doubt that the October Revolution in Russia in 1917 and the revolution in Yugoslavia in 1941, by their very character, have much in common. In both countries, the working masses came to power through revolution. But, setting aside for the moment the differences in the development of these two revolutions, it is necessary to point out that the Yugoslav revolution was built on a far wider basis than the October Revolution in Russia.

The October Revolution rallied the people against the war, calling upon them to abandon the front line; the Yugoslav revolution was carried out during the Second World War, calling people to the front to defend their fatherland. In the war of liberation, patriotism and social discontent were allied, and as a direct result, the masses entered directly into the struggle. While, especially at the beginning, the Russian revolution embraced the working masses in only a few large centres, the Yugoslav revolution enlisted broad masses of peasantry, the poor and even the rich, under the leadership of the working class. Furthermore, the majority of the intelligentsia joined the ranks of the revolution, while in Russia they held back. In Yugoslavia, the revolution won the support of a part of the clergy, if only the lower clergy of the Serbian-Orthodox and Moslem communities; the Russian clergy remained hostile.

Through its national character also, the basis of the revolution was broader in Yugoslavia. While in the revolution in Yugoslavia (a multi-national state) all five Yugoslav peoples took part, the revolution in Russia (also a multi-national state) was carried out primarily in a few large proletarian centres, where the population consisted largely of Russian inhabitants. . . .

In every revolution, at the outset, it is necessary to create a centralized State apparatus so that the aims of the revolution may be protected and successfully defended against attempts at counter-revolution. This apparatus is, in fact, inevitable and at first progressive, but at the same time it forms the principal source of bureaucracy. Therefore the functions of the State should begin to wither away from the moment the working masses take power. But in backward countries, as Russia was, there is always the danger that the State apparatus will begin as the servant of the community and end as its master. . . .

In Yugoslavia the development has been different. The achievements of the revolution are being protected, in so far as no return to the old conditions will be permitted, no return to the defeated and discredited classes, the exploitation of man by man. The French Revolution has proclaimed: no freedom for the enemies of freedom. But the development in Yugoslavia, on the other hand, is more in the direction of a socialist democracy, towards the withering away of the State, towards debureaucratization and decentralization, towards less and less interference with the work and life of individuals. In this respect the basic thing is the rights of the producers; whether they may freely decide about their surplus labour, or whether this is done by State officials. . . .

Before Yugoslavia lies still another vast problem to be reckoned with — the problem of the village. It is clear that it would result in sheer economic catastrophe if the village were permitted to consist of small producers with their primitive agricultural equipment. A terrific disproportion between industry and agriculture is already emerging. . . .

The problem of the village in socialism is the basic problem with which the Yugoslavs now have to deal. They are fully aware that the solution lies in some form of co-operative, but the proper form — one which would harmonize the interests of the peasant-producers with the interests of the community, which would stimulate the villages as the factories have been stimulated — this has not yet been found.

Tito enumerates the differences between the Yugoslav and Soviet social systems as follows:

"The first difference, the principal one, is that we are building genuine socialism, while in the Soviet Union the building up of socialism has degenerated into State capitalism under the leadership of a dictatorial bureaucratic caste.

"Second, socialist democracy in Yugoslavia is beginning to dominate the country's entire social life, and nothing impedes an even more rapid development except the lack of technology and a too-slow increase of tempo in socialist consciousness on the part of the citizens of our country. Yet, while in our country this democratic development is noticeable from day to day, in the Soviet Union there is no democracy at all. . . .

"Third, here in Yugoslavia the national question has been correctly solved, both formally and in substance, and a federative State has been created out of six republics, based on an equality in which the various peoples freely decide their lives and their futures. A national community has been created in which there is no leading nation to impose its will on the others, nor to suppress other peoples. In the Soviet Union, the national question has been solved on paper, but in substance nothing has been carried out except a formal creation of different republics governed by one nation — the Russian nation. By decree of the bureaucratic leaders in Moscow, not only entire republics but whole nations are being forcibly moved and exposed to annihilation. . . ."

As we see, in Yugoslavia the State is withering away, and a socialist democracy is developing. But what of the Communist Party? What of the one-party system in Yugoslavia? I remember a discussion on this question between Tito . . . on one side and an outstanding socialist leader of Western Europe on the other. . . .

The Western socialist asked if the Communist Party in Yugoslavia were withering away.

"The Communist Party cannot continue to function in the same old way if at the same time the State is withering away," Tito replied. "If the State does not wither away, then the Party becomes, in a certain sense, an instrument of the State, a force outside of society. If the State really withers away, the Party necessarily withers away with it. Many of our own people do not realize this fact yet. We have to explain to them gradually what this withering away consists in, and we have begun to do so."

Visitor: "As far as we can see, the Yugoslav masses understand very well two practical aspects of the withering away of the State: the decentralization and debureaucratization. They well understand these specific steps, but have they truly understood the second, theoretical part of the problem: the withering away of the Party?"

Tito: "This process will take a little longer." . . .

"I would like to point out the unsoundness of objections based on our so-called one-party system. We do have one revolutionary party which leads the country and provides its entire theoretical and practical line. But united in our People's Front we have all the citizens of our country who are in agreement with the final aim and programme of the Communist Party. These are not necessarily Communists; they are people who desire a change, who want a socialist society. . . .

"But you must also consider that in a revolutionary period it is absurd to speak about a multi-party system. What does such a system mean? Several parties mean several programmes, and here in our country, there is only one programme: to create a socialist society. This programme unites the vast majority of the citizens of our country. Those opposed to this programme cannot be permitted to impede its realization." . . .

In the West it is often believed that since 1948 Yugoslavia has been creating a new ideological line, a so-called "Titoism." Some people even have gone so far as to compare Tito with Luther, with Stalin in the role of the Pope.

I once brought this matter up with Tito. "Titoism as a separate ideological line does not exist," he answered at once. "To put it as an ideology would be stupid. I do not say that out of modesty. It is simply that we have added nothing to Marxist-Leninist doctrine. We have only applied that doctrine in harmony with our own situation. Since there is nothing new, there is no new ideology. Should 'Titoism' become an ideological line, we would become revisionist; we would have renounced Marxism. We are Marxists, I am a Marxist and therefore I cannot be a 'Titoist'. Stalin is the revisionist: it is he who has wandered from the Marxist road." . . .

This is Tito's opinion. But, if "Titoism" as an ideology of its own does not exist, it is not entirely meaningless if this term is used to reflect the desire of individual countries to resist the expansion of the great powers. This expression is in particular much applied in the case of Eastern European countries which are exposed to the oppression of the Soviet Union. For the very fact that Yugoslavia exists as an independent socialist country after more than four years of open conflict with the USSR, that Yugoslavia continues to find its own way to socialism — these facts are a nightmare to the Kremlin. . . .

In essence, "Titoism" is identical with the right of every nation to equality with others and to the right of independent development. That is, in reality, the basis of the foreign policy of Yugoslavia. It is based on the principles of the Charter of the United Nations.

For that reason Yugoslavia did not want to join any bloc or union, because it considers that the Charter and its system of collective security is the fundamental source of its international rights and obligations; that the sources of aggression are not different ideologies but the expansionism of States. . . .

Peter Pastor

Official Nationalism

Stalinist rule wrought major upheaval on the societies of Eastern Europe. Following the death of Stalin, Soviet leaders attempted to ameliorate the worst aspects of the system. Their actions only worsened the strain in Hungary, where Stalinists like Mátyás Rákosi still held power and the Communist party was deeply resented. In 1956 the Hungarian people rose against communist rule, but the Soviet military promptly crushed their revolt. In the aftermath of the uprising, János Kádár, who had sided with the Soviets, took control. Initially seen as a betrayer of the Hungarian nation, Kádár set out to chart a "separate road to socialism" with the approval of then Soviet leader Nikita Khrushchev.

Peter Pastor, a historian, describes how Hungarian communist intellectuals sought to gain some legitimacy for the regime by dis-

"Official Nationalism in Hungary Since 1964" by Peter Pastor from *Nationalism in the USSR and Eastern Europe,* ed. by George Simmonds, University of Detroit Press, 1977, pp. 410–416.

cussing the meaning of the nation and its place in a socialist society. A combination of toeing the Soviet line on foreign matters, accepting anyone not openly against the regime, and promoting national pride were the main elements in an attempt at an official nationalism called "socialist patriotism." Although recourse to the national past helped, it was the regime's efforts to improve material conditions that brought it and Kádár a measure of acceptance.

Hungarian nationalism and Marxism have been strangely intertwined from the very first explosion of romantic nationalism in Hungary in 1848–49. The efforts of Louis Kossuth[1] and the other Hungarian revolutionaries to bring about Magyar domination in a multi-national state carried the support of the founder of Marxism — Karl Marx himself. For Marx, the Magyars had the right to limit the national aspirations of the non-Magyar nationalities, who were labeled as reactionary and immature. The survival of the Hungarian imperium was justified by Marx on the grounds that it was a historic state.

The lost war and the collapse of the Austro-Hungarian Empire in 1918, however, seemed to turn the Marxian model upside down. The peacemakers in Paris in 1919 aimed at reducing Hungary to an ethnically pure "Magyarie." This was to be accomplished by the detachment of even ethnically Magyar territories from the Magyar heartland. The Hungarian heirs to Marx's legacy came to the defense of the "realm of Saint Stephen."[2] The Hungarian Soviet Republic which was born in March 1919 was the result of national exasperation and the Marxist slogans adopted spoke of an international war against "Entente Imperialism". . . .

The collapse of the Hungarian Soviet Republic and the subsequent Peace Treaty of Trianon did create the kind of peace the Peace Conference wanted with an ethnically Magyar Hungary

[1]Louis Kossuth (1802–1894) was a liberal nationalist who led the Hungarians in the revolutionary events of 1848–1849. — Ed.

[2]The realm of Saint Stephen comprised the historic territories of the Hungarian Kingdom before World War I. — Ed.

surrounded by multi-national states with Magyar *irredenta*. Only Austria, Hungary's western neighbor, was an exception. The revisionist nationalism of the interwar Horthy era with its anti-communism continued the struggle initiated by Béla Kún.[3] The issue of revisionism was finally settled with a second defeat of Hungary in the course of World War II. This time, however, it was Marxist Soviet Russia and its dictator J. V. Stalin who established the boundaries of the Hungarian state, which were similar to the ones which were rejected by the Hungarian communists in 1919.

In the process Hungary became, ethnically, almost purely Magyar again, but it also became the virtual colony of the Soviet Union. One of the duties of Stalin's puppet in Budapest, Mátyás Rákosi, was to eliminate the ideology of nationalism. In its place he attempted to shape a new communist Magyar subservient to the whim of Stalin's great Russian chauvinism. . . . Instead of nationalism, the Hungarians were to embrace socialist patriotism. The new patriot was to count out the nation which, according to Stalin, was a historic unit doomed to disappear in the Socialist stage of history. Thus, socialist patriotism was the ideology of the working class, overriding national interest. . . .

The relatively brief but traumatic Stalin era came to its end with Khrushchev's thaw. This new policy was necessitated by the power struggle in the Soviet Party presidium and by the mechanism of the modernization process which could no longer function along Stalinistic totalitarian lines. In the struggle for his own survival and for the survival of the Soviet bloc, now on the verge of economic chaos, Khrushchev saw national communism as the panacea. His . . . recognition of "many roads to communism" was hoped to generate popular consensus behind the East European leaders, while discrediting hard-line Stalinists everywhere.

Khrushchev, however, miscalculated and, in October 1956, the Hungarian national communists, pressured by the nationalism and the Russophobia of the masses, opted for an end to Hungary's colonial status. The revolutionary government of October 1956 was an heir to the Kún régime. . . .

---

[3]Béla Kún was a Hungarian communist who attempted to create a Soviet-style socialist state in Hungary in 1919. — Ed.

What was missing from the ideology of national communism of 1956, however, was . . . territorial revisionism. . . . The defeat of the Hungarian revolutionaries and the subsequent execution of Imre Nagy[4] and some other Hungarian national communists indicated clearly that the Hungarian road to socialism was still to be mapped out by the Soviet Union. Definitions of the national components of socialism still had to be arrived at with Moscow's approval, if not by its initiative. The lesson for Khrushchev's man in Budapest, János Kádár, was clear: Hungary must toe the Soviet line when it comes to international issues, and for the Soviets, nationalism was an international issue. . . . The events of 1956 did not mean, however, that Hungary had to accept the exact Soviet internal model. Rather, the Soviet Union was still willing to accept differences as long as they did not threaten the existing relations of this east European country with Moscow. . . .

In Hungary, following the process of retribution and party reorganization (1957–1959), the Hungarian communists were ready to tackle the issue of nationalism with Khrushchev's blessings. Thus, aspects of what Professor Peter Sugár calls "*apparatchik* nationalism" were adopted in Hungary, too. Still labeled as socialist patriotism, this warmed-over ideology now stressed its national aspects, which were arrived at through the usual communist method — debate.

The debate was opened in 1960 by the dean of Marxist historians, Erik Molnár. The repentant Stalinist now revised the former view that nationalism was bad. It was now characterized as fit for a multi-class historic epoch. In a one class system of socialism, patriotism was serving socialist national interest while simultaneously serving international interests too. With this new definition, the socialist patriot could have his cake and eat it, too.

Developments in Hungary were closely scrutinized by Khrushchev — who was a frequent visitor to Hungary — as if to prove his point that socialism can work in Hungary. Improvements in the standard of living because of the halt of pre-1956

---

[4]A reform-minded communist, Nagy was prime minister at the time of the 1956 uprising. He was arrested by Soviet authorities and later executed. — Ed.

type exactions were identified with the success of communist leadership and with Khruschev's political acumen. The braggart Soviet leader had even coined the phrase "goulash socialism," ostensibly to identify Hungary's unique trek to socialism. . . . In Hungary, the Magyars were encouraged to contribute to economic well-being through the call of Kádár; "he who is not against us is with us."

The coup d'état of October 1964 which brought about the Brezhnev, Kosygin ascendancy did not mean the fall of Kádár, Khrushchev's favorite East European, nor of Khrushchev's East European policies. Instead, the momentum initiated under Khrushchev was accelerated during the next three years while the Soviet leadership was in a transition. . . .

In Hungary, debates on the meaning of nation and patriotism did not abate either. Changes in Soviet nationalities policies following the 23rd Party Congress of March 1966 gave the Hungarians new freedom to follow the old path. The Khrushchevian party program for the Soviet nationalities projected the imminent merger of the nationalities. The new program, responding to the needs of the new leadership opted for a *"rapprochement"* of the nationalities in an undated future. . . .

As a consequence, the Hungarians rediscovered their Magyar brethren in Transylvania, where forced assimilation was the Romanian policy. No doubt, in addition to the decisions of the Soviet Party Congress the cooling of Soviet-Romanian relations also contributed to this new Magyar interest. The debate form was used again as Hungarian writers reviewed the Magyar literature in neighboring countries. Their message was that Magyar authors in Hungary had a responsibility to aid Magyar culture in the neighboring countries. As the Romanians were becoming more independent of Moscow, the Hungarians became more interested in Transylvania. In 1971, the nationalities issue was brought up openly in the Budapest parliament. . . .

The literary debate in 1968 had another significance. It signaled the broadening of the discussion on the meaning of the nation and patriotism by a larger segment of the intelligentsia. With this development the popularizing stage of the debate was reached. . . . There was a revival of the discussion of pros and cons of interwar nonrevisionist varieties of nationalism — the populist-urbanist debate. The question centered on whether the national heritage is best preserved in the peasant culture or in the intellectual culture of the cities. It is significant to point out, however, that revisionism [was] not a part of the discussion. Soviet Russian attitudes on the sanctity of East European borders would exclude the reappearance of this type of nationalism. . . .

In the nationalism debate one of the most notable contributions came from the prominent Hungarian author, the late Péter Veres. In his essay, which appeared in the Party daily *Népszabadság*, Veres rejected the Marxist meaning of the nation as defined along class lines. This view states that in Hungary's past only the exploiting feudal and later capitalist minorities formed the nation, while in the uni-class socialist state everyone belongs to the nation. Veres argued that the nation was always a collective, irrespective of class lines. Thus, Veres, a populist, reiterated his belief in the "eternal nation," which he claimed still existed in Hungary. . . .

. . . The party leaders . . . claim that it is this traditional nationalism which is responsible for anti-Soviet feelings in Hungary. . . . In reality, however, hostility to the Soviet Union is a more recent phenomenon in Hungary which could be traced back to the liberation of 1945, which turned out to be an occupation. Even if one uses the Marxist yardstick for Hungarian nationalism, one could see an "inevitable" rise of national feelings. The Marxists claim that in Hungary's past the struggle against foreign oppressors brought the privileged classes of the nation together with the unprivileged "patriotic" masses, creating nationalism. Today, a foreign oppressor is visibly there and official social patriotism is unsuccessful in its fight against the virulent Russophobia which exists in Hungary, and which fuels traditional nationalism.

The Soviet presence is clearly in the mind of all debaters. The Hungarian communists who need to encourage national pride in order to ensure their success at home are in a difficult position when they have to justify their policy before their masters. Loyalty to Moscow has to be stated and of course the "moderates" in the Soviet nationality debates have to be supported, since it is the moderate line which preserves Hungarian interests. It also justifies the existence of the NEM,[5] which was rejected by the Russians as a method for the Soviet economy. In the long run it is clear, therefore, that the question of nationalism is an issue of politics and not of intellectual mental gymnastics.

The final say-so on nationalism and patriotism, therefore, had to come from the Party, and it did come in the Fall of 1974. . . . In September the Cultural-political Subcommittee of the Central Committee of the Hungarian Socialist Labor Party issued its position paper, "The Timely Questions of Socialist Patriotism and International Socialism." . . .

Naturally the document praised socialist patriotism while "bourgeois nationalism" was branded as an attempt to undermine socialist internationalism and integration. . . . The committee called for the preservation of national traditions, but it gave warning that these traditions could also feed the forces of nationalism and provincialism. Its criticism of petty bourgeois egoism also sounded the end for the populist-urbanist debate. Both tendencies were identified as "petty bourgeois." . . .

While the tone of the policy paper seems to indicate that the debate on nationalism has come to an end, it is also a testimony to the fact that contemporary policies on nationalism in Hungary were found acceptable by the Russians. It is evident, therefore, that for Hungary there has been no radical break between Khrushchev and Brezhnev.

The Kádár régime was the creation of Khrushchev as a result of Russian intervention. The right of Soviet intervention in the affairs of its satellites had been reinforced by the Brezhnev doctrine. The position paper recognizes the validity of the Brezhnev doctrine when it states:

> *The national interest of the socialist states must be synthesized with the international interests of socialism. If the assumed or the*

[5]The New Economic Mechanism (NEM) was an economic-reform plan implemented in Hungary in 1968. It aimed to improve productivity through decentralization of the economy and incentives for enterprise effort, to provide more consumer goods, and to make Hungarian products competitive in the international market. — Ed.

> *temporarily real national interest would compromise international interest, then not only international but in the final outcome the national interest of socialist society is damaged. In its historic meaning, not one socialist country could profit at the expense of another.*

The party document also had to deal with the anti-Russian feelings of the Magyars. The committee's solution was education through which the socialist achievements in the Soviet Union would be described "in a richer and more truthful way." Anti-Sovietism was also identified as an imperialist ideological diversion to break up the socialist world. It is of little surprise that the Hungarian Party reiterated its loyalty to socialist patriotism. . . .

In spite of all these expressions of socialist patriotism, it is evident that, at its worst, it is merely an empty propaganda phrase and, at best, a new pattern of nationalism. As a pattern of nationalism it could be labeled as "utopian nationalism," which found few adherents in Hungary. . . . The régime's call for the incorporation of "national traditions" in socialist patriotism is, actually, a tacit recognition that socialist patriotism must be propped up by traditional patterns of nationalism, such as political nationalism, economic nationalism, and romantic nationalism. . . .

Kádár, as ruler, managed to gain some semblance of affection among his compatriots, who recognize that in the shadow of Soviet bayonets he succeeded in furthering the thaw in totalitarianism. His policy also helped to improve the standard of living, which is among the highest in Eastern Europe and surpasses the Russian one. Still, one could claim that Hungarian devotion to him is only skin deep. . . . Since Kádár's source of power emanates from the system, his strength has not been built on firm foundations.

Kádár's successes in the economic sphere, however, have indeed contributed to national pride in Magyar talents. Kádár's attempt to utilize the COMECON[6] as a "Common Market" rather than an integrated economic unit seem to smack of economic na-

---

[6]The Council for Mutual Economic Assistance (COMECON) was created in 1949 by the U.S.S.R. in response to the Marshall Plan. Its purpose was not to create a common economic market in Eastern Europe but to coordinate the economic plans of the member communist states. — Ed.

tionalism. The relatively high standard of living achieved via the New Economic Mechanism contributes to economic nationalism. Although the Soviet Union indicated disapproval of the Hungarian economic model which stresses decentralization, and although the Hungarians in turn promised to mend their way by firing some NEM proponents from the government, the economic system remained the same. . . .

As the Hungarian Party leaders perceived, economic nationalism as a tool of the establishment also has limits. The average Magyar worker just has to look toward the West to note that recession notwithstanding his peer in the West enjoys a higher standard of living. Thus, the Party needs to stress the attack on "consumerism."

Romantic nationalism as a pattern reinforcing socialist patriotism can best be seen in Hungary in the revival of pseudohistorical debates among the historians of Hungary and its neighbors. Closely related to this development is the revival of what George Mikes called *gatya nationalism,* named after the white, freely flowing trousers which were worn by Hungarian horsemen of the nineteenth century. As the term may suggest, it is the regime's attempt at nostalgia.

The use of romantic nationalism has its dangers, which had been recognized and denounced. Most significantly, Russophobia has recently been most virulently expressed on anniversary celebrations of the 1848 revolution. On recent March 15ths Hungarian students, identifying with the youth of March 1848, have demonstrated against Soviet occupation. The result is that March 15 is still a working day and students must show medical excuses in order to miss school on that day.

. . . [It] is simple to conclude that official Hungarian policies on nationalism have closely followed the policy approved by the Brezhnev-Kosygin leadership, the masters over the Kádár regime. The policy of the last ten years indicates a continuity of practices initiated during the Khrushchev era. Socialist patriotism, the new pattern of nationalism, is successful so long as it exhibits characteristics which, like the proverbial emperor's clothes, are much like traditional patterns of nationalism. Socialist patriotism as an international doctrine has been a failure because it merely camouflages the Brezhnev doctrine. . . .

George Klein

Socialist Crises and Nationalist Politics

In the 1960s, the communist regimes in Eastern Europe, at the urging of Khrushchev and later Brezhnev, attempted to provide more consumer goods and better living conditions for their peoples while boosting economic productivity. Soviet leaders hoped that making such improvements would validate the claim that socialism offered a better way for society to develop. In Czechoslovakia those who still believed in this ideal began with proposals for economic reform and went on to advocate changes in all aspects of society by the spring of 1968. In Yugoslavia Tito committed the League of Yugoslav Communists to further economic reform and political decentralization. Czechoslovakia's hope of creating "socialism with a human face" led to a massive invasion by Warsaw Pact countries in August 1968. The changes in Yugoslavia sparked political ferment in the republic of Croatia that eventually brought a crackdown by Tito and the federal authorities. George Klein, a political scientist, demonstrates how nationalism figured in the political crises in both of these multinational states supposedly dedicated to internationalism.

Yugoslavia and Czechoslovakia [were] multinational states where the ethnic question [was] intertwined with almost all political issues. The Croat and Slovak questions [were] the focus of political concern for both states since their formation in the aftermath of World War I. The political dynamics of ethnicity differ[ed] in the two states, however. . . .

The atmosphere of ferment which permeated Czechoslovakia

"The Role of Ethnic Politics in the Czechoslovak Crises of 1968 and the Yugoslav Crisis of 1971" by George Klein, from *Studies in Comparative Communism*, v. 8, no. 4 (Winter 1975), pp. 339–369, Butterworth Scientific Ltd.

in 1968 and Yugoslavia in 1971 reached far beyond the problems of ethnic demands, but ethnicity played a vital role in all the events in both states. . . .

The Czechoslovak and Yugoslav events resulted from the activities of reforming coalitions, which had been instrumental in changing the quality of political life in both states over a period of years. In the aftermath of liberalism in both states, the respective Communist parties moved toward greater orthodoxy. Because the status quo had been far more conservative in Czechoslovakia than in Yugoslavia during the previous two decades, the Party discipline reimposed there has been quite different from that in Yugoslavia. In Yugoslavia, a federal government intervened in the political life of one of the constituent republics. There were no breaches of international legality, and the Yugoslav events remained a purely internal matter. In Czechoslovakia, the termination of the Prague Spring by Soviet intervention was in clear contempt of Czechoslovak sovereignty. . . .

In both states, the political processes were not permitted to run their full course; the democratization of the existing system was by no means the only possible outcome. The federal leadership of Yugoslavia obviously feared for the integrity of the state and for the continued role of the League of Communists within it. Ultimately, the Soviet leadership justified the Soviet entry into Czechoslovakia on a very similar basis.

Ethnicity and the Organization of Czechoslovakia and Yugoslavia

Yugoslavia ha[d] been a federation since 1945, when the Partisan leadership carried out its wartime pledge to create a federal state. Czechoslovakia, on the other hand, a unitary state since its inception in 1918, . . . rendered only token recognition to Slovak autonomy. Until Novotný's surrender of power in 1968, the Czechoslovak Communists followed the established centralist tradition. . . .

The Yugoslav tradition under Communism [was] substantially different. The Yugoslav Constitution of 1946 established a federal state based on Soviet practice and the Soviet Constitution of

1936. The Yugoslav leadership implemented federalism only after the promulgation of workers' self-management in June 1950. To justify Yugoslavia's existence outside the Cominform,[1] the Yugoslav leadership presented self-management and the subsequent decentralization as being in accord with the principles of Marxism-Leninism. The "withering" of power at the center was hailed as the prelude to the withering of the state.

In Czechoslovakia, by contrast, centralism was the universally proclaimed policy, subscribed to by all, including the secretaries of the Slovak Communist Party. All deviations from this centralist position were persecuted as bourgeois nationalism. . . .

Ethnic Conflict in Perspective

The fundamental psychological orientation of the Croats and Slovaks toward their respective major nationalities differed vastly. Slovakia joined the Czechoslovak Republic in 1918 at a far less developed stage than the Czech lands and became a fertile field for directed development. The Czechs cultivated colonial attitudes toward the Slovaks, while the Slovaks suffered from inferiority feelings vis-à-vis the Czechs. On the other hand, the Croats' self-image as part of the Hapsburg domains was one of cultural superiority toward the Serbs and they viewed themselves as the carriers of superior Western culture. The ideal of Yugoslavia and Yugoslavism had wide currency among the South Slavs of the Austro-Hungarian Empire but was far less a part of the political culture of the Slavs of Ottoman territories. Misconceptions originated with the very formation of the Kingdom of Serbs, Croats, and Slovenes. The Croat leaders believed that they were joining an enlightened South Slavic federation, while the Serbs thought that the other nationalities should welcome their inclusion in an expanded Serbian state. This fundamental misunderstanding,

---

[1]The Communist Information Bureau (Cominform) was founded in 1947 and used by Stalin to impose order and control the communist parties in Eastern Europe. It was abolished in 1956 in light of the new policy of "peaceful coexistence" enunciated by the Soviet Union in relations with the Western powers. — Ed.

which afflicted the leaders of both nationalities, created the conflict that remained unsettled until the collapse of the Yugoslav
Kingdom in 1941. The Croats developed and nurtured a siege
mentality based on both real and imagined exploitation by the
Belgrade politicians, whom they held responsible for all the political and economic ills that befell interwar Croatia. The Serbs in
turn resented the Croats' legalistic obstructionism.

The Croat case has been complicated by the presence of a
substantial Serbian minority within the borders of Croatia, constituting 14 percent of the population of the republic. The Serbs of
Croatia were subject to forceful conversion or extermination in
the Independent State of Croatia set up under the aegis of the
German occupation. Since World War II, the Serbian population
of Croatia has ardently supported the present system. The question of the Serbian minority in Croatia has agitated both the
Serbs and the Croats — the Serbs because they were unwilling to
see their co-nationals in Croatia treated as a minority in a republic
where nationalism was in ascendance, the Croats because the
presence of the Serbian minority has given Serb leaders cause for
legitimate concern.

In contrast to the relatively high development of Croatia
within the Yugoslav state, Slovakia and Ruthenia were the most
undeveloped portions of the Czechoslovak Republic. The Slovaks
emerged out of feudalism only after World War I. The record of
the First Republic in Slovakia was quite positive, if viewed in
terms of nation-building. For the first time, Slovakia was endowed
with a viable system of public education and, until the advent of
the Great Depression, industrialization made modest economic
gains. Czechoslovakia carried out extensive land reform, which altered the feudalistic social structure in the Slovak countryside and
wrought changes ranging from electrification to improved sanita-
tion. In the process of development, Czechs came to Slovakia as
businessmen, administrators, and teachers and held most of the
key positions in civil service. Thus, the Czechs came to develop a
paternalistic attitude toward the Slovaks, a characteristic common
to majority-minority relationships.

During the interwar period Croat and Slovak politics tended
to be centered on, and mobilized around, the ethnic problem. In

Slovakia, the People's Party of Father Hlinka gained substantial support with its demands for Slovak autonomy. In Croatia, [Ante] and Stjepan Radić organized the Croat Peasant Party as the main parliamentary vehicle for the articulation of Croat griev-ances. The outlawed Ustasha movement advocated the destruc-tion of the Yugoslav state and the establishment of an indepen-dent Croatia. Both the Hlinkists and Ustasha accelerated nationalist trends in Slovakia and Croatia, and both used Roman Catholicism as a rallying point. In Croatia, religion was the major cultural distinction between Croat and Serb and the nationalist movement received its special edge of fanaticism by proclaiming Croatia a bastion of Western culture against the "Byzantine" Or-thodox Serbs. In Slovakia, the principal leaders of the People's Party were Catholic clergymen, who borrowed some of their techniques and ideology from fascism. These two movements eventually provided the governments of the Slovak and Croat puppet states, which the Axis occupation created after the dis-memberment of the Czechoslovak and Yugoslav states. Both puppet states dealt harshly with their former majority nationality. This was especially true in Croatia, where the Ustasha regime led by Ante Pavelić concentrated on creating a purely Croat state by subjecting the Serb population to forceful conversion to Catholi-cism or sporadic exterminations. Slovak atrocities never reached that depth, although the Slovak "state" handed over its Jews to the Germans for extermination. At the end of World War II, both Slovakia and Croatia were integrated into a reestablished Czechoslovakia and Yugoslavia. Thereafter, in both states, Slovak and Croat nationalism was held in low esteem. No Slovak or Croat political leader, regardless of political origins, could stress the nationality issue lest he be compromised by association with the recent past. . . .

The revival of the nationality issue in both states during the 1960s was the direct result of the increasingly tolerant political at-mosphere within both societies. Both parties made an effort to draw wide publics into the political process. The point of origin of liberalization in both societies differed widely. Czechoslovakia did not effectively emerge from monolithism until January 1968. From 1948 to 1968, the Czechoslovak leadership clung stubbornly to the ideological bequests of the Stalinist era. Czechoslovakia did not experience major changes of leadership as the result of Khrushchev's de-Stalinization. . . .

The Slovak Party leaders played a very active role in the events preceding the Prague Spring. In general, they remembered and resented Novotný's[2] attitudes toward the Slovaks, most particularly Novotný's contention that any assertion of a separate Slovak identity was a manifestation of bourgeois nationalism. Gustáv Husák[3] and other Slovak Party intellectuals felt that they had been singled out for special attention in the trials, which led at least indirectly to Novotný's ascent. . . .

The more liberal atmosphere that prevailed in Slovakia in the mid-1960s could be traced to the emergence of Alexander Dubček as First Secretary of the Slovak Communist Party in 1963. Dubček's success in liberalizing Slovakia gave the Slovak Party leadership an entrée into the ranks of the reformers, who were becoming increasingly active on the Czechoslovak political scene. The reforming intellectuals could be found in all spheres of scientific and political activity. In coalition with the Slovaks, they engineered the coup that overthrew Novotný in December 1967. The coalition was the direct result of the economic stagnation of the early 1960s which forced the Novotný leadership to seek solutions from intellectuals and intellectual institutions. This brought the intellectuals a status that had been denied to them during the previous era. As a result, many intellectuals moved into positions of strategic importance from which they could influence public opinion and gradually erode the position of the existing leadership. By contrast, Yugoslav liberalization policies evolved gradually in accordance with the processes established by the League. Liberalization in Yugoslavia was not a consistent unilinear move-

[2]Antonín Novotný was a staunch Stalinist and unimaginative leader of the Czechoslovak Communist Party from the mid-1950s until January 1968, when he was ousted in favor of the reformist Slovak Alexander Dubček.—Ed.

[3]Gustáv Husák, a leading Slovak communist, was imprisoned in the 1950s for his nationalist sentiment. He replaced Alexander Dubček as head of the party in 1969, a position that he held until 1987. He also served as president of the country until he resigned because of the revolution in 1989.—Ed.

ment; rather, it proceeded by fits and starts and accelerated rapidly after the dismissal of Vice-President Aleksandar Ranković[4] in 1966. Nevertheless, the general course toward liberalization was fairly consistent over a twenty-year period and was brought to a peak by the constitutional amendments of 1971.

The devolution of power at the center encouraged the growth of grass-roots politics in Yugoslavia and entrenched the principles of federalism. The republics became the constituencies of active, regionally based politicians who owed little of their career either to the federal government or to central League organs. The Yugoslav Constitution of 1963 provided for contested elections, which further diluted League control over politics. . . . Local politicians derived their legitimacy from the support of their home constituencies, which were in general bounded by ethnic identifications. Given these political dynamics, the efforts of the political leaderships to broaden their support within their constituencies were quite logical. Thus, they increasingly turned to non-Party sources for support and drew on non-Party publics outside the accepted scheme of Yugoslav politics. The Croat crisis was the logical outcome of weakened League authority coupled with the involvement of non-Party groupings in a political process that rested more and more on local bases of power.

Economic Factors

Croatia and Slovakia occupied very different economic positions in their respective states. Croatia ranks second in per capita income within the Yugoslav federation, following Slovenia. Both republics are more developed than Serbia and the other republics. By contrast, Slovakia has always lagged economically behind the Czech lands. Both Croatia and Slovenia received a substantial portion of the available Yugoslav investment capital because their more developed infrastructure was more efficient. . . . In theory, this state of

---

[4]Aleksandar Ranković (1909–1982), a leading communist during World War II, was seen as a supporter of Serbian interests in Yugoslavia. He served as minister of interior and head of the secret and military police. He lost his position and was expelled from the party in 1966 for abusing his power. — Ed.

affairs should have been satisfactory to the Croats, but many felt that the price exacted by the federal government for the maintenance of Yugoslavia was too high. Although the developed republics fought for the maximum retention of funds, the underdeveloped areas, where most Yugoslavs live, demanded that the federal government assume a more active role in the distribution of development money. Intense competition among the republics for investment funds led to a growth of regional nationalism, and the rhetoric of politics and economics tended to merge. . . .

. . . The Croat sense of being exploited economically is as old as Yugoslavia. Croat economic complaints have frequently been advanced for the purpose of achieving political ends. In November 1971, the economic and political issues merged into a demand for Croat autonomy. . . .

In Czechoslovakia, the economy did not emerge from rigid central planning until 1968, despite some cautious experimentation in the mid-1960s. As Czechoslovak economists have pointed out, the planners applied the Soviet model with little regard for the highly industrialized nature of the Czech lands. The Soviet model tended to work far better in Slovakia, where conditions were more appropriate. The relative success of industrialization in Slovakia is borne out by the statistics; the high rate of Slovak growth has been a source of national pride. The complaints of the Slovak leaders centered far more on the methods used in the industrialization of Slovakia than on the results; published criticisms were largely directed at the paternalism of the Czechs. In the later 1960s Slovak economists demanded that the plans for Slovak development be generated within Slovakia and be managed by Slovaks. . . . The economic issue was less intense for the Czechs and Slovaks than for the Croats and Serbs.

The Political Crisis: Czechoslovakia, 1968, and Yugoslavia, 1971

With the removal of Ranković in 1966, the pace of change in Yugoslavia accelerated. The subsequent curbing of the secret police removed a very persuasive threat system, and the political consequences were soon felt. . . . With the blessings of the

League, the foci of power had shifted from federal to republic institutions. . . . As a result, the Party lost influence over federal and regional governmental institutions. . . . The weakening of Party discipline in a changed political environment permitted the Croat crisis to occur. The reformers sought to equalize the political status of all the republics and provinces, and thus to defuse the charges of Serbian dominance. Increased republic autonomy tended to institutionalize strong regional Party machines at the expense of the federal government and Party organs. Once regional leaders were freed from Party discipline, they were able to develop virtually independent bases of power within their respective areas. Decentralization and a reversed flow of power were therefore the direct result of choices made at the highest Party levels.

By contrast, the Prague Spring took place within perhaps the most centralized and egalitarian state in the Communist bloc and the period of liberalization was compressed into eight months. . . . The reform leadership lacked the institutions and resources that would have enabled them to direct the changes in a rational way. Consequently, the major changes in Czechoslovakia took place within cultural institutions and other agencies over which neither Party nor government exercised direct control. In Czechoslovakia, unlike Yugoslavia, there was no charismatic figure who could control the processes that so frightened the Soviet leaders. The legitimacy of Dubček's leadership was based on his ability to satisfy the pent-up demand for change. The reformers could not resort to arbitrary actions, lest they be accused of reverting to past discredited methods. . . .

The Yugoslav situation is in sharp contrast; once Tito decided to intervene in Croatia, he did not lack the means to implement his policies. The state security organs and the army supported his policy and could be mobilized to back the federal position. The Croat events cast a disturbing shadow in a number of republics, and the intervention had few opponents outside of Croatia.

Within Czechoslovakia, however, the reform movement enjoyed the overwhelming support of all sections of the country. . . . In the Czechoslovak instance, the government was moving fast to implement the changes outlined by the April Program.[5] . . . The abolition of censorship, the complete freedom granted to the press, including the freedom to be irresponsible, and statements by the military leaders all strengthened hard-line elements in the Soviet leadership and contributed to the Soviet decision to intervene. In Czechoslovakia, unorthodox liberalization was a truly national movement uniting the more nationalist elements within the Slovak Party with those voicing the almost universal demand for liberalization.

In Yugoslavia, the Croat events did not possess such a national character. The Croat drive for greater autonomy was a divisive issue. Although decentralization was initially supported by Serb intellectuals within and outside the League, the Croat events divided the Serb community and eventually even the Serb liberals became alarmed at the vehemence of the Croat demands. . . .

The mass support in Croatia expressed by student movements, religious actions, and the media at least partially articulated separatist aims. In Czechoslovakia, both the Slovaks and the mass organizations were dedicated to the support of the federal authorities. The demand for Slovak autonomy within a federal state was a minor movement within the general wave of reform. In Yugoslavia, federal-regional conflict was at the heart of the issue. . . .

One of the more interesting phenomena common to the Yugoslav and Czechoslovak situations was the relative passivity and uninvolvement of the working class. Their interests tended to center on bread-and-butter demands, which they were content to articulate through established channels. The thrust of the Czechoslovak demands was toward the establishment of workers' self-management along the lines of the Yugoslav model. In Yugoslavia, most changes were adopted in the name of workers'

[5]The Action Program was published in April 1968. Reflecting the views of the reform members of the party, the program called for greater economic freedom and promised full civil liberties. — Ed.

self-management and the opposing factions were always described as the opponents of workers' self-management. Both the nationalist leaders and the supporters of the intervention waved the flag of workers' self-management. In both countries, the principal actors in the events could be found among the intelligentsia. The principal target seemed to be the arbitrariness of the central authorities rather than the Party or economic systems per se. The two main issues in the Yugoslav crisis were the status of Croatia within the Yugoslav federation and the degree of citizen participation in the democratization of the system. These issues were prominent in the Czechoslovak situation as well. . . . Both the Slovak and Croat leaders acknowledged implicitly the leading role of the Party by operating from positions of highest Party authority. . . .

Ultimately, the crucial question revolved around the intended role of the Czechoslovak Communist Party and the Yugoslav League of Communists. In the reform period, both were caught between nascent pluralism and near anarchy. The aim of the reformers was to abolish the monistic role of the respective parties. In this regard, both experiments failed because they failed to provide a substitute for the leading role of the Party. Yet any recentralization would necessitate a return to reliance on the very elements that had been discredited during the previous era. Neither the Soviet leaders nor the remnants of the Czechoslovak reform leadership wanted to turn the clock that far back. The Yugoslav leaders also wished to preserve the substance of many of the reforms. . . .

While most of the reformers were content to liberalize the existing systems, there were also many who participated in the reform movement in the hope of eliminating the role of the Party. These opponents viewed reform as a transitory stage toward the eventual abolition of the Party monopoly. . . .

The termination of both crises was marked by an attempt to restore Party influence. In Yugoslavia, Tito publicly repudiated the long path travelled by the League of Communists since 1952. The Tenth Party Congress of May 1974 restored democratic centralism and Party discipline. In Czechoslovakia, a similar course was dictated by post-entry realities. In view of the differential points of departure of both societies on the scale of liberalization, the Yugoslav recentralization is still behind Czechoslovakia's. . . .

In the wake of the crises, both states cleansed Party ranks. In Yugoslavia, the purge was far less drastic than in Czechoslovakia, where the number of those cast out of the Party may number 500,000. The Czechoslovak Party was much larger, however, especially considering the smaller population base, and the effect of the purge on the political atmosphere of the country was far more drastic. Most of the intellectuals who participated in the Prague Spring were forced out of politics. . . .

The proclamation of new constitutions and the revisions of the liberalized Party statutes marked the end of the Yugoslav and Czechoslovak crises. . . .

Conclusions

Yugoslavia

1. The crisis in Yugoslavia developed as a result of a nationalistic movement in the Republic of Croatia, which appeared to have support outside the League of Communists. The federal authorities were uncertain whether the Croatian League retained control of the republic's policy. The primary focus of the Croat crisis was on nationalism.

2. The Croat crisis was brought about by a coalition of reforming Communist liberals and nationalist elements. This combination was inherently unstable because the nationalist elements . . . thinly concealed particularistic aims; their version of reform would have brought a radical change in the system. The liberalizing elements in the League merely wanted some limited reforms within the framework of the system. Without federal intervention, these disparate elements would surely have clashed.

3. In Yugoslavia, federalism was legally established and institutionalized through the continuous evolution of the system. Republic and local organs control their own funds. Thus, the central organs had few institutional means of curbing nationalism short of the drastic measure they took—namely, dismissing the reformist leadership of the Croat League.

4. The Croat situation brought about a crisis in the relation-

ship between the federal organs of the Yugoslav government, on the one hand, and the League, on the other. Subsequent dismissals of Party personnel affected most republics, as the central government paved the way for the reestablishment of a more centralist regime. . . .

5.   Yugoslav federal institutions and the emphasis on legally sanctioned ethnic particularism has had the effect of economically benefiting the more prosperous republics of Yugoslavia to the detriment of the poorer. The ideology of Communism does not easily accommodate to the fact of income differences among the republics. . . .

Czechoslovakia

1.   Slovak nationalism played a relatively minor role in the broad national movement known as the Prague Spring. Slovak nationalism was the catalyst for the ouster of the Novotný regime, but the goals of the nationally supported movement ranged far beyond the Slovak nationality question. The naming of a Slovak to the post of First Secretary of the Party and his leadership of the liberalization created broad binational support for the movement and a general sense of euphoria. The Czech liberals did not see the federalization of the state as a threat and therefore supported it actively.

2.   The Slovak issue developed out of the lack of governmental or Party institutions capable of articulating Slovak national aspirations. Many Slovak Communists therefore participated in the reform movement for narrow nationalist reasons, with the specific aim of establishing parity between Slovaks and Czechs within the state. These Slovak Communists did not share the liberal leanings of their Czech counterparts. Once their demands for autonomy had been fulfilled, they broke the solid front of the reform movement by advocating a return to greater orthodoxy.

3.   The Czechoslovak events were not the result of a continuous and planned political evolution toward liberalization but originated in a political coup within the central leadership.

4.   The forces led by Dubček never fully controlled the events of the Prague Spring. The state security forces remained a Novotný stronghold. Dubček's resolution not to use forceful or

extralegal methods against his opponents left important areas in
the hands of the opposition. The army was disorganized by a series of internal scandals. Thus, the new regime lacked the capacity
to defend itself from internal and external challenges.

Katherine Verdery

Why National Ideology Under Socialism?

Though espousing the ideal of proletarian internationalism, all the
communist regimes in Eastern Europe sought popular support by
identifying themselves to some degree with their nation's past. The
communists did this despite the fact that they had come to power
vowing to overcome the national question. They sought to develop a
"socialist consciousness" among the people while allowing only cultural national manifestations—being what they termed "nationalist
in form but socialist in content."

Many scholars have argued that the communists were forced to
lean on the national pillar in their search for legitimacy. Katherine
Verdery, an anthropologist, has examined the regime that perhaps
more than any other in Eastern Europe developed and extolled the
national element in its ideology—that of Nicolae Ceauşescu in Romania. Verdery believes that the Romanian communists did not just
use nationalism for support, but that they were pushed to do so by
the very nationalist tradition in Romania that they were trying to
overcome, and by the fact that the society they had shaped was weak
and fragmented. Far from being suppressed, nationalism was necessary for the survival of the regime.

From *National Ideology Under Socialism* by Katherine Verdery, University of California Press, 1991, pp. 121–134. Reprinted by permission of University of California Press.

. . . Why did a Marxist-Leninist regime employing a symbolic-ideological mode of control give so much weight to an ideology that was *national?* This question has been handled at greater or lesser length by a number of political scientists, most of whom see the answer in the regime's need for public support, either in general or in its quarrel with the Soviet Union. Nationalism, it is argued, was the Ceaușescu leadership's main instrument for legitimating its rule with the populace and for keeping the intellectuals co-opted or subservient. . . .

I do not adopt this line of argument. I see the national ideology that became a hallmark of Ceaușescu's Romania as having several sources, only one of which was its purposeful instrumentalization by the Party. To a considerable extent, I argue, the Party was *forced* onto the terrain of national values (not unwillingly) under pressure from others, especially intellectuals, whom it could fully engage in no other manner. These intellectuals were drawing upon personal concerns and traditions of inquiry that made the Nation a continuing and urgent reality for them despite its official interdiction. They were also engaged in conflicts among themselves for which, as before, the Nation provided a basic idiom. . . . In addition, I see the national ideology as having an elective affinity, beyond any leadership's conscious manipulation, with certain inherent characteristics of Romanian socialism. Although I do not reject arguments . . . that Ceaușescu realized the necessity of fusing nationalism and socialism, . . . I think the story is much more complicated than that.

The most obvious source of the restored national values was, of course, the quiet revolt of the high Party elite from Soviet supervision, as they insisted upon controlling Romanian society and not being dictated to by someone else. . . . Soviet rule entailed the wholesale imposition of a language, Marxism-Leninism, that was native to almost none in Romania and congenial to few. From factional struggles and purges an ethnic Romanian leadership had emerged that, despite its genuine adherence to Marxist ideas, was also heir to two centuries of politics couched in a language of national identity — the dialect, as it were, natural to Romanian political life.

Romanians were not the only ones to reply to Soviet domination in a national dialect: it was evident in Hungary in 1956, in

Poland then and even more so in 1968. But Romanian leaders replied to Soviet rule in that language more often than others, culminating in Ceaușescu's famous speech on the Soviet invasion of Czechoslovakia:

> *The penetration of the troops of the five socialist countries into Czechoslovakia constitutes a great mistake and a grave danger to peace in Europe, and to the fate of socialism in the world. It is inconceivable in today's world, when peoples are rising up in struggle to defend their national independence and their right to equality, that . . . socialist states should transgress the liberty and independence of another state.*
>
> *. . . The problem of choosing the roads of socialist construction is a problem for each individual Party, each State, each people. No one can pose as an adviser, as a guide to the way in which socialism is to be built in another country. . . .*
>
> *Among the measures that the [Romanian] Central Committee, the Council of Ministers and the State Council have decided to take are . . . the formation of armed patriotic detachments of workers, peasants, and intellectuals, defenders of the independence of our socialist homeland. We want our people to have its armed units in order to defend its revolutionary gains. . . . The entire Romanian people will not permit anyone to violate the territory of our homeland. . . .*
>
> *Be sure, comrades, be sure, citizens of Romania, . . . that we [communist leaders] shall never betray our homeland, we shall never betray the interests of our people.*

It is true that after this speech thousands of Romanians flocked to join the Party who would never have conceived of such a thing the day before. At least one of Ceaușescu's motives, I nonetheless believe, was not this but a Romanian national reply to Soviet domination, a reply born of both interest and sentiment.

The forces underlying its national form, however, included both institutionally embedded traditions and the active pressure of national sentiment from below. Something like this informs Hugh Seton-Watson's observation that because both the Romanian and the Polish communist leaders of the 1950s enjoyed so little popular support relative to other East European Party leaderships, they were on the one hand more dependent on the Soviet Union for their position, but, on the other, more vulnerable to upward seepage of the universal anti-Russian sentiments of their own masses. The presence of a "solid layer of middle-level, devoted, indoctrinated cadres" would have impeded this seepage, but such a layer did not exist. In consequence, both of these Party leaderships ended by identifying more with the national sentiments of their populations than with their Soviet patrons.

Seton-Watson's insight is particularly apt for the relation between Party leaders and the educated stratum, with its privileged opportunity (compared with the "masses") to spread concepts and ideas. The university students, the cadres-in-training, or the youths who headed for the new Writers' School, were people deeply socialized into patriotic attachment. Many of them were fresh from a Transylvania recently dismembered, its northern part returned to Hungary in 1940 and rejoined to Romania in 1944 after much suffering; others were from a Moldavia whose Bessarabian portion the Soviet Union had just amputated. The national sentiments of such people were freshly aroused, and they entered an intellectual and political environment from which it had been impossible to extirpate all remnants of the "bourgeois nationalist" practices. . . . These people did not share the vantage point of the top political circles, who perhaps believed (as some argue) that only by silencing national discourse, thus convincing Stalin that his former opponents on the battlefield were now his staunchest allies, could Romania be sure of retaining Transylvania with its large Romanian population and its crucial industrial resources. . . .

. . . Although Ceauşescu may have brought the national discourse back into public usage, he assuredly did not do so from a position of dominance over its meanings. Rather, he presided over the moment when the Marxist discourse was decisively disrupted by that of the Nation. From then on, the Party struggled to maintain the initiative in the use of this rhetoric. If national ideology struck outside observers as the most salient feature of Romanian politics, this was not because the Party emphasized nothing else but because the Nation was so well entrenched discursively in Romanian life. It was the one subject that was guaranteed to get Romanians' attention, because so many of them were using it themselves.

These underlying sources of prevalent nationalism were augmented by others during the 1970s and 1980s, when . . . the leadership's assault on cultural institutions politicized the entire field of cultural production. As the Party's attempt to monopolize cul-ture sharpened conflict among the producers of symbols and images, different groups began to compete by recourse to national values. . . .

Although it is true that some of the impetus for this manipulation of the Nation by intellectuals in the decades of the 1970s and 1980s was, precisely, the favor shown to national values by the Ceauşescu leadership (itself resuming this language, I have suggested, partly because of the intellectuals' ongoing attachment to it), I do not think the role of identity questions under Ceauşescu is adequately explained by this "regime use of nationalism." These questions had already achieved their own autonomy; the Party could not simply appropriate them and wave them about at will. Intellectuals who engaged in arguments about national identity were not doing so because they were told to, or because they were allowed to (although that was of course a necessary ingredient): they were doing so because by these means they could give vent to passionately held resistance to Soviet and/or Marxist-Leninist rule and, at the same time, lay claim to a larger share of resources in a political world in which national values had only briefly ceased to carry weight. Their arguments filled the air with national talk that increased from barely audible in the 1950s to deafening in the 1980s. Even the Party sometimes had trouble being heard above the din. Perhaps it would not be too much to say that the Party's own national exaggerations reflect, precisely, the effort that was required to assert some authority over the national idea.

It is this utilization in argument, this discourse and counter-discourse, definition and counterdefinition, that made national ideology so salient in Romania. Few other ideas launched by the Party, no matter how incessantly repeated, managed to enter into such a dialogue. Contestation, not mere repetition, is the vehicle of ideology: a word or symbol is a means for forming conscious-ness only if it arouses a counterword, a reply. The words and symbols that did this in Ceauşescu's Romania — not because a Party leadership wanted legitimacy but because different kinds of human beings differently situated in the social world cared about those particular significances — were words about national identity. This is why Ceauşescu's regime found itself compelled, despite the Marxist-Leninist orthodoxy its leaders might have preferred, to base its symbolic-ideological mode of control on an ideology that was national. And because that regime participated in it, the national discourse was further invigorated for the politics of a post-Ceauşescu era.

Considerations such as these might be sufficient in themselves to account for the durability of national talk in Romania, but they were augmented as well by systemic tendencies within the Romanian form of socialist political economy: an economy of shortage, a system dynamic maximizing the apparatus's control over resources for redistribution, and a weak state trying to project the appearance of strength. Some of these tendencies increased after the early 1970s, reproducing national ideology through time well after its initial "causes" had been superseded.

The link between national ideology and an economy of shortage . . . can be provisionally summarized as follows. Within a system of shortage, consumers at all levels of the system — firms, households, hungry individuals — enter into competition to acquire the goods they need. Unlike capitalist "demand-constrained" economies, in which a premium is placed on mechanisms that facilitate *selling* goods, the premium in supply-constrained socialist systems is on mechanisms facilitating *acquisition.* Any device that expels potential competitors for goods plays a highly functional role in such a system, from the consumer's point of view. National ideology is such a device: it bounds the community, defining clearly who is in and who is out. Significantly, this use of national ideology does not emanate primarily from the top but flows throughout the ranks of disadvantaged purchasers lower down. It is in the interests of average folks, not the top elite, to reduce the pool of competing purchasers by keeping matters of identity firmly in mind. . . .

A related factor that *does* emanate from the top, or at least from the Party bureaucracy as it extends downward into society, is that national ideology serves well the systemic tendency of the political apparatus to maximize the resources under its control. . . . For these purposes it is not just any national ideology that serves, but a definition of national identity that is indigenist. Such a definition focuses on *local* production of values and their *local* appropriation: Romanian values for a Romanian apparatus. Indigenism creates a Romanian genealogy with no foreign cousins who might have claims on the output. . . . [I]ndigenism is precisely the definition the Romanian party leadership came increasingly to prefer.

A final set of points concerning the durability of Romanian nationalism, especially in the austerity-ridden 1980s (in which, of course, the validity of the two above points is enhanced), relates to the weakness of socialist states and their representation or symbolic projection of themselves as strong. . . . [M]ost Leninist regimes have passed [through two phases], Consolidation and Inclusion. . . .

. . . What the Romanian case seems to present us with, rather, is a regime that went from Consolidation (the late 1940s and 1950s) to Inclusion (the 1960s) and back to Consolidation (the 1970s and 1980s). I prefer the notion of modes of control, which in the Romanian case shifted from an initial period of coercive control to a brief experiment with remunerative/symbolic control, then to a mode at first symbolic-ideological and subsequently more and more coercive.

. . . Consolidation regimes with their "castle" mentality and images of contamination are obsessed with the problem of identity, a problem about which national ideologies have a lot to say. We can see how the Nation entered into the problem of regime identity for Romania by noting, in the third period even more clearly than before, a system of concentric circles—two tiers of sacrality and contamination. First was the continuing division between "sacred" Party and "contaminating" Romanian society, evident above all in the sovereign disdain with which the high priests of Romanian politics treated the pagans who were their unfortunate subjects; but in addition, the Party identified itself entirely with the Nation and saw contamination as coming from *beyond* the national borders. . . . In other words, Romanians were superior to the contaminating nomadic tribes (Hungarians and Slavs) that surrounded and debased them.

This construction of a unitary Romanian Party-Nation as an extreme instance of symbolic control was taking place, I note, in the context of centrifugal tendencies perhaps worse than those of the interwar years, . . . seeking to transfer the advantages of blocwide mechanical solidarity to the next level down, it applied a policy of "self-provisioning" . . . at the level of each county and, insofar as possible, to commune units within them. Each unit was expected to be maximally self-sufficient in the foodstuffs and other materials it required—within the constraints of heavy central planning, of course: this was not part of a decentralizing reform. Counties and even cities bartered with one another in kind to make up shortfalls. . . . Counties came to resemble independent fiefdoms, held together by the unending peregrinations of Ceauşescu much as Charlemagne unified his kingdom in medieval times. . . .

If these examples suggest an erosion of internal central control, the late 1980s eroded something else equally upsetting to the leadership: Romania's economic independence from the socialist bloc. While the 1960s and 1970s were the era of growing connections with the West, the 1980s saw the country's reincorporation into the East. . . . Without the Soviet market, less demanding than western ones, Romania's trade would have been in serious difficulty. These reversals accompanied battered relations with western states—the withdrawal of U.S. Most-Favored-Nation status and of some European ambassadors, for example—connected with western reassessments of Ceauşescu's human rights policies.

Here, then, are all the elements of a weak state presiding over a fragmented society and suffering a renewed Soviet dependency, yet speaking as loudly as possible of the unity and independence of the Nation. To understand this speech as simply a manipulation of popular support impoverishes what was in fact a much more urgent and consequential project: to constitute, through discourse, wholeness for a reality that was in fragments and sovereignty for a vassal—to constitute a wholeness and a sovereignty that were imaginary. Years of trying to build up a state resting on a teleology of progressive change and an ideology of internationalism (with the acceptance of internal diversity) had ended in the realization that the state could adequately construct itself only in terms of what it had at first denied: a teleology of national continuity and an ideology of national values, premised on internal uniformity. Through national ideology, the leadership represented its weak state and regime as the embodiment of a strong, autonomous, unified will. . . .

I have tried to show here why I think one must see a national discourse in Romania as more than something used instrumentally by the Communist party but as, rather, inscribed in and emanating from many quarters of Romanian society. Because of its force in other quarters, because others used it in their own battles and sought to impose their own meanings on it, the Party had to strive as well to control the image of Romanian identity and to defend this image as adequately representing and protecting the Nation's interests. These efforts produced and reproduced Romanian national ideology, as a field of contention whose symbols were always open to other uses. . . .

Milan Kundera

Identity Beyond Nationalism and Communism

The Prague Spring, the 1968 reform movement in Czechoslovakia, came to an abrupt, harsh end at the hands of the Soviet Union and other Warsaw Pact military forces in August of that year. This defeat led many people in east central Europe to abandon hope that communism was capable of real change. Many simply went on with their daily lives as long as the system provided for them. A few, such as the Czech writer Vaclav Havel, took the path of moral protest.

Havel's countryman, Milan Kundera, had his first novel published during the Prague Spring. After the Soviet intervention, Kundera's works were proscribed in Czechoslovakia, and he moved to France in 1975. With the development in the 1970s of détente — the accommodation between the West and the East — Kundera feared that nations like his were now permanently under Soviet domination.

"The Tragedy of Central Europe" by Milan Kundera from *The New York Review of Books*, 31:7 (April 26, 1984), pp. 33–38. Reprinted by permission of the author.

In this essay, which reflects his hopelessness, he depicts Europe as divided into two civilizations—the West and the East—the latter which he identified with Russian culture and the Soviet Union. Kundera asserted that the nations of east central Europe were inextricably linked with the West culturally. But now, he feared, they faced the danger of losing their identity to the alien eastern civilization. He hoped that the West would not abandon the small, western-oriented nations of east central Europe but somehow would help them to break free from the Soviet orbit.

1.

In November 1956, the director of the Hungarian News Agency, shortly before his office was flattened by artillery fire, sent a telex to the entire world with a desperate message announcing that the Russian attack against Budapest had begun. The dispatch ended with these words: "We are going to die for Hungary and for Europe."

What did this sentence mean? It certainly meant that the Russian tanks were endangering Hungary and with it Europe itself. But in what sense was Europe in danger? Were the Russian tanks about to push past the Hungarian borders and into the West? No. The director of the Hungarian News Agency meant that the Russians, in attacking Hungary, were attacking Europe itself. He was ready to die so that Hungary might remain Hungary and European. . . .

2.

In fact, what does Europe mean to a Hungarian, a Czech, a Pole? For a thousand years their nations have belonged to the part of Europe rooted in Roman Christianity. They have participated in every period of its history. For them, the word "Europe" does not represent a phenomenon of geography but a spiritual notion synonymous with the word "West." The moment Hungary is no longer European—that is, no longer Western—it is driven from its own destiny, beyond its own history: it loses the essence of its identity.

"Geographic Europe" (extending from the Atlantic to the Ural Mountains) was always divided into two halves which evolved separately: one tied to ancient Rome and the Catholic Church, the other anchored in Byzantium and the Orthodox Church. After 1945, the border between the two Europes shifted several hundred kilometers to the west, and several nations that had always considered themselves to be Western woke up to discover that they were now in the East.

As a result, three fundamental situations developed in Europe after the war: that of Western Europe, that of Eastern Europe, and, most complicated, that of the part of Europe situated geographically in the center — culturally in the West and politically in the East.

The contradictions of the Europe I call Central help us to understand why during the last thirty-five years the drama of Europe has been concentrated there: the great Hungarian revolt in 1956 and the bloody massacre that followed; the Prague Spring and the occupation of Czechoslovakia in 1968; the Polish revolts of 1956, 1968, 1970, and of recent years. . . . [W]e can no longer consider what took place in Prague or Warsaw in its essence as a drama of Eastern Europe, of the Soviet bloc, of communism; it is a drama of the West — a West that, kidnapped, displaced, and brainwashed, nevertheless insists on defending its identity.

The identity of a people and of a civilization is reflected and concentrated in what has been created by the mind — in what is known as "culture." If this identity is threatened with extinction, cultural life grows correspondingly more intense, more important, until culture itself becomes the living value around which all people rally. That is why, in each of the revolts in Central Europe, the collective cultural memory and the contemporary creative effort assumed roles so great and so decisive — far greater and far more decisive than they have been in any other European mass revolt. . . .

3.

One could say: We'll admit that Central European countries are defending their threatened identity, but their situation is not unique. Russia is in a similar situation. It, too, is about to lose its identity. In fact, it's not Russia but communism that deprives nations of their essence, and which, moreover, made the Russian people its first victim. . . .

In Central Europe, the eastern border of the West, everyone has always been particularly sensitive to the dangers of Russian might. And it's not just the Poles. Frantisek Palacky, the great historian and the figure most representative of Czech politics in the nineteenth century, wrote in 1848 a famous letter to the revolutionary parliament of Frankfurt in which he justified the continued existence of the Hapsburg Empire as the only possible rampart against Russia. . . .

Central Europe, according to Palacky, ought to be a family of equal nations, each of which — treating the others with mutual respect and secure in the protection of a strong, unified state — would also cultivate its own individuality. And this dream, although never fully realized, would remain powerful and influential. Central Europe longed to be a condensed version of Europe itself in all its cultural variety, a small arch-European Europe, a reduced model of Europe made up of nations conceived according to one rule: the greatest variety within the smallest space. How could Central Europe not be horrified facing a Russia founded on the opposite principle: the smallest variety within the greatest space? . . .

This is why the countries in Central Europe feel that the change in their destiny that occurred after 1945 is not merely a political catastrophe: it is also an attack on their civilization. The deep meaning of their resistance is the struggle to preserve their identity — or, to put it another way, to preserve their Westernness.

5.

There are no longer any illusions about the regimes of Russia's satellite countries. But what we forget is their essential . . . tragedy: these countries have vanished from the map of the West.

Why has this disappearance remained invisible? We can locate the cause in Central Europe itself.

The history of the Poles, the Czechs, the Slovaks, the Hungarians has been turbulent and fragmented. Their traditions of statehood have been weaker and less continuous than those of the larger European nations. Boxed in by the Germans on one side and the Russians on the other, the nations of Central Europe have used up their strength in the struggle to survive and to preserve their languages. Since they have never been entirely integrated into the consciousness of Europe, they have remained the least known and the most fragile part of the West—hidden, even further, by the curtain of their strange and scarcely accessible languages. . . .

6.

So is it the fault of Central Europe that the West hasn't even noticed its disappearance?

Not entirely. At the beginning of our century, Central Europe was, despite its political weakness, a great cultural center, perhaps the greatest. And, admittedly, while the importance of Vienna, the city of Freud and Mahler, is readily acknowledged today, its importance and originality make little sense unless they are seen against the background of the other countries and cities that together participated in, and contributed creatively to, the culture of Central Europe. . . .

A question arises: was this entire creative explosion just a coincidence of geography? Or was it rooted in a long tradition, a shared past? Or, to put it another way: does Central Europe constitute a true cultural configuration with its own history? And if such a configuration exists, can it be defined geographically? What are its borders?

It would be senseless to try to draw its borders exactly. Central Europe is not a state: it is a culture or a fate. Its borders are imaginary and must be drawn and redrawn with each new historical situation. . . .

In the nineteenth century, the national struggles (of the Poles, the Hungarians, the Czechs, the Slovaks, the Croats, the Slovenes, the Rumanians, the Jews) brought into opposition nations that—insulated, egotistic, closed-off—had nevertheless lived through the same great existential experience: the experience of a nation that chooses between its existence and its nonexistence; or, to put it another way, between retaining its authentic national life and being assimilated into a larger nation. . . .

The twentieth century has witnessed other situations: the collapse of the Austrian empire, Russian annexation, and the long period of Central European revolts, which are only an immense bet staked on an unknown solution.

Central Europe therefore cannot be defined and determined by political frontiers (which are inauthentic, always imposed by invasions, conquests, and occupations), but by the great common situations that reassemble peoples, regroup them in ever new ways along the imaginary and ever-changing boundaries that mark a realm inhabited by the same memories, the same problems and conflicts, the same common tradition. . . .

Central Europe as a family of small nations has its own vision of the world, a vision based on a deep distrust of history. History, that goddess of Hegel and Marx, that incarnation of reason that judges us and arbitrates our fate—that is the history of conquerors. The people of Central Europe are not conquerors. They cannot be separated from European history; they cannot exist outside it; but they represent the wrong side of this history; they are its victims and outsiders. . . .

Thus it was in this region of small nations who have "not yet perished" that Europe's vulnerability, all of Europe's vulnerability, was more clearly visible before anywhere else. Actually, in our modern world where power has a tendency to become more and more concentrated in the hands of a few big countries, *all* European nations run the risk of becoming small nations and of sharing their fate. In this sense the destiny of Central Europe anticipates the destiny of Europe in general, and its culture assumes an enormous relevance. . . .

8.

Today, all of Central Europe has been subjugated by Russia with the exception of little Austria, which, more by chance than necessity, has retained its independence, but ripped out of its Central European setting, it has lost most of its individual character and all of its importance. The disappearance of the cultural home of Central Europe was certainly one of the greatest events of the century for all of Western civilization. So, I repeat my question: how could it possibly have gone unnoticed and unnamed?

The answer is simple: Europe hasn't noticed the disappearance of its cultural home because Europe no longer perceives its unity as a cultural unity.

In fact, what is European unity based on?

In the Middle Ages, it was based on a shared religion. In the modern era, in which the medieval God has been changed into a *Deus absconditus*, religion bowed out, giving way to culture, which became the expression of the supreme values by which European humanity understood itself, defined itself, identified itself as European.

Now it seems that another change is taking place in our century, as important as the one that divided the Middle Ages from the modern era. Just as God long ago gave way to culture, culture in turn is giving way.

But to what and to whom? What realm of supreme values will be capable of uniting Europe? Technical feats? The marketplace? The mass media? (Will the great poet be replaced by the great journalist?) Or by politics? But by which politics? The right or the left? Is there a discernible shared ideal that still exists above this Manichaeanism of the left and the right that is as stupid as it is insurmountable? Will it be the principle of tolerance, respect for the beliefs and ideas of other people? But won't this tolerance become empty and useless if it no longer protects a rich creativity or a strong set of ideas? Or should we understand the abdication of culture as a sort of deliverance, to which we should ecstatically abandon ourselves? Or will the *Deus absconditus* return to fill the empty space and reveal himself? I don't know, I know nothing about it. I think I know only that culture has bowed out. . . .

10.

The last direct personal experience of the West that Central European countries remember is the period from 1918 to 1938.

Their picture of the West, then, is of the West in the past, of a West in which culture had not yet entirely bowed out.

With this in mind, I want to stress a significant circumstance: the Central European revolts were not nourished by the newspapers, radio, or television—that is, by the "media." They were prepared, shaped, realized by novels, poetry, theater, cinema, historiography, literary reviews, popular comedy and cabaret, philosophical discussions—that is, by culture. . . .

That's why, when the Russians occupied Czechoslovakia, they did everything possible to destroy Czech culture. This destruction had three meanings: first, it destroyed the center of the opposition; second, it undermined the identity of the nation, enabling it to be more easily swallowed up by Russian civilization; third, it put a violent end to the modern era, the era in which culture still represented the realization of supreme values.

This third consequence seems to me the most important. In effect, totalitarian Russian civilization is the radical negation of the modern West, the West created four centuries ago at the dawn of the modern era: the era founded on the authority of the thinking, doubting individual, and on an artistic creation that expressed his uniqueness. The Russian invasion has thrown Czechoslovakia into a "postcultural" era and left it defenseless and naked before the Russian army and the omnipresent state television. . . .

11.

After the destruction of the Austrian empire, Central Europe lost its ramparts. Didn't it lose its soul after Auschwitz, which swept the Jewish nation off its map? And after having been torn away from Europe in 1945, does Central Europe still exist?

Yes, its creativity and its revolts suggest that it has "not yet perished." But if to live means to exist in the eyes of those we love, then Central Europe no longer exists. More precisely: in the eyes of its beloved Europe, Central Europe is just a part of the Soviet empire and nothing more, nothing more.

And why should this surprise us? By virtue of its political system, Central Europe is the East; by virtue of its cultural history, it is the West. But since Europe itself is in the process of losing its own cultural identity, it perceives in Central Europe nothing but a political regime; put another way, it sees in Central Europe only Eastern Europe.

Central Europe, therefore, should fight not only against its big oppressive neighbor but also against the subtle, relentless pressure of time, which is leaving the era of culture in its wake. That's why in Central European revolts there is something conservative, nearly anachronistic: they are desperately trying to restore the past, the past of culture, the past of the modern era. It is only in that period, only in a world that maintains a cultural dimension, that Central Europe can still defend its identity, still be seen for what it is.

The real tragedy for Central Europe, then, is not Russia but Europe: this Europe that represented a value so great that the director of the Hungarian News Agency was ready to die for it, and for which he did indeed die. Behind the iron curtain, he did not suspect that the times had changed and that in Europe itself Europe was no longer experienced as a value. He did not suspect that the sentence he was sending by telex beyond the borders of his flat country would seem outmoded and would not be understood.

As socialism collapsed in Yugoslavia, the country disintegrated. Ethnic conflict erupted in Bosnia-Herzegovina where Serbs refused to join with Muslims and Croats to form a new state. Serb nationalists besieged areas, seizing territory and driving out the people. A UN truck evacuates residents from the Muslim enclave of Srebrenica in March 1993. (AP/Wide World Photos)

The Collapse of Communism and the Return of Nations

Václav Havel

Dilemmas of Postcommunist Development

Once the euphoria over the collapse of the communist regimes in Eastern Europe wore off, the serious business of creating pluralist political systems and market economies began in earnest. It quickly became apparent that in some countries nationalist politics complicated and even hindered this process.

Václav Havel, a leading Czech dissident in the 1970s and 1980s,

"The Post-Communist Nightmare" by Václav Havel from *New York Review of Books*, May 27, 1993, pp. 8–10. Reprinted by permission.

was elected the first president of postcommunist Czechoslovakia. Despite his pleading, Slovak nationalists pressed their demands on the central government, and soon the country separated, albeit peacefully, into two states. Havel sees this and other such events as natural responses to the legacy of communist rule. In his view, nationalism fills a void left by a system that attempted to impose uniformity in the name of an internationalist ideology. Nationalistic feeling is inherent in people's desire to renew and assert an often submerged identity. Moreover, as they face unfamiliar and often unwelcome social and economic change, people turn to nationalism as a way to cope with their frustrations. Havel believes, however, that although the reality of nationalism must be recognized, it is not the solution. Individuals need to understand their problems in a larger, world context. Havel expresses his hope for such a widened outlook in his concern about the very reasons for the upsurge in nationalism.

For long decades, the chief nightmare of the democratic world was communism. Today—three years after it began to collapse like an avalanche—it would seem as though another nightmare has replaced it: postcommunism. There were many, not just in the West, but in the East as well, who had been looking forward for years to the fall of communism, and who had hoped that its collapse would mean that history had at last come to its senses. Today, these same people are seriously worried about the consequences of that fall. Some of them may even feel a little nostalgic for a world that was, after all, slightly more transparent and understandable than the present one.

I do not share sentiments of that kind. I think we must not understand postcommunism merely as something that makes life difficult for the rest of the world. I certainly didn't understand communism that way. I saw it chiefly as a challenge, a challenge to thought and to action. To an even greater extent, postcommunism represents precisely that kind of challenge.

Anyone who understands a given historical phenomenon merely as an inconvenience will ultimately see many other things that way too: the warnings of ecologists, public opinion, the vagaries of voters, public morality. It is an easy, and therefore seductive, way of seeing the world and history. But it is extremely dangerous because we tend to remain aloof from things that inconvenience us and get in our way, just as some of my acquaintances avoided me during the Communist era. Any position based on the feeling that the world, or history, is merely an accumulation of inconveniences inevitably leads to a turning away from reality, and ultimately, to resigning oneself to it. It leads to appeasement, even to collaboration. The consequences of such a position may even be suicidal.

What in fact do we mean by postcommunism? Essentially it is a term for the state of affairs in all the countries that have rid themselves of communism. But it is a dangerous simplification to put all these countries in one basket. While it is true that they are all faced with essentially the same task—that is, to rid themselves of the disastrous legacy of communism, to repair the damage it caused, and to create, or renew, democracy—at the same time, and for many reasons, there are great differences between them. . . .

. . . I will mention only some of the root causes of the phenomena that are arousing the greatest concern in the democratic West, phenomena such as nationalism, xenophobia, and the poor moral and intellectual climate which—to a greater or lesser extent—go along with the creation of the new political and economic system.

The first of these causes I see in the fact that communism was far from being simply the dictatorship of one group of people over another. It was a genuinely totalitarian system; that is, it permeated every aspect of life and deformed everything it touched, including all the natural ways people had evolved of living together. It profoundly affected all forms of human behavior. For years, a specific structure of values and models of behavior was deliberately created in the consciousness of society. It was a perverted structure, one that went against all the natural tendencies of life, but society nevertheless internalized it, or rather was forced to internalize it.

When Communist power and its ideology collapsed, this structure collapsed along with it. But people couldn't simply absorb and internalize a new structure immediately, one that would correspond to the elementary principles of civic society and democracy. The human mind and human habits cannot be transformed overnight; to build a new system of living values and to identify with them takes time.

In a situation where one system has collapsed and a new one does not yet exist, many people feel empty and frustrated. This condition is fertile ground for radicalism of all kinds, for the hunt for scapegoats, and for the need to hide behind the anonymity of a group, be it socially or ethnically based. It encourages hatred of the world, self-affirmation at all costs, the feeling that everything is now permitted and the unparalleled flourishing of selfishness that goes along with it. It gives rise to the search for a common and easily identifiable enemy, to political extremism, to the most primitive cult of consumerism, to a carpetbagging morality, stimulated by the historically unprecedented restructuring of property relations, and so on and so on. Thanks to its former democratic traditions and to its unique intellectual and spiritual climate, the Czech Republic, the westernmost of the post-Communist countries, is relatively well off in this regard, compared with some of the other countries in the region. Nevertheless we too are going through the same great transformation that all the post-Communist countries are and we can therefore talk about it with the authority of insiders.

Another factor that must be considered in any analysis of post-Communist phenomena is the intrinsic tendency of communism to make everything the same. The greatest enemy of communism was always individuality, variety, difference—in a word, freedom. From Berlin to Vladivostok, the streets and buildings were decorated with the same red stars. Everywhere the same kind of celebratory parades were staged. Analogical state administrations were set up, along with the whole system of central direction for social and economic life. This vast shroud of uniformity, stifling all national, intellectual, spiritual, social, cultural, and religious variety, covered over any differences and created the monstrous illusion that we were all the same. The fall of communism destroyed this shroud of sameness, and the world was caught napping by an outburst of the many unanticipated differences concealed beneath it, each of which—after such a long time in the shadows—felt a natural need to draw attention to itself, to emphasize its uniqueness and its difference from others. This is the reason for the eruption of so many different kinds of old-fashioned patriotism, revivalist messianism, conservatism, and expressions of hatred toward all those who appeared to be betraying their roots or identifying with different ones.

The desire to renew and emphasize one's identity, one's uniqueness, is also behind the emergence of many new countries. Nations that have never had states of their own feel an understandable need to experience independence. It is no fault of theirs that the opportunity has come up decades or even centuries after it came to other nations.

This is related to yet another matter: for a long time, communism brought history, and with it all natural development, to a halt. While the Western democracies have had decades to create a civil society, to build internationally integrated structures, and to learn the arts of peaceful international coexistence and cooperation, the countries ruled by communism could not go through this creative process. National and cultural differences were driven into the subterranean areas of social life, where they were kept on ice and thus prevented from developing freely, from taking on modern forms in the fresh air, from creating, over time, the free space of unity in variety.

At the same time many of the nations suppressed by communism had never enjoyed freedom, not even before communism's advent, and thus had not a chance to resolve many of the basic questions of their existence as countries. . . . It is truly astonishing to discover how, after decades of falsified history and ideological manipulation, nothing has been forgotten. Nations are now remembering their ancient achievements and their ancient suffering, their ancient suppressors and their allies, their ancient statehood and their former borders, their traditional animosities and affinities—in short, they are suddenly recalling a history that, until recently, had been carefully concealed or misrepresented.

Thus in many parts of the so-called post-Communist world, it is not just the regional order (sometimes referred to as the Yalta order) that is being corrected. There are also attempts to correct certain shortcomings in the Versailles order, and even to go farther back into history and exploit the greatest freedom some of them have ever had to make farther amends. It is an impossible desire, of course, but understandable all the same.

If we wish to understand the problems of the post-Communist world, or some of them at least, then we must continually remind ourselves of something else. It is easy to deny the latent problems, ambitions, and particularities of nations. It is easy to make everything the same by force, to destroy the complex and fragile social, cultural, and economic relationships and institutions built up over centuries, and to enforce a single, primitive model of central control in the spirit of a proud utopianism. . . . But it is infinitely more difficult to restore it all, or to create it directly. . . .

What are we to do if we don't wish to understand postcommunism simply as a new inconvenience that would be better avoided by sticking our heads in the sand and minding our own business?

I think the most important thing is not just to take account of external and more or less measurable phenomena like the gross national product, the progress of privatization, the stability of the political system, and the measurable degree to which human rights are observed. All of these things are important, of course, but something more is necessary. There must be an effort to understand the profound events taking place in the womb of post-Communist societies, to take note of their historical meaning and think about their global implications. The temptation must be resisted to adopt a disparaging and slightly astonished attitude, one based on a subconscious feeling of superiority on the part of observers who are better off. Just as Czechs should not sneer at the problems of Tadzhikistan, so no one should sneer at the problems of the Czech Republic. It is only against this background of understanding that meaningful ways of assistance can be sought.

It seems to me that the challenge offered by the post-Communist world is merely the current form of a broader and more profound challenge to discover a new type of self-understanding for man, and a new type of politics that should flow from that understanding. As we all know, today's planetary civilization is in serious danger. . . .

I see only one way out of this crisis: man must come to a new understanding of himself, of his limitations and his place in the world. He should grasp his responsibility in a new way, and reestablish a relationship with the things that transcend him. We must rehabilitate our sense of ourselves as active human subjects, and liberate ourselves from the captivity of a purely national perception of the world. . . .

We live in a world in which our destinies are tied to each other more closely than they ever have been before. It is a world with a single planetary civilization, yet it contains many cultures that, with increasing vigor and singlemindedness resist cultural unification, reject mutual understanding, and exist in what amounts to latent confrontation. It is a deeply dangerous state of affairs and it must be changed. The first step in this direction can be nothing less than a broad-based attempt by people from these cultures to understand one another, and to understand each other's right to existence. Only then can a kind of worldwide, pluralistic metaculture . . . evolve. It is only in the context of such a metaculture that a new sense of political responsibility—global responsibility—can come into being. And it is only with this newly born sense of responsibility that the instruments can be created that will enable humanity to confront all the dangers it has created for itself.

The new political self-understanding I am talking about means a clear departure from the understanding of the world that considers history, foreign cultures, foreign nations, and ultimately all those warnings about our future, as a mere agglomeration of annoying inconveniences that disturb our tranquility. A quiet life on the peak of a volcano is just as illusory as the notion I talked about at the beginning: that by avoiding an encounter with a dissident in the street, we can avoid the problem of communism and the question of how to deal with it.

Ultimately, I understand postcommunism as one of many challenges to contemporary man—regardless of what part of the world he lives in—to awaken to his global responsibilities, and to awaken to them before it is too late. . . .

In today's world, everything concerns everyone. Communism also concerned everyone. And it is also a matter of concern to everyone whether or not, and in what way, we manage to build a new zone of democracy, freedom, and prosperity on its ruins. Every intellectual and material investment in the post-Communist world that is not haphazard, but based on a deep understanding of what is happening there, will repay the whole world many times over.

And not only that: it will also be one more step on the thorny pilgrimage of the human race toward a new understanding of its responsibility for its destiny.

Adam Michnik

Nationalism

The resurgence of the national idea in the postcommunist era in Eastern Europe is a Janus-faced phenomenon for writer Adam Michnik. A historian, a dissident who was imprisoned in Poland, and a leading supporter of the Solidarity trade-union movement, Michnik perceives both a positive and negative side to expressions of nationalist sentiment. To struggle for one's national rights — for the right to remember the past, preserve cultural identity, and live in an independent state — is an acceptable and even laudable aim. But to Michnik nationalism is something else — a dangerous force. It encourages an exclusive concentration on one's own people at the expense of tolerating others, an unwillingness to confront both good and bad in the nation's past, and a closed, inwardly focused view of one's society. Most troubling to Michnik is the fact that both former communists and anticommunists have resorted to the negative form of the national idea — nationalism — in their pursuit of political power.

I recently took part in a meeting of writers organized by the PEN Club in the beautiful little Slovenian town of Bled. What was discussed there were processes that are raising fears today. . . . Yugoslavia is a condensed miniature of a whole set of problems char-

"Nationalism" by Adam Michnik from *Social Research*, v. 58, no. 4 (Winter 1991), pp. 757–763. Reprinted by permission of the New School for Social Research.

acteristic of the postcommunist states. One of the Serbs I spoke with, frightened by the growing chauvinism, reminded me of a phrase by a poet of the last century, Grillparzer, who, observing the successive stages of the Spring of the Nations,[1] spoke of the path from humanism, through nationalism, to bovinism. It sounds like a warning for each of our countries and for each nation.

In these countries a revolution is taking place. Bloodless, peaceful—but a revolution nevertheless. Every revolution has its phases. After the phases of the struggle for freedom from the old regimes comes the struggle for power within the camp of the victors. And the fight for revenge against the defeated. In the first phase, the ideology which binds the opposition together is always the slogan "Freedom Against Dictatorship." Fighting for one's own freedom, for that of one's nation or one's movement, one uses the slogans of universal freedom, tolerance for those who think differently, rights for minorities. Afterward, internal divisions arise, and along with them a quest for the language of ideological differences.

Communism aspired to the role of a worldview that explained everything. After communism there remained an ideological vacuum; and the end of communism meant the opening of a Pandora's box. Into that vacuum began to creep demons from bygone epochs: ideologies proclaiming chauvinism and xenophobia, populism and intolerance.

The word *nationalism* is tainted by a multiplicity of associations. . . . Let us state then, that—in our opinion—the aspirations to reclaim the national memory, to defend cultural identity, to have an independent state do not qualify as nationalism. Nationalism is not the struggle for one's own national rights, but a disregard for someone else's right to national and human dignity. Nationalism represents a certain vision of the world in which nations are condemned to an animal struggle for survival. Nationalism is a degenerate form, after all, of a natural need to live with national dignity and in an independent national state, since nationalism amounts to intolerance: it allows the rejection of another person because of his otherness.

---

[1] The revolutions of 1848 were known as the Spring of the Nations. — Ed.

Nationalism is the last word of communism. A final attempt to find a social basis for dictatorship. . . . [Slobodan] Milošević, the leader of Serbia's communists, [is a] good illustration of that.

Yet nationalism is also an articulation of the opposition to communism. Communism tramples national dignity and destroys national tradition, violates national sovereignty. Nationalism then becomes a distorted form of national self-defense, and this distortion comes all the more easily, the greater the repression. Self-defense—let's say it again—is not nationalism. Nationalism comes only with the conviction that my—suppressed—nation is superior to some other one. Obviously, there is nationalism and there is nationalism. Lenin was right when he distinguished the nationalism of a conquered nation from the nationalism of the occupying nation. The nationalism of the colonizer is always the ugliest and the most worthy of condemnation. In their polemic with the nationalism of Greater Russia, Ukrainian and Lithuanian, Estonian and Georgian writers often write about the imperial psychology of Greater Russians. Yet the matter of Russian nationalism is not so simple either. The Russian nationalist will say that no other nation was harmed by communism in a manner equally cruel: a destroyed culture, religious persecution, the massacre of the intellectual and industrial elites and the elites of cities and villages, along with hunger, enslavement, and despair. The Russian nationalist will construct a theory of the Russian nation as victim. One cannot speak—he will say—about Russia's responsibility for Bolshevism, because Marxist theory is an invention of the West and the revolutions are the work of foreigners: Jews, Poles, Latvians. Communism is not our fault but our misfortune, the Russian nationalist will answer. And that will not be such an absurd answer at all. It will just be an answer that disregards the question of responsibility for one's own and others' misfortunes.

Why do intellectuals so often accept such intellectual shallowness? Because intellectuals living within the communist system have a complex about their own guilt and weakness, their isolation from their own people. Nationalism is an illusion, an attempt to break this isolation and find common emotional and historical values. It refers to what is noble, because it is a deformation of authentic needs. Caring for the national culture, reclaiming the historical memory—all of these indicate an attitude of responsibility.

National identity and responsibility give the right to pride in one's own nation when this is possible, and an obligation to be ashamed when that is necessary. The one is inseparably connected with the other. If—being a German—I feel proud because of Goethe, Heine, and Thomas Mann, even though it wasn't I who wrote their books, I also have to feel shame because of Hitler, Himmler, and Goebbels, even though I never had any sympathy for that ensemble. This is what responsibility consists of.

Nationalism is usually a technique of escaping from responsibility for the past. Strangers are guilty—that is the conviction of a nationalist.

Nationalism is also a technique for building an image of one's own nation—foreign tribesmen do not belong to the nation. Within the framework of nationalist thinking one can point out someone's Jewish background, hunt down cosmopolitan ideas in the culture, proclaim the slogans "Russia for the Russians," "Poland for the Poles," "Bulgaria for the Bulgarians." One may also demand the expulsion of foreigners, as did the authors of the graffiti on the walls of Leipzig, *"Polen 'raus!"* One can finally organize pogroms, as proven by the blood of the Hungarians murdered in Transylvania.

Beyond those emotions there is the dilemma of which path to choose. What next? Where do we go from here? Some say, "We are returning to Europe." While others say, "We are returning to our roots." These need not be contradictory postulates, but they are becoming such as their outlines become sharpened through confrontation. It is a classic dispute within societies that are backward and have a feeling of degradation resulting from their backwardness: to follow in the footsteps of rich and liberal Europe, or to seek their own authentic, though anti-European, path. Nationalism becomes the ideological equipment of the anti-European option. . . .

It is often said that in contemporary Russia the dispute between [Westernizers] and Slavophiles has been recreated.[2] I do

---

[2]Westernizers and Slavophiles were two groups of intellectuals in mid-nineteenth century Russia. The Westernizers believed that Russia had to follow the path of Western civilization. They criticized the Russian political system and demanded more enlightenment. The Slavophiles believed in the superiority of Russian culture, which was based on the Orthodox faith, over Western civilization.—Ed.

not think this is true. I see in this above all a dispute between democracy . . . and the anticommunist "Black Hundreds."[3] The dispute is in essence banally simple: Why do I reject communism? Is it because it violates elementary human rights, the rights of all people? Or is it because it was dragged in from outside, is foreign, Russian, German, Jewish, Masonic, cosmopolitan?

. . . A person with the Black Hundred mentality wants his Russia or his Poland pure, but how easily he loses himself in inconsistencies, denying some the right to be Russian (for example, Jews), or denying others the right not to be Russian (for example, the Ukrainians), because he questions their national identity and distinctiveness.

Each postcommunist country has its "Black Hundred." Whoever says he is free of that sickness is infected in a special way. The Black Hundreds' picture of the world is simple, just as simple as that proposed by a primitive communism. This is why it so easily takes root in the heads of people who witness the collapse of communist dogmas, regarded for decades as inviolable and eternal.

The Polish situation is specific. Poland is a one-nation country within the borders designated by Stalin; a country whose euphoria experienced after the defeat of communism is clouded by the deep crisis of its economic structure. In Poland one can see most clearly what the "Black Hundreds" is about — it is not, after all, about struggling with ethnic minorities, which are not threatening anybody with anything. It is about the shape of Poland itself, the nation and its culture, the state and its guiding principles. It is a dispute neither between the right and the left, nor between Christian democracy and social democracy. None of those designations makes much sense today. It is a dispute between two ideas of nation and state: between the idea of a civil society and an open nation on the one hand and, on the other, the idea of a "Catholic State of the Polish Nation" and intolerance toward those who are different. The former uses the language of democ-

---

[3]Black Hundreds was an antirevolutionary and anti-semitic organization founded in Russia at the time of the 1905 revolution that was opposed to change — Ed.

ratic debate; the latter, the language of insinuation and hatred. For the former, the nation is a community of culture; for the latter, a community of blood. . . .

I am an intellectual engaged in politics. I look at processes which are taking place today from a particular perspective: with joy and hope, but also with sadness and anxiety. How many times did we think about this big holiday celebration of the end of communism? And here, before our very eyes, right next to what is most precious, monsters are creeping out from their hiding places. We still believe that they are marginal, the remnants of bygone times. And that the times which are coming will unfold under the banner of democracy. Are we right?

Steven L. Burg

The Nationalist Appeal and the Remaking of Eastern Europe

After 1989 an "end of empire" mood once again spread among the peoples of Eastern Europe, as it had at the end of World War I. Nationalities such as the Slovenes and Slovaks sought independence rather than remain part of larger states. As new or remade leaders strove to garner popular support at a time when it was impossible to meet the material expectations of their people, they turned to nationalism to legitimate their governments. Steven Burg, a political scientist, sees the transition from one-party rule under communism to a pluralist society impeded by the ethnic conflict that has arisen in Eastern Europe. This conflict stems from the rekindling of national antagonisms that hark back to the end of the nineteenth century as

"Nationalism Redux: Through the Glass of the Post-Communist States Darkly" by Steven Burg from *Current History*, April 11, 1993, pp. 162–167. Reprinted with permission from Current History, Inc.

well as from demands for the redress of recent grievances over status and power. The mobilizing appeal of nationalism has attracted even governments committed to democracy. But in the process, smaller groups have suffered discrimination in the name of the majority. Nationalism has thus challenged both the inviolability of territorial frontiers and the legitimacy of governments.

The wanton violence of the fighting taking place in the Balkans and the Caucasus (Armenia, Azerbaijan, and Georgia) has brought death and destruction to Europe on a scale not seen since the end of World War II; it threatens to destabilize not only the continent but other international communities. Because political boundaries rarely match ethnic boundaries, conflicts based on calls for ethnic self-determination inevitably threaten to involve neighboring states. And, as has been seen in the Balkans and Caucasus, once initiated, the violence of ethnic-based conflicts is easily escalated by individual acts of brutality into widespread death and destruction. . . .

The appeals of nationalist-separatist groups to the principle of national self-determination challenge the principles of state sovereignty, territorial integrity, inviolability of borders, and noninterference that have been central to the post–World War II international system. This challenge must be addressed if peaceful mechanisms for the resolution of ethnic conflicts are to be established, and the stability of the international system is to be preserved. This will inevitably require the careful redefinition of these postwar principles and the obligations arising out of them. The conflict between nationalism and democracy in the post-Communist states also presents a direct challenge to the ability of the United States to make human rights principles central to the international system.

From Containment to Involvement

As long as the Communist leadership in Moscow exercised hegemony over the states of eastern Europe, the United States and its allies had only limited involvement in the region. . . . Although the United States adopted a strategy of "containment," it consistently refrained from becoming directly involved in the internal affairs of the Soviet bloc countries. Even when faced with outbreaks of popular unrest or mass opposition to Communist rule (as was the case in Hungary in 1956, in Czechoslovakia in 1968, and in Poland in 1979 and 1980), the West refrained from intervening directly. Paradoxically, it was the onset of détente and the collaborative Soviet-American effort to ratify the status quo that created new opportunities for change in eastern Europe.

In 1975, 35 countries—including those from the Soviet bloc, western Europe, and the United States—concluded the Helsinki Final Act. Although the Helsinki agreement ratified the international status quo, it also provided the basis on which the West and, more important, domestic groups in the Communist states, could pursue political changes in eastern Europe. The Helsinki Final Act included 10 basic principles that were to be used to evaluate the actions of the signatory countries. These included some that ratified the post-war configuration of states in Europe by establishing their sovereignty and territorial integrity, affirming the inviolability of their borders, and mandating nonintervention in their internal affairs. Other principles committed the signatories to peaceful relations by disavowing the threat or use of force and calling for the peaceful settlement of disputes; the principles also committed them to respect "human rights and fundamental freedoms" and "the equal rights of peoples and their right to self-determination." The act further established the right of peoples to determine their political status. In effect, the Helsinki principles made Western concepts of individual liberty and collective democracy the political standard, and applied that standard to all the signatory states, from the countries of North America to the Soviet Union.

One consequence of the Helsinki agreement, certainly unanticipated in the East and perhaps in the West as well, was the formation in the Communist countries of small but active dissident grass-roots political organizations to uphold these political standards. The increase in cultural contacts between East and West that followed the act also reinforced a process already under way among the broader, nondissident social elites in the East: the development of increasingly liberal political values and growing national consciousness. This liberalization of values and new emphasis on national identity contributed—once Soviet President Mikhail Gorbachev's attempt to reform the Soviet system had introduced new opportunities for grass-roots political activity —to the re-emergence of national movements aimed at the establishment of independent states; in the end it also contributed to the collapse of communism. . . .

. . . The implosion of the Soviet domestic political order, the emergence of independent states in the former territory of the Soviet Union, and the emergence of new regimes in eastern Europe has produced [a] devolution of power to the state. As a result, nationalism has again become a powerful legitimating force for new governments with uncertain bases of popular support. It remains to be seen whether these post-Communist regimes will be able to transform the bases of their legitimacy from nationalist to democratic principles. The increased salience of nationality has rekindled many of the ethnic issues of the late nineteenth and early twentieth centuries. . . .

A Bad Fit: Nationalism and Democracy

The commitment and ability of a government to guarantee individual rights is a necessary element in solving any ethnic conflict. . . . Such protection is essential to ending the threat felt by individuals in situations of intergroup conflict and establishing interethnic peace. . . .

The development of democratic regimes in eastern Europe and the former Soviet Union, and the construction of a new framework for Euro-Atlantic security, are best served by linking Western aid to local efforts to establish democracy. . . . The loosening and even abandonment of state censorship and state-imposed limits on individual expression have indeed permitted the emergence of a multitude of citizens organizations of varying size and interests. And the introduction of competitive electoral politics has stimulated the formation of independent political parties. These expanded freedoms of expression, participation, and organization are essential to the democratization process. But the degree to which government institutions are becoming instruments for the representation of social interests and can impose accountability on the national leadership, not to mention the extent to which individual rights are protected, varies greatly from state to state. . . .

Nationalism is distinguished from social movements that arise among other aggrieved groups by the powerful emotions associated with it. In extreme cases, nationalist movements evoke a willingness to fight and die on behalf of the cause. This derives from the notion that what is at issue is group "survival." Nationalist movements, however, cannot be understood as solely "primordial" in nature. They are most often also organizational vehicles for the articulation of arguments over rights, goods, status, power, and other material and political issues. . . . Their ultimate solution . . . must involve the redress of grievances over rights, status, and power that also motivate and mobilize the populations—and especially their leaders—in these conflicts.

The strength of nationalist political movements, the popular appeal of avenging long-held ethnic grievances, and the resultant escalation of ethnic conflict impede the transition from authoritarianism to democracy. . . . Nationalist conflict suppresses the importance and, in some cases, even the emergence of multiple issues, demands, and interests as nationalist leaders try to subordinate all other issues. Nationalist movements usually demand autonomy and seek a separate existence, denying the reality of commonalities, shared interests, or even mutual dependence. Ethnically based claims to autonomy thus strike at the heart of the process of democratization, since they compete with individual rights-based legitimation of a liberal democratic order.

The political organizations characteristic of nationalist movements, and the state institutions and processes they spawn are therefore ill-suited to the conciliation of competing demands. They tend to adopt exclusivist rather than inclusivist policies, and tend to extremism rather than moderation. In this way the politics of nationalism are contrary to the essence of the liberal democratic process.

The enormous hardships that have been imposed on the people of eastern Europe and the former Soviet Union by the transition from central planning and state ownership to market-based economies make it difficult, if not impossible, for governments to win popular support on the basis of the material benefits they can deliver. This heightens the effectiveness of a government's appeals to national sentiments. The declaration of "sovereignty," the establishment of cultural supremacy, or even the threat of military action are promises more easily delivered than an improvement in the standard of living. Moreover, such acts strengthen the state's power and secure the positions of political incumbents far more effectively than efforts to institutionalize civil liberties, which would facilitate criticism of the government and the activities of an opposition.

Attempts to legitimate even democratically elected governments through appeals to nationalism may unsettle relations between neighboring states. Expressions of concern for minority communities of ethnic brethren in neighboring countries, no matter how carefully constructed, may raise the specter of irredentist claims and stimulate nationalist responses among the neighboring ethnic majority. Given the changing historical/political status of territories throughout eastern Europe and the former Soviet Union, real and imagined irredentist issues claims represent sources of potentially serious interstate conflict.

Nationalist legitimation of new states may also lead to actions that impede the development of internal democracy. Several post-Communist governments have attempted to redress the ethnic grievances of the majority or eponymous population through legislation that effectively discriminates against minorities. Already, new citizenship laws, laws on language rights, voting rights laws, and other legislation have heightened tensions between dominant and minority groups. . . .

The post-Communist regimes are experiencing a broad, multidimensional transition from the enforced integration, artificial homogeneity, and stability of communism to the more open and pluralistic patterns of public discourse and behavior associated with incipient democracy. . . . With only a few notable exceptions, political organizations and institutions in these states have yet to bring together diverse groups and reconcile their conflicting interests. Their inability to do so may reflect the absence of interests that bind their populations together. At the very least it suggests that such interests are now far less important to the population than those that divide them.

Even where common economic interests, for example, might provide a pragmatic basis for linking constituencies to a common administrative and political center, the power of nationalist-separatist sentiments among the populace makes it difficult for local leaders to act on them. Indeed, even the distribution of economic interests and resources themselves may be in dispute, held to be illegitimate legacies of the old regime for which contemporary compensation is due. . . . The perception of material conflicts in ethnic terms by the mass populace, the acceptance or exploitation of such ethnic definitions by elites, and the frequency with which conflicts defined this way produce violence, make the resolution of differences over the distribution of government functions and over economic and other issues much more difficult to achieve. . . .

The Ties That Didn't Bind

In the post-Soviet states, the former Yugoslav states, and in Czechoslovakia, the transition from authoritarianism was turned into a simultaneous "end of empire" process. Once seen this way, intellectual, economic, and other groups who might otherwise have been inclined to support a transition to democracy were drawn toward more nationally determined positions. The Slovenian and Croatian challenges to rule from Belgrade, for example, stimulated a conservative and even reactionary response among some Serbs, whose earlier support for democratization proved less powerful than the appeal of Serbian nationalism. Similarly, the opportunity to establish an independent state proved more appealing to democratic activists in Slovenia than the task of democratizing a common Yugoslav state. In Czechoslovakia, the alliance of Czechs and Slovaks opposed to communism soon disintegrated and electoral support in both Slovakia and the Czech Republic shifted to leaders and parties intent on pursuing regional interests at the expense of continued federation.

The rush to redress long-suppressed national grievances has also led in some cases to the partial legitimation, or re-legitimation of the antidemocratic aspects of national political history. The Fascist and Nazi collaborationist regimes established in Hungary, Slovakia, and Croatia during World War II have been the object of public, and in some instances de facto official re-valuation by nationalist leaders. New governments in Lithuania and Slovenia have pardoned Nazi collaborators. These actions are one dimension of the reaffirmation of collective identities, and a reflection of the powerful urge to reject any negative judgments of them. They also reflect, however, how weak concerns are for individual and human rights in the contemporary politics of the region. The still overwhelming strength of collective identities makes efforts to distinguish between national-cultural communities and the actions of individuals, especially when they are government officials, very difficult. And such distinctions are essential to the success of a transition from nationalist to democratic bases of legitimation. . . .

Democratically inclined leaderships in the region are, therefore, confronted with the task of establishing an enforceable boundary between democratically acceptable and unacceptable political behavior. This is an immensely difficult political challenge. Debate over this issue continues in the United States even after 200 years of institutionalized democratic experience. It should not be surprising, therefore, that this is so difficult to achieve in the post-Communist states. It is clear that these states cannot depend on either a mass civic culture or on their own accumulated legitimacy to insulate them from popular discontent; moreover, they do not have the resources to deliver sufficient benefits to their people to counterbalance the social, economic, and political hardships that confront them.

Lenard J. Cohen

The Destruction
of Yugoslavia

After more than forty years of communist rule, Yugoslavia collapsed. Its disintegration ignited violence unparalleled in Europe since World War II. Lenard Cohen, a political scientist, sees the two developments as linked. The country's fragmentation and the resulting devastation both had roots in lingering, historically derived ethnic animosities as well as the failure of the communist regime to resolve them through its nationality policy and program for modernization. The cooperation of the South Slav peoples in a Yugoslav state foundered on divergent views of the nature of the polity—was it a federation or a unitary national government? Attempts under Tito's leadership to recognize cultural and historical diversity did not bring the desired unity of peoples. Instead, when economic distress buffeted the country in the 1980s, it only heightened nationalist political grievances.

Two important and complex issues have troubled observers in relation to the catastrophic events that unfolded in the Balkans during the early 1990s. First, and perhaps the less difficult of the two issues, is the matter of why the "Second Yugoslavia" (1945–1991) collapsed. Second, there is the related and perplexing question as to why the disintegration of the federation generated so much violence and suffering. In addressing the first issue, [the] focus [must be] primarily on the failure of political leaders—newly elected or reelected to power during the "pluralist revolution" of 1990—to agree upon a revised model of political and economic coexistence that could have preserved some form of state unity among the

Reprinted from *Broken Bonds: The Disintegration of Yugoslavia* by Lenard Cohen, 1993, pp. 265–270, by permission of Westview Press, Boulder, CO 80301.

peoples of Yugoslavia but would also have permitted expanded sovereignty for the former federation's constituent territorial and ethnic groups. Serious difficulties stemming from interelite mistrust and elite-led ethnic nationalism, or what [can be] referred to . . . as "the politics of intransigence," did not begin with the disintegration of the League of Communist's monopoly in early 1990. Once multiparty pluralism and competitive elections emerged, however, issues related to transcending disagreements among regional elites became far more complex and serious. Not only did the number of centrist parties — mainly reconfigured communist-nationalists and noncommunist nationalists — multiply but a large number of ultranationalist parties and movements also emerged on the scene.

Most of the country's major civilian and military leaders recognized the danger of impending state disintegration and political violence if they failed to reach agreement on a new constitutional model, but they proved woefully inept in finding a way out of the looming disaster. After months of elite posturing and stalemate in the negotiations regarding the intractable federation-confederation dispute, saber rattling by all sides, and leadership mishandling or outright manipulation of the explosive "Serbian question," it became impossible to sustain the cohesion of a perennially fragile country afflicted with a history of deep ethnic and regional enmities. External factors — particularly German and Austrian support for the secessionist goals of Slovenia and Croatia, and the "pasted together diplomacy" exhibited by the United States and EC when handling Yugoslav affairs — certainly played an important role in the collapse of the federation but the major responsibility rests with the quarrelsome nationalist leaders of Yugoslavia's republics.

Explanations for the collapse of the Yugoslav federation are closely linked but are still separate from the second issue raised here, namely, why state disintegration spawned such widespread, protracted, and barbarous violence. Three closely related factors . . . are particularly significant for understanding the intense violence associated with the dissolution of the Yugoslav federation: first, the persistence and intensification of deep-seated animosities among the country's diverse ethnic and religious groups, who lived together rather uneasily in the Balkan region for centuries but who shared membership in a common state from only 1918 to 1991; second, the desire of many Yugoslav citizens to redress grievances arising from the violent bloodletting among ethnic groups during World War II; and, finally, the failure of the communist regime's nationality policy and modernization programs to resolve outstanding, albeit temporarily submerged, interethnic grievances and to engender a substantial basis for long-term interethnic tolerance. The combined impact of the preceding three factors not only contributed substantially to the elite intransigence that led to the demise of the Second Yugoslavia, but in the particular circumstances and traditions endemic to the Balkans, also unleashed extremely violent interethnic strife.

Consideration of the policies and strategies conducted by successive political regimes is crucial to an understanding of the deep intergroup antagonisms in Balkan society. Indeed, throughout much of Balkan history the region's intrinsic heterogeneity was nurtured and utilized as a basis for maintaining authoritarian political rule. For example, the contending Ottoman and Hapsburg empires, which asserted hegemony over the various South Slav ethnic groups between the late fourteenth and early sixteenth centuries, maintained political control of their multiconfessional and multiethnic Balkan domains up to the early twentieth century by means of various divide-and-rule strategies, including the segmentation of religious communities. Although some members of the nonruling intelligentsia did endeavor to forge closer ties among different ethnically related communities — for example, the "Yugoslav idea," elaborated in Croatian elite circles during the first part of the nineteenth century . . .—such notions enjoyed only shallow and uneven support from the region's ethnically and religiously divided population.

Notwithstanding its limited popular support, a unified Yugoslav state was created in 1918, bringing together several South Slavic and non-Slavic ethnic groups within a single territorial framework. Although the new state's Belgrade-based political

regimes largely abandoned earlier imperial policies of group segmentation, their various attempts to induce a pan-ethnic "Yugoslav" consciousness during most of the next 73 years, though
contrasting with the policies of their imperial predecessors,
tended to aggravate the general pattern of ethnic antagonisms.
Thus the imperatives of central political rule once again con-
strained the free expression of ethnic and religious differences.
Whether under the Serbian-dominated unitary state between the
two world wars or under the more ethnically balanced but opposi-
tionless communist federation established by Tito, ethnic grievances continued to accumulate and fester into potential sources
of political instability.

Short-lived periods of political contestation or liberalization —
such as the fragmented multiparty system of the 1920s, and the
factionalized one-party socialist pluralism reluctantly permitted
by Tito in the second part of the 1960s — proved to be episodes of
chaotic ethnopolitical rivalry that offered little opportunity for the
sustained reconciliation of intergroup animosities. Thus although
precommunist and communist political elites in Belgrade did
manage to constrain the outbreak of widespread ethnic conflict
for substantial periods of time, as did earlier rulers in Constantinople, Vienna, and Budapest, deep-seated ethnic resentments persisted as a vital latent force, simmering beneath the facade of con-
trived stability and cohesion.

Historically, the potential for ethnically and religiously based
violence in the Balkans was most evident during periods of regime
crisis and breakdown (e.g., the last phase of Ottoman control
which led to the Balkan Wars; the final throes of Hapsburg rule
just before and during World War I; the collapse and dismemberment of the Yugoslav state in 1941). Indeed, perceptive observers
of Balkan society have frequently noted the close relationship between regime breakdown, historically based ethnoreligious antagonisms, and intense violence. Discussing his native Bosnian society in the period just before World War I, Nobel-Prize-winning
author Ivo Andrić brilliantly captured how seemingly tranquil intergroup relations have traditionally exploded into an orgy of mutual bloodletting. In an illustrative case, Andrić describes the
"Sarajevo frenzy of hate" that erupted among Moslems, Roman

Catholics, and Orthodox believers following the assassination on June 28, 1914, of Archduke Franz Ferdinand in Sarajevo:

> *Adherents of the three main faiths, they hate one another from birth to death, senselessly and profoundly . . . often, they spent their entire lives without finding an opportunity to express that hatred in all its facets and horror; but whenever the established order of things is shaken by some important event, and reason and law are suspended for a few hours or days, then this mob or rather a section of it, finding at last an adequate motive, overflows into the town . . . and, like a flame which has sought and has at last found fuel, these long-kept hatreds and hidden desires for destruction and violence take over the town, lapping, sputtering, and swallowing everything, until some force larger than themselves suppresses them, or until they burn themselves out and tire of their own rage.*

Vera St. Erlich, a Zagreb sociologist, also emphasized the Balkan tradition of violent interethnic struggle, particularly in areas such as Bosnia-Hercegovina and other regions that have been under Turkish rule, when attempting to explain how a "determination to fight" was so quickly "revived" following the dismemberment of the Yugoslav state in 1941. In St. Erlich's view, the protracted resistance struggle waged by the South Slavs against Ottoman tutelage fashioned a "heroic value orientation," imprinting the collective conviction "that no force in the world can conquer fighters."

> *Generations of Yugoslavs from the fourteenth century until today grew up with this value orientation. Their character was formed through loyalty to resistance movements and not through conformity to an established culture and institutions. . . . As the old authorities collapse under enemy attack and invasion, the unity of society ceases to exist. From then on factions raise their claims, and the people divide into hostile camps, the individual is compelled to make his choice.*

The dismemberment of the "First Yugoslavia" (1918–1941), and the collapse of authority in that state, precipitated savage interethnic violence during World War II, which resulted in the death of approximately one-tenth of the country's population. Wartime atrocities and radically heightened political polarization left a pattern of emotional scars that were only superficially masked by the communist system's promising slogans (e.g., "Brotherhood and Unity," "Equality of Nations"), pan-ethnic strategies, and artificial political uniformity.

Although broad-ranging generalizations, such as those made by Andrić and St. Erlich, often neglect the important differences within and among particular ethnic groups and regions, they do serve to draw attention to the important historical factors that have conditioned Balkan and South Slav political life. The impact of historical factors on current Balkan development has also been recognized in more recent sociological research relating to the intensification of ethnic conflict in Yugoslavia during the 1980s and 1990s. For example, a comprehensive review by the Serbia-based sociologist Sergej Flere of various theoretical approaches seeking to explain the upsurge of ethnic antagonism in post-Tito Yugoslavia identified the historical perspective as the most convincing. Flere conceded that as recently as the late 1980s it appeared to most observers that modernization had largely eroded religious divisions and had contributed to Yugoslavia's "emancipation from tradition." By 1990 however, Flere argued, the role of traditional religions in generating ethnic conflicts—including resentments derived from the history of religious warfare and forced religious conversion in the Balkans—was already very pronounced.

Flere acknowledged, as many other analysts so often had in past years, the considerable changes in Yugoslav society during the post–World War II period and the existence of various potentially integrative factors (e.g., intermarriage by individuals belonging to different ethnic groups, substantial numbers of citizens self-identified as "Yugoslavs"), but he emphasized that socialist Yugoslavia remained "substantially unintegrated" and "retained a basically segmented quality." Buffeted and alienated by the severe economic crisis of the 1980s, the subsequent breakdown of the socialist federation, and lacking a strong sense of common identity and reciprocal trust, Yugoslavia's citizens—in both the economically developed and disadvantaged regions of the country—sought refuge in their only superficially or partially eradicated traditional ethnoreligious beliefs and resentments.

Thus viewed in historical perspective, particularly in the context of the Balkan region's traditional proclivity for ethnoreligiously based violence at times of regime breakdown, an explosion of intercommunal hatred and savagery was not at all surprising when ethnic elites proved tragically inept at peacefully resolving their differences.

Raising the national flag emblazoned with the *šahovnica*, the medieval Croatian emblem, Croatia's citizens demonstrate their support for their newly declared independent country. (© James Mason/Black Star)

PART

VI

The National Idea and Civic Community: The Past in the Future of Eastern Europe

From the Constitutions of the Czech Republic and the Republics of Slovakia, Croatia, and Macedonia

The Surge of Nations and the Making of New States

Following the breakdown of the communist system, some states in Eastern Europe fragmented, including the Soviet Union. For many peoples, the desire to assert their national sovereignty outweighed any thought of remaining within larger political units. The desire to

From the constitutions of the Czech Republic, Slovakia, Croatia, and Macedonia, from Blaustein and Flanz, eds., *Constitutions of the Countries of the World,* Oceana Publications, 5 (July 1994), 11 (July 1994), 17 (June 1993), Granville Publishers, Inc.

provide for the rights and institutions of civic community as well as to assert national identity is reflected in the founding documents of these newly independent states.

CONSTITUTION OF THE CZECH REPUBLIC

Preamble

We, the citizens of the Czech Republic in Bohemia, Moravia, and Silesia,
at the time of the renewal of an independent Czech state,
faithful to all the good traditions of the ancient statehood of the lands of the Czech Crown and the Czechoslovak statehood,
determined to build, protect, and develop the Czech Republic in the spirit of the inviolable values of human dignity and freedom, as a homeland to equal, free citizens who are conscious of their obligations toward others and of their responsibility toward the whole, as a free and democratic state based on respect for human rights and on the principles of a civil society, as a part of the family of European and world democracies,
determined to jointly guard and develop the inherited natural, cultural, material, and intellectual wealth,
resolved to abide by all the tested principles of a legal state,
adopt through our freely elected representatives this Constitution of the Czech Republic.

Chapter One
Fundamental Provisions

Article 1

The Czech Republic [are] a sovereign, unitary . . . and democratic law-governed state based on the respect for the rights and liberties of man and citizen.

Article 2

[1] The people [are] the source of all state power; they exercise through the medium of the legislative, executive, and judicial organs.

[2] A constitutional law may specify when the people exercises state power directly.

[3] State power serves all citizens and it can only be exercised in the cases, within the limits, and in ways established by law.

[4] Every citizen can do what is not forbidden by law and no one must be forced to do what is not established by law.

Article 3

The Charter of Fundamental Rights and Freedoms is part of the constitutional order of the Czech Republic. . . .

Article 5

The political system is based on the free and voluntary origin of political parties and their free competition respecting basic democratic principles and rejecting force as a means of enforcing one's interests.

Article 6

Political decisions originate from the will of the majority expressed in free voting. Decisions by the majority provide . . . for the protection of minorities. . . .

CHARTER OF FUNDAMENTAL RIGHTS AND FREEDOMS

. . .

Chapter One
General Provisions

Article 1

Humans are free and equal in their dignity and in their rights. The fundamental rights and freedoms are inherent, inalienable, nonprescriptive.

Article 2

[1] The State is founded on democratic values and must not be tied either to an exclusive ideology or to a particular religion.

[2] The power of the State may be asserted only in cases and within the limits established by law and in a manner specified by law.

[3] Everybody may do what is not prohibited by law and nobody may be forced to do what the law does not require.

Article 3

[1] Fundamental human rights and freedoms are guaranteed to everybody without distinction to gender, race, color, language, belief, religion, political or other persuasion, national or social origin, membership in a national or ethnic minority, property, birth, or other status.

[2] Everybody has the right to decide freely his nationality. Any form of influencing this choice is prohibited, just as any form of pressure aimed at denationalization. . . .

[3] Nobody may be caused detriment to his rights because he asserts his fundamental rights and freedoms. . . .

Chapter Two
Human Rights and Fundamental Freedoms

Part One
Fundamental Human Rights and Freedoms

. . .

Article 6

[1] Everyone has the right to life. Human life is worthy of protection already before birth.

[2] Nobody must be deprived to life.

[3] Capital punishment is inadmissible.

[4] It is not a violation of rights according to this article, if someone has been deprived of life in connection with an act which is not punishable under the law.

Article 7

[1] Inviolability of the person and privacy is guaranteed. It may be limited only in cases specifically by law.

[2] Nobody may be tortured or subjected to inhuman or degrading treatment or punishment. . . .

Article 10

[1] Everybody has the right to protection of human dignity, personal honor, good reputation, and name.
[2] Everybody is entitled to protection against unauthorized interference in his personal and family life.
[3] Everybody is entitled to protection against unauthorized gathering, publication or other misuse of personal data.

Article 11

[1] Everybody has the right to own property. The ownership right of all owners has the same statutory content and the same protection. Inheritance is guaranteed.
[2] The law shall specify which property is essential for securing the needs of the whole society, development of the national economy, and public interest may be owned only by the State, the community, or by specified judicial persons; the law may also specify that some things may be owned only by citizens or by judicial persons having their seat in the Czech . . . Republic. . . .

Article 12

[1] The sanctity of the home is inviolable. It may not be entered without permission of the person living there.
[2] A house search is permissible only for purposes of criminal proceedings on the basis of a written warrant by a judge. The manner in which a house search may be conducted is specified by law.
[3] Other interferences in the inviolability of the home may be permitted by law only if it is essential in a democratic society for protection of the life or health of individuals, for the protection of the rights and freedoms of others, or for averting a serious threat to public security and order. If a home is also used for a business enterprise or for the pursuit of other economic activity, the law may permit such interfer-

ences if this is essential for the realization of the duties of public administration. . . .

Article 15

[1] Freedom of thought, conscience and religious confession is guaranteed. Everybody has the right to change his religion or faith or to be without religious confession.
[2] Freedom of scientific research and of the creative art is guaranteed.
[3] Nobody can be forced to perform military service if it is [in] conflict with his conscience or religious confession. Detailed provisions are set by law. . . .

Division Two
Political Rights

Article 17

[1] Freedom of expression and the right to information are guaranteed.
[2] Everybody has the right to express freely his opinions by word, in writing, in the press, in pictures or in any other form, as well as to seek freely, receive and disseminate ideas and information irrespective of the frontiers of the State.
[3] Censorship is not permitted.
[4] The freedom of expression and the right to seek and disseminate information may be limited by law if it involves measures essential in a democratic society for the protection of the rights and freedoms of others, the security of the State, public security, public health, and morality. . . .

Article 20

[1] The right to associate freely is guaranteed. Everybody has the right to associate with others in clubs, societies and other associations.
[2] Citizens have the right to form political parties and political movements and to associate in them.
[3] The exercise of these rights may be limited only in cases spec-

ified by law, if it is essential in a democratic society for the security of the State, the protection of public security and public order, the prevention of crime, or for the protection of the rights and freedoms of others.

[4] Political parties and political movements, as well as other associations, are separated from the State. . . .

Article 22

The legal provisions governing all political rights and freedoms, their interpretation, and application must make possible and protect the free competition between political forces in a democratic society.

Article 23

Citizens have the right to resist anybody who would do away with the democratic order of human rights and fundamental freedoms, established by the Charter, if the work of the constitutional organs and effective use of legal means are made impossible.

Chapter Three
Rights of National and Ethnic Minorities

Article 24

The national or ethnic identity of anyone must not be used to his detriment.

Article 25

[1] Citizens who constitute national or ethnic minorities are guaranteed all-round development, in particular the right to develop with other members of the minority their own culture, the right to disseminate and receive information in their language, and the right to associate in national associations. Details are provided by law.

[2] Citizens belonging to national and ethnic minorities are also guaranteed under conditions set by law
  [a] the right to education in their language,

[b] the right to use their language in official contact,
[c] the right to participate in the settlement of matters concerning national and ethnic minorities.

CONSTITUTION OF
THE SLOVAK REPUBLIC

Preamble

We, the Slovak Nation,
mindful of the political and cultural heritage of our forefathers and of hundreds of years experience in the struggle for our national existence and our own statehood,
in the spirit of St. Cyril and St. Metod's tradition, and out of the legacy of the Great Moravian Empire, based on the natural right of nations to their self-determination,
together with the members of national minorities and ethnic groups living in the territory of the Slovak Republic, in the interest of everlasting and peaceful cooperation with other democratic countries,
striving to exercise democratic forms of government,
striving to guarantee a free life and development of our spiritual culture and economic prosperity,

Therefore We, the Citizens of the Slovak Republic herewith resolve,
through our representatives,
to establish this Constitution:

Chapter One

Section I
Fundamental Provisions

Article 1

The Slovak Republic is a democratic and sovereign state ruled by law. It is bound neither to an ideology, nor to a religion.

Article 2

(1) The power of the state comes from the people who exercise it either through their representatives or directly.
(2) The state authorities shall act only on the basis of the Constitution and to the extent and in the manner which will be stipulated by law.
(3) Everybody is free to do anything that is not prohibited by law and nobody shall be forced to do something that is not imposed by law.

Article 3

(1) The territory of the Slovak Republic is integrated and indivisible.
(2) The frontier of the Slovak Republic can only be changed by a constitutional act. . . .

Article 5

(1) The conditions for naturalization or deprival of state citizenship of the Slovak Republic will be regulated by law.
(2) No person shall be deprived of citizenship of the Slovak Republic against his own will.

Article 6

(1) The Slovak language is the state language in the territory of the Slovak Republic.
(2) The use of languages other than the state language in administrative relations will be regulated by law.

Article 7

The Slovak Republic may, by a free decision, enter a union with other states. The right of secession from such a union shall not be restricted. The joining of a union with other states or the secession from such a union shall be decided by a constitutional law and consequent referendum.

Chapter Two
Basic Rights and Freedoms

Section I
General Provisions

Article 11

The international agreements on human rights and basic freedoms which were ratified by the Slovak Republic and which have been declared legal, take precedence over its laws whenever they guarantee a wider scope of constitutional rights and freedoms.

Article 12

(1) The people are free and equal in their dignity and rights. The basic rights and freedoms are inalienable, imprescriptible and irreversible.
(2) The basic rights and freedoms are guaranteed to every person in the territory of the Slovak Republic irrespective of sex, race, colour, language, faith and religion, political and other views, national or social origin, nationality or ethnic origin, wealth, heritage or social position. On these grounds, no person shall be persecuted, favoured or discriminated against.
(3) Every person may freely decide his nationality. The decision in this respect must not be influenced in any way. Any form of pressure directed toward denationalization is prohibited.
(4) The exercise of basic human rights and freedoms must not be detrimental to the rights of any person who exercises them.

Article 13

(1) Duties may be imposed only on the basis of law, within the limits of law, at the same time respecting the basic rights and freedoms.
(2) The limitations of the basic rights and freedoms may be stipulated on conditions specified in this Constitution only by law.
(3) Any legal restriction of the basic rights and freedoms must have the same effect in all cases which comply with the legally designated conditions.
(4) Whenever a restriction will be enforced against the basic

rights and freedoms, their substance and sense must be respected. Such a restriction may be used only for specific purposes.

Section II
Basic Human Rights and Freedoms

Article 14

Every person is eligible for rights.

Article 15

(1) Everyone has the right to live. Human life is worthy of protection even before birth.
(2) No person shall be deprived of life.
(3) Capital punishment is unacceptable.
(4) The rights enforced by this article are not infringed upon if a person is deprived of his life by a legally unpunishable action. . . .

Article 17

(1) Personal freedom is guaranteed.
(2) No person shall be prosecuted or deprived of freedom other than for reasons and in the manner ordained by law. No person shall be deprived of freedom exclusively because of his inability to discharge contractual obligation. . . .
(4) No person accused shall be taken into custody without a well grounded injunction issued by [a] judge in writing. A person held in police custody shall be committed to court within twenty four hours. The judge must hear the person accused within twenty four hours from the time the accused has been committed to the court, and put the accused in custody or set the person accused free.
(5) A person shall be taken into custody only for legally ordained reasons and duration. . . .

Article 23

(1) The freedom of migration and the freedom of domicile are guaranteed.

(2) Every person staying legally in the territory of the Slovak Republic has the right to leave it freely.

(3) The freedoms listed in [Paragraphs] (1) and (2) may be legally restricted if such a restriction is necessary for the security of the state or necessary to maintain public order, to protect health or rights and freedoms of other persons and, in certain areas, to protect nature.

(4) Every citizen has the right to enter the territory of the Slovak Republic without restrictions. No citizen shall be forced to leave his homeland. No citizen shall be expelled or sent out to other countries. . . .

Article 24

(1) The freedom of thought, conscience, religion and creed are guaranteed. This right also includes the possibility to change one's religious affiliation or creed. Every person has the right to be religiously indifferent. Every person has the right to express his thoughts freely.

(2) Every person has the right to practice his religion privately or in public, individually or with others, through religious masses, offices or education. . . .

Article 25

(1) The defence of the Slovak Republic is a matter of honour for every citizen.

(2) No person shall be forced to serve in the army if this duty is at variance with his conscience or religious affiliation. The details will be specified by law.

Section III
Political Rights

Article 26

(1) The freedom of expression and the right to information are guaranteed.

(2) Every person has the right to express his opinions orally, in writing, in pictures, through the press or in other ways, as well

as the right to seek, receive and communicate ideas and information regardless of the state frontier. The press is not subject to state authority. Business activities in radio and television broadcasting may be subject to state authorization. The law will specify other details.

(3) Censorship is prohibited.

(4) The freedom of speech and the right to seek and broadcast information may be restricted by law if such a restriction is, in a democratic society, necessary for the protection of the rights and freedoms of other persons, for the security of the state and public, and for public health and morality.

(5) The state central authorities and the authorities of regional administrations must provide information about their activities in a reasonable manner and in state language. The conditions for the execution of this paragraph will be set by law. . . .

Article 29

(1) The right to unite freely is guaranteed. Every person has the right to be a member of a union, community, society or any other association.

(2) The citizens have the right to found political parties and movements and unite among themselves. . . .

Article 31

All political rights and freedoms shall be legally established, explained and exercised in such a manner that will facilitate and protect the free competition of political forces in a democratic society. . . .

Section IV
The Rights of National Minorities and Ethnic Groups

Article 33

The membership in any national minority or ethnic group whatsoever must not be detrimental to any person.

Article 34

(1) The universal advancement of citizens who are members of national minorities and ethnic groups shall be assured, first of all the right to develop their own culture with other members of the national minority, the right to broadcast and receive information in their mother tongue, the right to unite themselves in national associations and the right to found and maintain educational and cultural institutions. The law shall specify other details.

(2) Respecting the conditions ordained by law, the citizens who belong to national minorities and ethnic groups, in addition to the right to acquire their mother tongue, are also legally entitled:

    a) to education in their mother tongue

    b) to use their language in administrative relations,

    c) to participate in the solution of issues concerning the national minorities and ethnic groups,

(3) The exercise of the rights of the citizens who belong to national minorities or ethnic groups, and which are guaranteed by this Constitution, must not lead to the breach of integrity of the Slovak Republic or to discrimination against other citizens in Slovakia's territory. . . .

THE CONSTITUTION OF THE REPUBLIC OF CROATIA

I. Historical Foundations

Giving expression to the thousand-year old national identity and statehood of the Croatian nation, confirmed by the continuity of a series of historical events in various political forms and by the maintenance of the state-forming idea of the Croatian nation's historic right to full state sovereignty, which manifested itself:

— in the formation of Croatian principalities in the 7th century;

— in the autonomous medieval state of Croatia founded in the 9th century;

— in the Kingdom of Croats established in the 10th century;

— in the maintenance of the subjectivity of the Croatian state in the Croatian-Hungarian personal union;

— in the autonomous and sovereign decision of the Croatian Sabor[1] of 1527 to elect a king from the Habsburg dynasty;

— in the autonomous and sovereign decision of the Croatian Sabor to sign the Pragmatic Sanction of 1712;

— in the conclusions of the Croatian Sabor of 1848 regarding the restoration of the integrity of the Triune Kingdom of Croatia under the power of a *Ban*[2] . . . on the basis of the historic, state and natural right of the Croatian nation;

— in the Croatian-Hungarian compromise . . . of 1868 regarding the regulation of relations between the Kingdom of Dalmatia, Croatia and Slavonia and the Kingdom of Hungary, on the basis of the legal traditions of both states and the Pragmatic Sanction of 1712;

— in the decision of the Croatian Sabor of October 29, 1918, to dissolve state relations between Croatia and Austro-Hungary, and in the simultaneous accession of independent Croatia, in accordance with its historic, natural and national right, to the State of Slovenes, Croats and Serbs, proclaimed on the theretofore territory of the Habsburg Monarchy;

— in the fact that the Croatian Sabor never sanctioned the decision of the National Council of the State of Slovenes, Croats and Serbs to unify with Serbia and Montenegro in the Kingdom of Serbs, Croats and Slovenes (December 1, 1918), later on (October 3, 1929) proclaimed as the Kingdom of Yugoslavia;

— in the establishment of the Banovina of Croatia in 1939 by which Croatian state identity was restored;

— in laying the foundations of state sovereignty during the Second World War through decisions of the Antifascist Council of the National Liberation of Croatia (1943), as contrary to the proclamation of the Independent State of Croatia (1941), and subsequently in the Constitution of the People's Republic of Croatia (1947), and later in the Constitution of the Socialist Republic of Croatia (1963–1990).

---

[1]The Sabor was the assembly or parliament. — Ed.
[2]The Ban was the governor. — Ed.

At the historic crossroads marked by the rejection of communism and changes in the international order in Europe, the Croatian nation confirmed in the first democratic elections (1990) by the freely expressed will of its thousand-year long identity as a state and its resolution to establish the Republic of Croatia as a sovereign state.

Proceeding from the above-presented historical facts, and from generally accepted principles in the modern world and the inalienability and indivisibility, nontransferability and imperishability . . . of the right to self-determination and state sovereignty of the Croatian nation, including the inviolate right to secession and association, as the basic preconditions for peace and stability of the international order, the Republic of Croatia is established as a national state . . . of the Croatian nation and a state of members of other nations and minorities who are its citizens: Serbs, Moslems, Slovenes, Czechs, Slovaks, Italians, Hungarians, Jews and others, who are guaranteed equality with citizens of Croatian nationality and the realization of national rights in accordance with the democratic norms of the United Nations Organization and the countries of the free world.

Respecting the will of the Croatian nation and all citizens, resolutely expressed in free elections, the Republic of Croatia is hereby formed and develops as a sovereign and democratic state in which the equality and freedoms and rights of man and the citizen are guaranteed, and their economic and cultural progress and social welfare fostered.

DECLARATION ON THE ESTABLISHMENT OF THE SOVEREIGN AND INDEPENDENT REPUBLIC OF CROATIA

I

Proceeding from the thirteen centuries old state-law tradition on its territory between the Adriatic Sea and the rivers of Drava and Mura, the Croatian nation has preserved the consciousness of its identity and its right to identity and independence in the independent and sovereign State of Croatia.

Due to the coincidence of historical circumstances and to its position on the dividing line between Eastern and Western Christianity, of two frequently opposed civilizations and cultures with differing political, economic and other interests, the Croatian nation was throughout centuries compelled to defend its national state, simultaneously defending the nations living to the west of its territory. The Croatian nation was governed by its national rulers and by its Sabor, either as an independent state or in unions with other nations, always vigilant in defending the identity and sovereignty of its state. Even under the most difficult historical circumstances, Croatia succeeded in retaining part of its national territory and its capital Zagreb, with all the features of Croatian sovereignty.

After the times of the Croatian rulers, the Croatian Sabor and the Croatian Ban (exercising the authority of vice-roy during state unions with other nations) took over the role of guardians and proponents of Croatia's sovereignty. The Croatian Sabor has preserved the traditions of Croatian historical law and maintained the identity of Croatian statehood throughout history, which makes the Croatian nation one of the oldest politically statenations of Europe.

II

The centralist, totalitarian system imposed by the Socialist Federal Republic of Yugoslavia hindered the Republic of Croatia from promoting and protecting its political, economic, cultural and other interests, which led to an increasing desire on the part of the Croatian people to disassociate themselves from the Yugoslav state.

Today we are confronted with attempts to destroy law and order and the integrity of the Republic of Croatia by organized outlawry and terrorism instigated from outside the republic. This is aimed at obstructing the realization of the will of the Croatian nation and all citizens of the Republic of Croatia, expressed at the elections and sanctioned by the Constitution of the Republic of Croatia, particularly at the referendum on Croatia's sovereignty and independence in relation to the remaining constituent republics of the Socialist Federal Republic of Yugoslavia and other adjoining countries.

The Croatian nation, together with all citizens who consider the Republic of Croatia as their homeland, is resolute in defending its independence and territorial integrity from any aggression, no matter where it comes from.

III

The Republic of Croatia is a democratic, social state based on the rule of law, whose highest constitutional values are: freedom, equal rights, national equality, love of peace, social justice, respect for human rights, pluralism, inviolability of ownership, conservation of nature, the rule of law and a democratic, multiparty system.

The Republic of Croatia guarantees to Serbs in Croatia and to all national minorities living on its territory respect of all human and civil rights, particularly freedom of speech and the cultivation of their own languages and promotion of their cultures, and freedom to form political organizations.

The Republic of Croatia protects the rights and interests of its citizens regardless of their religious or ethnic affiliation or race.

The Republic of Croatia in its capacity of the legal successor of the former Socialist Federal Republic of Yugoslavia guarantees to all states and international organizations that it will fully and conscientiously exercise all rights and perform all obligations in the part relating to the Republic of Croatia.

IV

The Constitutions of the Federal People's Republic of Yugoslavia and of the Socialist Federal Republic of Yugoslavia granted the Republic of Croatia the right to self-determination and secession.

Being established as an independent and sovereign state the Republic of Croatia, which has up until now realized part of its sovereign rights together with the other constituent republics and autonomous provinces of the Socialist Federal Republic of Yugoslavia, is now changing its status and its state-law relations with the Socialist Republic of Yugoslavia, and agrees to take part in its individual institutions and functions of common interest conducive to the disassociation process.

In the course of the disassociation process it is necessary to establish the rights and obligations, i.e., the share of the Republic of Croatia in the total movable and immovable property and the rights of the former Socialist Federal Republic of Yugoslavia.

By proclaiming the Constitutional Decision on Independence, the Republic of Croatia has started the process of disassociation from other republics of the SFRY, and wants to terminate this process as soon as possible in a democratic and peaceful manner, respecting the interests of all republics and autonomous provinces making up the SFRY.

By proclaiming the Constitutional Decision on Independence, conditions have been created for the recognition of the Republic of Croatia as an international legal entity, for which purpose the President and the Government of the Republic of Croatia will take all the necessary steps.

By the Constitutional Decision the present borders of the Republic of Croatia have become state borders with other republics and with the countries adjoining the former Socialist Federal Republic of Yugoslavia.

Only laws which have been adopted by the Sabor of the Republic of Croatia shall apply on the territory of the Republic of Croatia, with the exception of the federal regulations which have not been repealed pending the termination of the disassociation process.

All questions that cannot be resolved immediately, such as the position of the Yugoslav People's Army, federal diplomacy, the division of mutual rights and obligations, other federal units and the Socialist Federal Republic of Yugoslavia in the course of the disassociation process. The Republic of Croatia will recognize only those federal institutions in which decisions are reached on the basis of parity and agreement.

Federal agencies may not operate on the territory of the Republic of Croatia unless given specific and temporary authority by the Government of the Republic of Croatia.

The Republic of Croatia shall withdraw its representatives from the Federal Chamber of the SFRY Assembly, as its term has expired and its existence rendered unnecessary in the process of disassociation.

The Republic of Croatia considers that the Chamber of

Republics and Provinces is an appropriate forum for parliamentary debate on the problems involved in disassociation. . . .

CONSTITUTION OF
THE REPUBLIC OF MACEDONIA[1]

Preamble

Taking as the points of departure the historical, cultural, spiritual and statehood heritage of the Macedonian people and their struggle over centuries for national and social freedom as well as for the creation of their own state, and particularly the traditions of statehood and legality of the Krushevo Republic and the historic decisions of the Anti-Fascist Assembly of the People's Liberation of Macedonia, together with the constitutional and legal continuity of the Macedonian state as a sovereign republic within Federal Yugoslavia and the freely manifested will of the citizens of the Republic of Macedonia in the referendum of September 8th, 1991, as well as the historical fact that Macedonia is established as a national state of the Macedonian people, in which full equality as citizens and permanent co-existence with the Macedonian people is provided for Albanians, Turks, Vlachs, Romanies and other nationalities living in the Republic of Macedonia, and intent on:

— the establishment of the Republic of Macedonia as a sovereign and independent state, as well as a civil and democratic one;

— the establishment and consolidation of the rule of law as a fundamental system of government;

— the guaranteeing of human rights, citizens' freedoms and ethnic equality;

— the provision of peace and a common home for the Macedonian people with the nationalities living in the Republic of Macedonia; and on

---

[1]The name "Macedonia" for the country is not universally recognized. It became a member of the United Nations in April 1993 as the Former Yugoslav Republic of Macedonia (FYROM).—Ed.

— the provision of social justice, economic well-being and prosperity in the life of the individual and the community.

the Assembly of the Republic of Macedonia
adopts

I. Basic Provisions

Article 1

The Republic of Macedonia is a sovereign, independent, democratic and social state.

The sovereignty of the Republic of Macedonia is indivisible, inalienable and nontransferable.

Article 2

Sovereignty in the Republic of Macedonia derives from the citizens and belongs to the citizens.

The citizens of the Republic of Macedonia exercise their authority through democratically elected Representatives, through referendum and through other forms of direct expression.

Article 3

The territory of the Republic of Macedonia is indivisible and inviolable.

The existing borders of the Republic of Macedonia are inviolable.

The borders of the Republic of Macedonia may be changed only in accordance with the Constitution.

Article 4

Citizens of the Republic of Macedonia have citizenship of the Republic of Macedonia.

A subject of the Republic of Macedonia may neither be deprived of citizenship, nor expelled or extradited to another state.

Citizenship of the Republic of Macedonia is regulated by law.

Article 5

The state symbols of the Republic of Macedonia are the coat of arms, the flag and the national anthem.

The coat of arms, the flag and the national anthem of the Republic of Macedonia are adopted by law by a two-thirds majority vote of the total number of Assembly Representatives.

Article 6

The capital of the Republic of Macedonia is Skopje.

Article 7

The Macedonian language, written using its Cyrillic alphabet, is the official language in the Republic of Macedonia.

In the units of local self-government where the majority of the inhabitants belong to a nationality, in addition to the Macedonian language and Cyrillic alphabet, their language and alphabet are also in official use, in a manner determined by law.

In the units of local self-government where there is a considerable number of inhabitants belonging to a nationality, their language and alphabet are also in official use, in addition to the Macedonian language and Cyrillic alphabet, under conditions and in a manner determined by law.

Article 8

The fundamental values of the constitutional order of the Republic of Macedonia are:

— the basic freedoms and rights of the individual and citizen, recognised in international law and set down in the Constitution;
— the free expression of national identity;
— the rule of law;
— the division of state powers into legislative, executive and judicial;
— political pluralism and free, direct and democratic elections;
— the legal protection of property;
— the freedom of the market and entrepreneurship;

— humanism, social justice and solidarity;
— local self-government;
— proper urban and rural planning to promote a congenial human environment, as well as ecological protection and development; and
— respect for the generally accepted norms of international law.

Anything that is not prohibited by the Constitution or by law is permitted in the Republic of Macedonia.

II. Basic Freedoms and Rights of the Individual and Citizen

1. Civil and Political Freedoms and Rights

Article 9

Citizens of the Republic of Macedonia are equal in their freedoms and rights, regardless of sex, race, colour of skin, national and social origin, political and religious beliefs, property and social status.
All citizens are equal before the Constitution and law.

Article 10

The human right to life is irrevocable. . .

Article 34

Citizens have a right to social security and social insurance, determined by law and collective agreement. . . .

Article 36

The Republic guarantees particular social security rights to veterans of the Anti-Fascist War and of all Macedonian national liberation wars, to war invalids, to those expelled and imprisoned for the ideas of the separate identity of the Macedonian people and of Macedonian statehood, as well as to members of their families without means of material and social subsistence.
The particular rights are regulated by law. . . .

Article 48

Members of nationalities have a right freely to express, foster and develop their identity and national attributes.

The Republic guarantees the protection of the ethnic, cultural, linguistic and religious identity of the nationalities.

Members of the nationalities have the right to establish institutions for culture and art, as well as scholarly and other associations for the expression, fostering and development of their identity.

Members of the nationalities have the right to instruction in their language in primary and secondary education, as determined by law. In schools where education is carried out in the language of a nationality, the Macedonian language is also studied.

Article 49

The Republic cares for the status and rights of those persons belonging to the Macedonian people in neighbouring countries, as well as Macedonian ex-patriates, assists their cultural development and promotes links with them.

The Republic cares for the cultural, economic and social rights of the citizens of the Republic abroad. . . .

On January 6, 1992 the Assembly adopted two amendments which state:

Amendment I

1. The Republic of Macedonia has no territorial claims against neighbouring states.
2. The borders of the Republic of Macedonia could be changed only in accordance with the Constitution, and based on the principle of voluntariness and generally accepted international norms.
3. Item 1 of this Amendment is added to Article 3; and Item 2 replaces paragraph 3 of Article 3 of the Constitution of the Republic of Macedonia.

Amendment II

1. The Republic shall not interfere in the sovereign rights of other states and their internal affairs.
2. This Amendment is added to Paragraph 1 Article 49 of the Constitution of the Republic of Macedonia.

Julie Mostov

The National Idea and Democracy: Congruence or Confrontation?

Governments in Eastern Europe have proclaimed their commitment to pluralist politics and the strengthening of civic institutions, including individual rights. However, the national idea has remained the most popular and persistent political principle to bind governments and their peoples together. The notion that liberal civic institutions and a sovereign national community constitute a natural and complementary basis for modern societies has existed since the nineteenth century. Yet as the states in Eastern Europe develop in the postcommunist era, there is serious concern about the compatibility of these two political ideals. Julie Mostov considers both the promise and the challenge of securing civic rights in societies where politics to a large extent have revolved around national identity. She examines three interrelated political issues that highlight the problem: the criteria for citizenship, the relationship between collective and individual rights, and the idea of self-determination.

"Democracy and the Politics of National Identity" by Julie Mostov from *Studies in East European Thought*, v. 46 (1994), pp. 9–31. Reprinted by permission of Kluwer Academic Publishers.

Political and economic changes taking place in Eastern Europe and the countries of the past Soviet Union promise both possibilities for the liberalization and democratization of society and significant challenges to these processes. An important factor affecting the potential for democratic transformation and creating dangerous obstacles to a democratic practice of social cooperation in these regions is what I am calling the politics of national identity. A politics defined primarily by identification with a particular national community is in itself not incompatible with commitment to democratic principles or institutions. The environment in which national or ethnic identification plays a dominant role in the articulation of interests and the design of institutions and policies will be decisive here. In an environment in which national or ethnic identity provides the basis for the distribution of social goods, in which the political community is reduced to the nation, and political subjects are limited to nationally or ethnically defined collectivities, the politics of national identity is incompatible with democracy.

For the purposes of this argument, I assume that there is general agreement upon the following: democracy requires that political participation and government offices be open to all citizens without distinction, that all citizens be similarly afforded the rights and protections associated with political liberty and equal citizenship, that restrictions on citizenship be minimal, consistent, and impartial, and that social choices be made through public decision processes that support and promote the equality and independence of citizens. . . .

The fragility or absence of such frameworks in much of Eastern Europe and the ex-Soviet Union and a predisposition to recognize collective rather than individual actors as the constitutive elements of a political community have helped to create an environment in which a politics of national identity poses a threat to democratization. This is particularly the case in those countries or communities in which the state is designated as the "national state" of a particular people or nation. The phrase national state refers both to those states that explicitly define themselves in constitutional law as national homelands or the embodiment of longheld national goals of statehood and those states whose political policies and practices reveal similar aspirations despite the lack of explicit words to this effect in their founding or other legal documents. . . .

In order to analyze the obstacles to democratization arising from a politics of national identity, I focus on three interrelated aspects of this process. The first concerns the criteria for citizenship; the second, the relationship between collective and individual rights; and the third, the notion of self-determination. It is important to remember that while I separate these three aspects for the purpose of analysis, they are intimately tied in practice. I draw many of my examples in this work from the former Yugoslavia, where the consequences of such a politics are available in broad relief and are being played out in tragic form. . . .

Criteria for Citizenship

The emergence of new states and the radical restructuring of others pose practical questions about the criteria for citizenship. The question of who is a citizen could be relatively simple, but it is complicated by more abstract notions of membership and belonging. . . .

Here we need to look at what it means to talk about national identity. On a minimalist account, all of the people of a particular country who share a sense of common past and future as occupants of a territory, subjects of a common law, and possible participants in law-making make up the nation and, with few exceptions, all are eligible for citizenship. . . .

If common ancestry or shared cultural, linguistic, and historical ties define the parameters of the nation and membership in the nation is the primary criterion for citizenship, birth or long-time residency in a particular country may no longer be sufficient to secure enjoyment of citizenship rights for those who are not members of the dominant nation. At the same time, membership in the nation may be a sufficient claim to citizenship. Accordingly, some argue that the state has an abiding interest in the well-being of people beyond its borders, citizens or potential citizens of other countries (or potentially independent countries). Indeed, political leaders eager to demonstrate their commitment to the nation and their readiness to promote the welfare of its members address themselves to citizens beyond present state borders, claim to represent the interests of these members of the diaspora, and even attempt to regain historically contested territories currently within the boundaries of other states. In these neighboring states, such ties, concerns, and claims are seen as potential threats to their own sovereignty and territorial integrity.

The vow to unite all members of the nation in one state or to protect their right to develop and express their national identity is an important part of a national leader's program. Serbian President Slobodan Milošević began his serious climb to power by deploring the position of Serbs in Kosovo and promising to protect them while regaining full control of this 'cradle' of Serbian culture. He continued to consolidate political power by vowing to protect the interests and rights of Serbs in Croatia. Prime Minister Jozsef Antall of Hungary stirred up his neighbors' old suspicions of Hungarian territorial ambitions, by claiming to speak not only for the citizens of Hungary but also for Hungarians who are citizens of other countries. . . .

With the unraveling of federal relations and the creation of new states in the former Yugoslavia and Soviet Union, members of the old communities must reestablish their citizenship. This would pose no particular problem if citizenship were merely a function of choice and primary residence. But many of the new political entities identify themselves as the national states of particular national groups. Because of this identification, the ethnic composition of the inhabitants of these countries significantly affects the criteria for citizenship. . . .

In the ex-republic of Macedonia, while slavic Macedonians are still in the majority, the number of Albanians living on the territory has increased over the last years, bringing its share to approximately 33% of the population. Members of the Macedonian nationalist party (VMRO-DPMNE) feel that the criteria for citizenship must take into consideration the ethnic or national composition of the state in order to preserve its national 'character.' Thus, they have argued for longer residency requirements, hoping to limit the number of Albanians who would be granted immediate citizenship in the new state. . . .

The breakdown of the old regimes and the constitution of new national states has left some people without a 'legitimate' identity. Many of those who identified themselves earlier, for example, as Yugoslavs, must find a new identity and a new place of citizenship. Again, if taking citizenship did not also mean assuming a national identity that carries with it both a range of associations and social consequences, this change might call for little more than getting a new identity card and passport. However, for many having to (re)qualify for citizenship now on the basis of ethnic origins or loyalty to nationally defined interests has become a form of oppression.

As we will see in the next section, citizenship is problematic for the above members of nationally defined communities, because individuals are not recognized as political subjects. People are recognized only as members of collectivities. The collectivities that count here are nationally or ethnically defined ones. . . . National identity and ethnic origins are often readily acknowledged by individuals, but they may also be assigned to people independent of their choice. Persons of Serbian 'descent' who reject the national identity crafted by the leaders of the Serbian community and wish to participate in politics as individuals or through civic parties or coalitions, do not present an alternative Serbian or civic identity. They are merely traitors to the nation, characterized in the media as self-haters or collaborators with the enemy. Members of the peace movement in Serbia are good examples. . . .

Collective and Individual Rights

. . . The tension between individual and collective rights appears different depending on one's relative position of power. From the perspective of the dominant group, legitimate claims are claims to those things necessary (or considered necessary) to a particular kind of life defined by its community history, cultural practices and values, and vital interests. The latter are identified as interests essential to the continued integrity of the whole/group. Individual rights are seen as secondary and contingent on the realization of these collective rights. The priority of collective rights is rarely explicit in the text of the constitution, but implicit in the language of the document and the tone or spirit set by the preamble or accompanying arguments and in the application of law in policymaking. A collective national good that conflicts with the enjoyment of democratic freedoms may, thus, guide policy despite the inclusion of traditionally recognized individual rights in constitutional and other relevant legal documents.

A brief consideration of the new constitutions of Croatia, Macedonia, and Romania helps to clarify this. In the new Croatian Constitution of 1990, the constitution is said to be the realization of the thousand year dream of the Croatian people to establish a sovereign state. . . . It historically grounds the right of the Croatian people to self-determination and state sovereignty. . . .

Even if the rights of other national and ethnic groups are respected as outlined in this document, this statement might still give non-Croatians cause to worry. This is because of the emphasis on the national/ethnic character of the state and its attachment to the collective historical goal of the Croatian people. The rights of non-Croatian citizens are guaranteed them as members of collectives, that is, as members of non-Croatian, non-majority groups. Those Serbs, Hungarians or Italians who are recognized as citizens are recognized as members of a minority collectivity. . . .

This way of perceiving individuals as members of collectivities, gives way to mutual suspicions. Serbs or Hungarians must declare their loyalty to the Croatian People's state and accept their status not as individuals who happen to live on the territory of Croatia, whose ancestors may have, in fact, long lived there, but as Serbs or Hungarians. . . . These Serbs or Hungarians or Slovenes living in Croatia, then, begin to see themselves threatened as members of a group, likely to lose jobs in local government or important institutions and relegated to permanent minority status in nationally oriented multiparty politics in the Croatian Parliament. . . .

In Macedonia, the framers of the draft constitution were particularly conscious of the consequences of constructing a nationally defined constitution and the threat to democratization posed by recognizing citizens first and foremost as members of ethnically or nationally defined collectivities. They proposed a civil constitution to the Macedonian parliament, which defined citizenship in terms of residence on the territory of the republic. Individuals as inhabitants of Macedonia were designated the bearers of the rights and duties outlined in the document. The framers had hoped to pass this law with relative ease, given what they assumed were strong democratic arguments in its favor. However, the nationalist party (VMRO-DPMNE), which held close to a half of the seats in parliament, strongly objected to this idea of a civil constitution. They wanted the desire for statehood long held by the Macedonian people to find its expression in the document. They wanted . . . to define the future Macedonia as the national state of the Macedonian people. As such it would be a home to Macedonians, wherever they may live. In a compromise with the nationalist party's demands, the constitutional committee proposed a preamble that included a short history of the struggles of the Macedonian people and the contributions of the other ethnic or national groups within the present territory of Macedonia. . . .

This solution made no one happy. The framers defended the compromise, by emphasizing that the preamble was merely symbolic and not constitutional law. The Albanian Parliamentary Coalition that had originally accepted the draft, with some reservations about its provision of cultural autonomy and local self-government, rejected these additions. . . . Moreover, once the nationalists injected this approach into the process, the Albanian parties began to make greater demands on the provision and protection of collective cultural rights and the administration of education in areas in which Albanians are predominant. The VMRO nationalists who had already balked at the notion of collective rights for non-slavic Macedonians and the mention of others so prominently in the preamble, threatened to walk out if any concessions were made to the Albanians. In the end, the Albanian Coalition walked out and the Constitution was barely passed.

The Human Rights Commission of the European Community was impressed by the Constitution, its civil orientation, and its guarantees of individual liberties and gave it high marks as well on the recognition of collective rights. But its preamble stirred up the suspicions of neighboring Greece, because of its mention of Macedonia as a homeland to all Macedonians, angered Serbs, as the small Serbian population is not specifically mentioned in it as a national group, and encouraged Albanians to demand greater political autonomy in those areas in which they are the majority nation. . . .

From the perspective of members of ethnic or national

groups in the position of minorities, collective rights are claims to those things necessary to the expression of their respective national identities and to their integrity and well-being within the dominant political community and culture. These claims include the right to use one's own language and alphabet in local administration and in the public schools (at various levels); control of local school administration; cultural autonomy; local political autonomy; proportional representation in parliamentary bodies or local police and military bodies; and subsidies for newspapers, television and radio, journals, and other forms of expression in mother tongues.

These collective rights are viewed as attacks on the dominant culture and as special privileges that not only strain the national budget but also diminish the unity of administration and political power. Resentment about the provision of these entitlements among members of the majority or dominant national group supports denial of rights to cultural autonomy, which often amounts to the denial or violation of basic liberties such as freedom of speech and expression. Refusal to recognize or provide for enjoyment of collective 'minority' rights arouses fear among members of ethnic or national groups that their interests and needs will be effectively ignored or undermined in law and policymaking and that they will be treated as second class citizens. . . .

The point is not to reject the category of collective rights. Rather, it is to caution against structuring social and political relationships through collective rights. Individuals in minority positions within multi-national societies have legitimate concerns about the value of their citizenship and civil rights when there are no provisions for the enjoyment of cultural autonomy or protections against discrimination. Without a constitution that gives priority to individual rights, however, collective rights for those in the position of minorities have no stronger moral standing than those claims of the dominant national groups. Arguments about the equal value of liberties hold little weight except when there is a commitment to recognize the equality and independence of citizens in the processes of social choice.

Of course, it makes little sense to ignore the importance of national identity and its role today in politics in Eastern Europe.

Many people feel that they were robbed of their ethnic or national identities under the communist regimes in this region and that an important part of the process of liberalization and democratization is the opportunity to see their respective cultures flourish. But, it is equally important to recognize how relationships of power are developed and maintained through the assertion of collective rights. Reducing political conflicts to claims and counterclaims of nationally or ethnically defined groups, for example, structures power relations in ways that inhibit democratic development by narrowing the political agenda, limiting the number and kind of political actors, and blocking the formation of coalitions or compromise solutions. Democracy requires the possibility of shifting majorities, but the politics of national identity played out by a small number of collective subjects produces permanent majorities and minorities. This sense of permanent marginalization is expressed in the rejection of the term minority by different ethnic or national groups. The term 'minority' conveys a relationship of inequality: political marginality and inferiority. . . .

In an environment of radical social transition and rapidly deteriorating economic conditions people need to find some bearing and support. The vacuum left by the breakdown of old institutions and identities was quickly filled by 'recovered' networks of community and by historical collective identities. The idea of facing a new set of political and social institutions was daunting to people and nationally defined communities presented a positive vehicle through which to meet this challenge. Thus, while people were also eager to secure individual liberties they had been denied under the past regimes, many felt that they would be most secure when their claims were mediated by a strong collective subject. People had had little experience with political associations that normally provide important linkages or mediating networks for individuals in liberal democratic societies and had had little or no opportunity to try out their interactive skills in the political arena.

While it is a mistake to ignore the weight of national ties and the desire to foster cultural values and traditions in political practice, it is also a mistake to ignore the need for secure frameworks within which differences can find full political expression. When society is structured in terms of collective subjects, there are few or no institutions through which individuals can join together in expressing other interests and few mechanisms for social cooperation among individuals or fluid overlapping associations. . . .

National Self-Determination

. . . The claim to self-determination made by people living within a particular territory and political community to define the nature of their political association, to choose the members of their government and the terms of their participation in decision-making is generally recognized as an integral aspect of democratic development. However, the claim to self-determination based on the right of a people or nation, often part of a multi-ethnic or multinational community, to secure its cultural heritage and national interests as a 'national' state poses significant barriers to democratic development. The most obvious danger posed to democracy is the attempt to realize this right through the movement of populations, and the most tragic, violent expulsion of inhabitants, seizing of territory and civil war.

The force behind arguments for self-determination is the assumption that democratic polities are ones in which people ought to govern themselves. . . .

Generally speaking, in Eastern Europe and the former Soviet Union, the word 'nation' is used interchangeably with 'people' in making demands for national self-determination. Thus, those involved in promoting a nation's self-determination must first establish its legitimate claim to the title of nation in order to substantiate its right to self-governance. . . . Given their histories of changing borders, foreign domination or limited autonomy, and multi-ethnic composition, the quest for statehood by various communities in Eastern Europe and the former Soviet Union requires both an integrative process of 'nation-building' and an authenticating process establishing the 'natural' or ancient roots of the national community. . . . National leaders aspiring to statehood must provide histories of origins, national glory, and mythic heroes, and document suffering at the hands of others in order to establish historical continuity, mold a national character and will, revive bonds of loyalty. Finally, they must establish an indisputable claim to the territory over which they hope to rule. This may be said to require ensuring the numerical predominance of the nation and even engineering nationally 'pure' regions. . . .

The democratic version of self-determination based on the idea that people have a right to govern themselves is transformed into . . . a cultural based version. . . .

Justification of the right to national self-determination on this cultural version is based on the assumption that membership in a nation and the freedom openly to express and preserve one's national identity are essential human interests and that individuals cannot preserve their national identity unless they are able to express and practice it in a communal public space. . . .

It is only within a framework that accepts the democratic understanding of self-determination that cultural expression of national identity, and claims to public space for this expression, are secure within larger communities or do not exclude the expression of identity of other groups within new communities. . . . The collective right of a dominant national group to express its unique character does not provide the kind of legal or political framework in which individuals (members of other groups or nationals in disagreement with official national histories, values, or interests) are likely to feel secure in the enjoyment of their political and civil rights.

Of course, what guarantees are there that the decisions that are made through liberal democratic decision procedures will not also deprive individuals or groups of the free development of their national or ethnic identities or the pursuit of their economic and other interests? While the guarantees are formal, their articulation in legal documents and political debate and their repeated use or recognition in practice increase people's appreciation of their value. . . . When backed by a visible commitment by the state to uphold the rights of all, they provide an increasingly valued protection of everyone's security and liberty. . . .

. . . The process of historically grounding the need for a state, of explaining the inadequacy of other forms of political association, of demonstrating the impossibility of economic or democratic development in a community shared with others, and justifying the forced assimilation or expulsion of others provides a vehicle for establishing and consolidating political power. Being in a position to define the common character, goals, and values of the nation and further consolidating this hold by narrowing the scope of politics and limiting the number of legitimate players increases the power of national elites and decreases the arena for democracy. . . .

That people identify with a particular national group, common history, myths, and cultural values or recognize themselves and others as sharing common characteristics, language, or descent is reality. But that this identity ought to define the institutions and principles of the state that governs the territory considered 'home' to this national group, is an understanding of the politics of national identity that is incompatible with democracy, particularly as it is played out in the multi-national postcommunist countries in Eastern Europe and the ex-Soviet Union. Rather than attempting to set new criteria for defining what count as legitimate claims to self-determination today, a more successful approach might be to encourage the construction of civil constitutions that make national or ethnic groups feel less vulnerable in multinational communities and make their possible secession less ominous to people on either side of the new borders.

Gidon Gottlieb

A New Relationship Between States and Nations

After the demise of the empires in Eastern Europe following World War I, the states of the "New Europe" were proclaimed as embodying the principle of national self-determination. Some seven decades later, another imperial system, the Soviet Union, collapsed. The na-

"Nations Without States" by Gidon Gottlieb from *Foreign Affairs*, v. 73, no. 3 (May/June 1994), pp. 100–112. Reprinted by permission of Council on Foreign Relations, Inc.

tionalist movements and the tensions and conflict that have since arisen have led Gidon Gottlieb, a professor of international law, to question the validity of the principle that Woodrow Wilson championed. The idea that nations ought to have their own sovereign states is desirable, in principle, Gottlieb believes. But the ethnic complexity of areas like Eastern Europe makes defining national territorial units both impracticable and almost impossible without forcing peoples to move. Gottlieb argues that the way to accommodate the demand for recognizing ethnic rights, embodied in the national idea, is to take a "soft" approach in linking ethnic communities and states. The alternative, he fears, will be more political fragmentation and "ethnic cleansing."

Self-Determination Reconsidered

In the twentieth century, the great powers allocated territories and permitted the creation of new states on the basis of the Wilsonian principle of self-determination. They invoked ethnic principles for the equitable distribution of territories. The central element in this approach was the division of territories. Yet most of the national and ethnic conflicts that remain today cannot be settled by changing the boundaries of states to give each national community a state of its own.

States bent on extinguishing smoldering embers of ethnic strife without the traumatic surgery of secession must make it possible for restive nations to carry on their life free from alien rule. The principle of self-determination must be supplemented by a new scheme that is less territorial in character and more regional in scope. Such a "state-plus-nations" approach requires functional spaces and special functional zones across state boundaries, the creation of national home regimes in historical lands, the grant of a recognized status to national communities that have no state of their own, the design of unions between peoples —as distinct from territories—as well as an approach to issues of national identity and rights that differentiates between nationality and state citizenship. A states-plus-nations framework does not preclude territorial compromises; it widens the menu of options when territorial changes do not suffice or when they are altogether ruled out.

The map of the world in the twentieth century changed after every one of the three great conflicts, the two World Wars and the Cold War. Yet only on one occasion, at the end of the First World War, did the great powers make deliberate changes collectively. After the Second World War and the Cold War, the powers could do little to determine the shape of the peace. When World War II ended, they outlined at Yalta the Soviet Union's spheres of influence. When the Cold War drew to a close, they did little to direct the tide of the nationalist and ethnic forces that remade the map of Eurasia from Germany to Kazakhstan. The powers are now confronted once more with national questions that threaten the peace. A new framework is required where Woodrow Wilson's principles failed.

Beyond the Territorial Approach

In the abstract, a good case can be made for liberal nationalism and for the principle that every nation should have a state of its own. Homogeneous national entities may be more likely to evolve into peaceable democracies than states rent by harsh linguistic and cultural antagonisms. The peaceful breakup of repressive multinational entities might be desirable when the new states born of their demise are liberal in character. In practice, however, the revision of boundaries is likely to embroil entire regions in hideous strife similar to the Yugoslav war. Moreover, boundary changes offer no panacea to national communities scattered without geographical continuity across regions and empires.

In today's international order, the sharp divide between the status of statehood and all other forms of subordinate political organization elevates the value of territorial independence beyond what it might otherwise be. The emphasis on the formal equality of states contrasts with earlier, occasionally less violent phases of history when most rulers were subordinate in some way to popes, emperors or one of the other great sovereigns of the time. Statehood has become the ultimate prize of nationalists; their banner is self-determination and their demands are territorial. There are no halfway houses between subordination and equality, between independence and autonomy. Yet there should be some intermediate status between politically subordinate autonomy and territorial sovereignty that can ease the relationship of nations without a state of their own to the remainder of the world community.

The tide of nationalism and ethnic passions is still rising in a wide arc from central Europe to the heart of Asia. . . . For years to come, ethnic strife will continue to loom large in Eastern Europe, the Balkans and the former Soviet Union. It could overwhelm efforts to bring these former communist lands into closer ties with the West. Sustained ethnic strife could mire these countries in a brutish culture of xenophobia, racism and hatreds incompatible with Western political civilization. In countries where democracy is not deeply rooted, nationalism is emerging as the new organizing principle for authoritarian rule, with somber implications for international peace.

The troublesome circumstances inflaming the passions of nationalities throughout the former realms of the tsars, the Ottomans and the Hapsburgs cannot be resolved by having diplomats trace lines on maps, or by negotiating complex legal regimes for protecting communities that lack a state of their own. Regimes based on the protection of minorities failed and fell into disrepute between the two world wars. No boundaries could be traced to create homogeneous nation states; national communities were left stranded inside states bent on repression.

Many large national communities continue to find themselves living in trying conditions outside their own national state in countries at the edge of their homeland. . . .

In the Balkans, the gruesome bestiality of the wars waged by Serb nationalists highlights the ruthless passions of a nation divided by new borders in what it regards as its own homeland. These are the borders that the Muslim-dominated Bosnia inherited on independence. Serbia's assistance to the Bosnian Serbs encouraged them to create their own state within Bosnia, potentially as part of a Greater Serbia. It sank the country into the devastating war from which no exit is yet apparent.

The failure of the territorial approach is also evident elsewhere in the former Austro-Hungarian empire. The uneasy conditions of ethnic Albanians in Serbia and of Magyar inhabitants of the countries bordering Hungary stem from the First World War's peace settlement. They cannot be resolved by more border changes that would remake the map of these scarred lands without resorting to the forced transfer of entire minorities. . . .

. . . A similar problem arises in Kosovo, where the fate of the Christian Serb shrines and monasteries cannot be determined merely on the basis of the wishes of the province's predominantly Muslim population. Kosovo was the seat of the medieval Serbian Patriarchate and the scene of the battle at Kosovo Polje, where the Ottomans defeated Serbia's Czar Lazar in 1389. The site of the battle, which opened the era of Muslim domination, is endowed with a significance that outsiders are at pains to understand.

There is a need for fresh thinking of a kind not seen since the peace settlements of the 1920s. It is time for a new effort, to update Woodrow Wilson's scheme for new nation states. The need for an update, an *aggiornamento* of the state system, is underscored by the inability of the United Nations and NATO to safeguard the territorial integrity of Bosnia, which is a member of the United Nations, from the onslaught of Serb ethnic nationalism, or even to protect Bosnia's population from the barbaric massacres.

President Wilson's Fourteen Points do not resolve today, any more than they did 75 years ago, the enduring problems that are the legacy of the collapse of the Russian, Ottoman and Austro-Hungarian empires. No one contests these principles anymore, that "peoples and provinces must not be bartered about from sovereignty to sovereignty as if they were chattels or pawns in a game," that territorial questions should be settled "in the interests of the populations concerned," and that "well-defined national elements" ought to receive "the utmost satisfaction that can be accorded them without introducing new, or perpetuating old, elements of discord and antagonism." The trouble is that they do not address the hard issues of ethnic conflict and nationalist aspirations that unsettle a wide sweep of countries.

The States-Plus-Nations Framework

The age-old international order, which was limited to territorial states, needs to be expanded to make room for nations that are not organized territorially into independent states. A non-territorial system of nations has in fact existed for much of history, though it was never given a formal expression by states jealous of their sovereign authority. It consists of nations bound across borders and continents by ties of kinship, sentiments, affinity, culture and loyalty.

A deconstruction and rearrangement of rigid concepts of territorial borders, sovereignty and independence that originated in Western Europe has become a necessity in the East, where the creation of homogeneous nation states is out of the question. This deconstruction leads to "soft" solutions; it does not entail changes in international borders or the creation of new independent states. It reorders the standing of national communities on an internal constitutional plane as well as on the international diplomatic one along the lines outlined in the following sections.

Functional Spaces and Zones

Soft functional spaces are mere overlays added for limited purposes over existing boundary lines. They do not prejudice or modify internationally recognized borders. In the European Union, for example, there are sets of diverse "spaces" governing social policy, immigration and the free movement of persons. . . .

Historical Homelands

The notion of a special regime for a national or ethnic community in a historical homeland that lies across an international border would permit a soft exercise of national rights that does not entail a territorial rearrangement among states.

The depth of attachment of a nation to a historical homeland is not easily understood in secular societies, in which land is bereft of mystical significance and where the idea of a country blends into that of real estate. A national home is a concept that has its roots in history, culture and myth. The limits of a national or historical motherland often do not coincide with a state's boundaries. The ties of sentiment binding a people to its land must be treated with delicacy and acknowledged in a manner that does not preclude recognizing the ties of other people to the same land. . . .
The emotional nature of the ties between a nation and its

homeland renders them immune to legal claim and to notions of legitimacy and majority rule that are sometimes advanced to deny them. An internationally recognized regime must be devised to give expression to those ties without prejudicing the territorial settlement between the states of a region.

A homeland regime would define the rights that a community may exercise in areas it considers to be its historical or national home, astride the international borders that may bisect it. This can be done whether or not that community constitutes a majority in the region. A homeland regime could be crafted to place emphasis on national traditions, cultural rights and individual safety as well as on the disposition of land use questions at the local level. It could provide that no national would have the status of an alien in his or her national home even though not all might have the right to settle there. A regime of this nature would ideally involve a measure of local governance as well as the establishment of soft spaces across borders. It would have to be calibrated not to overly detract from the authority of the states in which it is established. Where the same territory is contested by two or more peoples, as in Bosnia, concurrent national home regimes could be created within a single region.

The Status of Nations

The lack of formal international status for nations and for ethnic communities that have no state of their own has been an object of constant concern in their struggle for recognition. The real stake in this struggle is support for the territorial claims of a national community implicit in the recognition of its status and the strain this inflicts on relations with affected states. But once international practice establishes that no such implications are warranted, granting recognition comes more easily. . . .

Nations that do not have a state of their own should be granted a formal non-territorial status and a recognized standing internationally, albeit one that differs from the position of states. The lack of international standing of communities that enjoy no territorial sovereignty can be mitigated with a soft approach, endowing them with privileges analogous to those that the regions of Europe have obtained in the European Community institutions and under the Maastricht treaty. Nothing in international practice, moreover, prevents granting representatives of non-territorial communities a standing and access to regional organizations like the Council of Europe or the Conference on Security and Cooperation in Europe. The colorful precedent of the Sovereign Order of the Knights of Malta, which has long maintained formal diplomatic relations with a number of Catholic states, supports the grant of diplomatic privileges and immunities to communities deprived of territorial jurisdiction. Modern statecraft is highly flexible with regard to the conduct of relations with communities other than states. . . .

National Identity and National Rights

The nationalist tensions in the former U.S.S.R. and the tragic wars in the Caucasus and the former Yugoslavia highlight the centrality of national rights for nations separated by international boundaries. Matters of national identity and citizenship are shrouded in great emotional and linguistic complexity. National identity is frequently confused with state citizenship. These issues involve separate but crosscutting realms of discourse, the social-psychological and the juridical. The assertion of a national identity is a political and cultural phenomenon. It can be given a formality distinct from that of citizenship, which is always legally determined. The laws on nationality and citizenship bear witness to a rich and diverse usage among countries. . . .

In the former Yugoslavia, it has become evident that states should allow nations and peoples to affirm a common cultural identity and kinship across international boundaries. States have no obligation to change their boundaries to accommodate the wishes of a minority community that may nonetheless predominate in a region. States should recognize the legitimate civil rights of members of national and ethnic communities as well as their social rights and entitlements, a recurring demand in the former Soviet Union. But the exercise of political rights is a different matter. It involves the relationship between a state and its citizens, a relationship built upon their undivided loyalty and mutual obligations.

Union of Peoples and Union of States

Soft forms of union between national communities divided by international frontiers could reduce tensions in stalemated conflicts. Such unions could grant a common nationality to persons of diverse citizenship and allow the exercise of political rights outside the state of a person's citizenship. A form of union that involves peoples rather than territories and that leaves international frontiers untouched could help resolve tensions in the Balkans, especially in Kosovo.

The arcane problems of Kosovo cannot be left to fester. This remote Serbian province, which borders on Albania, has a population that is 90 percent ethnic Albanian, and constitutes nearly half the Albanian nation. The struggle between Serbs and Albanians in the province threatens to unleash a wider Balkan war that could engulf Greece and Turkey. Seventy years after the final departure of the Ottoman Turks, the savage strife of Christian and Muslim populations in the former Yugoslavia is not over. In a sense, Kosovo is where the breakup of Yugoslavia began. It was there, in 1987, that Slobodan Milošević gained popularity by affirming Christian Serb supremacy over a largely Albanian and Muslim province.

A soft form of limited union between the ethnic Albanians of Kosovo and the people of Albania would leave the borders of Serbia unchanged. This union could define the rights, entitlements and privileges that Albania would grant ethnic Albanians. . . . The difficulty for Albania lies in its capacity to grant meaningful rights of any kind. Yet a union of sorts between Albanians on both sides of the border could be symbolically significant to the Albanian people. It could be expressed by granting Albanian "nationality" to ethnic Albanians. Such Albanian nationality would not modify the Serbian citizenship of Kosovo's ethnic Albanians. It need not prejudice Serb sovereignty or Serbia's historical rights in the province.

Up from Nationalism

A soft approach to managing the problems of nationalism corresponds to the profound changes that erode state sovereignty and reduce the all-importance of territoriality. These changes are characteristic of a global economy in which capital, technology and information flow unimpeded. Two contradictory trends—the integration and the fragmentation of states—are unfolding concurrently. The rise of free-trade areas that pushed states toward closer integration has paradoxically strengthened isolationist forces that nourish a revival of nationalism and ethnic strife. Nationalism is driven by the affinity-identity passions of ethnic communities and religious groups thirsting for self-esteem and dignity. These sentiments are strongest among laggards with hurt pride in the dark corners of fallen empires. . . .

Deep tides of nationalist feelings and powerful financial and market interests are running in opposite directions. These tides are running up against the politically driven forces of governments, which are jealous of the authority and jurisdiction that was traditionally theirs. They are slow to relinquish control over people and activities that were long in their grasp. The spontaneous emergence of market-driven "region states" across national frontiers has further inhibited government action and regulation. The region states are engines of growth that prosper only where state intrusion is minimal.

The reconciliation of these profoundly conflicting trends— the political and nationalist trends affirming state sovereignty, the economic trends forcing their wider association and the ethnically driven fragmentation trends threatening their unity—is a central task for modern statecraft. Soft forms of nationhood can help reconcile the forces of fragmentation. What is required is nothing less than a rethinking of self-determination; a revision of the Westphalian system, limited to states, from which other national communities are excluded; a readiness to update the peace settlements of 1919–23 with a scheme that reconciles the claims of national communities dispersed in the former empires of the east with the territorial integrity of existing states; a willingness to entertain national demands in terms broader than the protection of persons belonging to minorities and individual human rights; the adoption of diverse types of intermediate status between autonomy and territorial sovereignty; the elaboration of new kinds of regional standing for national communities that have no state of their own. All of this is within the reach of contemporary statecraft.

Suggestions for Additional Reading

The debate over the origins, nature, and role of nationalism in the history of the modern world continues unabated with numerous attempts to define it through an all-encompassing theory. As the number of works on nationalism in general grows, so does the feeling that its many manifestations cannot be explained neatly or conveniently, nor need they be. Evaluating its role in the development of Eastern Europe is even more difficult given the strong judgments that it has elicited from proponents and opponents. The reading suggestions for works in English listed below are intended to introduce and indicate the scope of the problem and the controversies that surround it.

Many writers see nationalism as a political phenomenon that originated in Western Europe during the early modern era. Its development and impact in Eastern Europe during the nineteenth century has therefore been considered distinctive in nature, often in a negative sense. Broad, historical treatments in this vein can be found in Carlton J. H. Hayes, *The Historical Evolution of Modern Nationalism*, NY, 1931, Russell and Russell reprint, 1968; and Hans Kohn, *The Idea of Nationalism*, NY, Macmillan, 1944. More recent accounts that accentuate the difference between Western and Eastern Europe as regards nationalism are Liah Greenfeld, *Nationalism: Five Paths to Modernity*, Cambridge, MA, Harvard University Press, 1992; and Elie Kedourie, *Nationalism*, London and NY, Hutchinson, 1960, 2nd ed, 1966. In the last two decades, scholarship in the social sciences has enlarged our understanding of nationalism while moving beyond a European perspective. A few examples are Benedict O. Anderson, *Imagined Communities*, London and NY, Verso, 2nd ed., 1991; John Breuilly, *Nationalism and the State*, Chicago, University of Chicago Press, 2nd ed., 1994; Ernest Gellner, *Nations and Nationalism*, Ithaca, Cornell University Press, 1982; Eric Hobsbawm, *Nationalism Since 1780*, NY, Cambridge University Press, 2nd ed., 1993; and Anthony Smith, *Theories of Nationalism*, NY and London, Harper and Row, 1971.

Good surveys of the course of the national idea in Eastern

Europe are Peter Sugar, ed., *Eastern European Nationalism in the Twentieth Century*, Lanham, MD, The American University Press, 1995; and Peter Sugar and Ivo J. Lederer, eds., *Nationalism in Eastern Europe*, Seattle, University of Washington Press, 1969, reprinted 1994. Though they examine Europe in general, the following items by Miroslav Hroch offer a useful framework: *Social Preconditions of National Revival in Europe*, NY, Cambridge University Press, 1985; and "From National Movement to the Fully-formed Nation," *New Left Review*, 198 (March/April, 1993), pp. 3–20.

The development of national movements in Eastern Europe during the nineteenth century is inextricably tied to the history and fortunes of the empires in the area. For East Central Europe, especially the Habsburg Monarchy, the following accounts provide good material on the debate over the role and significance of nationalism in the demise of the traditional states: *Austrian History Yearbook*, vol. 3, pts. 1–3 (1967), which brings together the papers of a conference on "The Nationality Problem in the Habsburg Monarchy in the Nineteenth Century: A Critical Appraisal"; Robert Kann, *The Habsburg Empire: A Study in Integration and Disintegration*, NY, Octagon Books, 1973; Robert Kann, *The Multinational Empire: Nationalism and National Reform in the Habsburg Monarchy 1848–1918*, 2 vols., NY, Columbia University Press, 1950; Robert Kann and Zdenek V. David, *The Peoples of the Eastern Habsburg Lands 1526–1918*, Seattle, University of Washington Press, 1984; Oscar Jászi, *The Dissolution of the Habsburg Monarchy*, Chicago, University of Chicago Press, 1929; C. A. Macartney, *The Habsburg Empire 1790–1918*, London, Weidenfeld and Nicolson, 1968; Andrei S. Markovits and Frank E. Sysyn, eds., *Nationbuilding and the Politics of Nationalism*, Cambridge, MA, Harvard Ukrainian Research Institute, 1982; Arthur J. May, *The Habsburg Monarchy, 1867–1914*, Cambridge, MA, Harvard University Press, 1960; Arthur J. May, *The Passing of the Hapsburg Monarchy 1914–1918*, 1966, 2 vols., Philadelphia, University of Pennsylvania Press; Lawrence D. Orton, *The Prague Slav Congress of 1848*, Boulder, CO, East European Monographs, 1978; Uri Ra'anan, Maria Mesner, Keith Ames, and Kate Martin, eds., *State and Nation in Multi-Ethnic Societies*, Manchester, Manchester University Press, 1991; Richard L. Rudolph and David F. Good, eds., *Nationalism and Empire*, NY, St. Martin's Press, 1992, which assesses the Habsburg and Soviet states; Alan Sked, *The Decline and Fall of the Habsburg Monarchy*, NY, Barnes and Noble, 1985; Victor L. Tapie, *The Rise and Fall of the Habsburg Monarchy*, NY, Praeger, 1971; A. J. P. Taylor, *The Habsburg Monarchy 1809–1918*, London, Hamish Hamilton, 1948; and Z. A. Zeman, *The Break-Up of the Habsburg Empire 1914–1918*, London, Oxford University Press, 1961. On the Russian Empire, there is Hugh Seton-Watson, *The Russian Empire 1801–1917*, Oxford, Oxford University Press, 1967.

Developments in the Ottoman Empire, including efforts at reform, are discussed in Niyazi Berkes, *The Development of Secularism in Turkey*, Montreal, McGill University Press, 1964; Roderic H. Davison, *Reform in the Ottoman Empire*, Princeton, Princeton University Press, 1963; William Haddad and William Ochsenwald, eds., *Nationalism in a Non-National State*, Columbus, OH, Ohio State University Press, 1977; Kemal Karpat, *An Inquiry Into the Social Foundations of Nationalism in the Ottoman State: From Social Estates to Classes; From Millets to Nations*, Princeton, Princeton University Press, 1973; David Kushner, *The Rise of Turkish Nationalism, 1876–1908*, London, Frank Cass, 1977; Bernard Lewis and Benjamin Braude, eds., *Christians and Jews in the Ottoman Empire*, 2 vols., NY, 1981; Bernard Lewis, *The Emergence of Modern Turkey*, London, Oxford University Press, 1961; Alan Palmer, *The Decline and Fall of the Ottoman Empire*, NY, M. Evans and Company, 1993; and Standford J. and Ezel K. Shaw, *History of the Ottoman Empire and Modern Turkey*, 2 vols., Cambridge, Cambridge University Press, 1977.

There are a number of works that discuss various aspects of the development of the national idea among the peoples of Eastern Europe during the nineteenth century. For the Poles, see Richard Blanke, *Prussian Poland in the German Empire*, Boulder, East European Monographs, 1981; Peter Brock, *Nationalism and Populism in Partitioned Poland: Selected Essays*, London, distr. Orbis Books, 1973; Norman Davies, *God's Playground, A History of Poland*, 2 vols., NY, Columbia University Press, 1982; R. F. Leslie, *Polish Politics and the Revolution of 1830*, London, University of London, 1956; Konstantin Symmons-Symonolewicz, *National Consciousness in Poland: Origin and Evolution*, Meadville,

PA, Maplewood Press, 1983; Andrzej Walicki, *The Enlightenment and the Birth of Modern Nationhood: Polish Political Thought From Noble Republicanism to Tadeusz Kosciuszko*, Notre Dame, IN, University of Notre Dame Press, 1989; Andrzej Walicki, *Philosophy and Romantic Nationalism: The Case of Poland*, Oxford, Clarendon Press, 1982; and Piotr S. Wandycz, *The Lands of Partitioned Poland 1795-1918*, Seattle, University of Washington Press, 1974.

Works on the Czechs and Slovaks are Peter Brock, *The Slovak National Awakening: An Essay in the Intellectual History of East Central Europe*, Toronto, University of Toronto Press, 1976; Bruce M. Garver, *The Young Czech Party, 1874-1901 and the Emergence of a Multi-Party System*, New Haven, Yale University Press, 1978; Stanley Kimbal, *Czech Nationalism: A Study of the National Theatre Movement 1845-83*, Urbana, IL, University of Illinois Press, 1964; Stanley Z. Pech, *The Czech Revolution of 1848*, Chapel Hill, NC, University of North Carolina Press, 1969; H. Gordon Skilling, *Thomas G. Masaryk: Against the Current, 1882-1914*, University Park, PA, Penn State Press, 1994; and Joseph Zacek, *Palacky: The Historian as Scholar and Nationalist*, The Hague, Mouton, 1970.

On the Hungarians, see George Barany, *Stephen Szechenyi and the Awakening of Hungarian Nationalism, 1791-1841*, Princeton, Princeton University Press, 1968; Istvan Deak, *The Lawful Revolution: Louis Kossuth and the Hungarians, 1848-49*, NY, Columbia University Press, 1979; Laszlo Deme, *The Radical Left in the Hungarian Revolution of 1848*, Boulder, CO, East European Monographs, 1976; and Gyorgy Szabad, *Hungarian Political Trends Between the Revolution and the Compromise, 1848-1876*, Budapest, Akademiai Kiado, 1977.

In southeastern Europe, national movements led to the creation of independent states during the nineteenth century. For general accounts, see Barbara Jelavich, *History of the Balkans*, 2 vols., Cambridge, Cambridge University Press, 1983, which includes coverage of the south Slav peoples in the Habsburg Monarchy; Charles and Barbara Jelavich, *The Establishment of the Balkan National States, 1804-1920*, Seattle, University of Washington Press, 1977; and L. S. Stavrianos, *The Balkans Since 1453*, NY, Holt, Rinehart, Winston, 1958.

Studies on the Romanian national movement are John C. Campbell, *French Influence and the Rise of Roumanian Nationalism*, NY, Arno Press, 1971; Keith Hitchins, *Orthodoxy and Nationality: Andreiu Saguna and the Rumanians of Transylvania, 1846-1873*, Cambridge, MA, Harvard University Press, 1977; Keith Hitchins, *The Rumanian National Movement in Transylvania, 1780-1849*, Cambridge, MA, Harvard University Press, 1969; Paul E. Michelson, *Conflict and Crisis, Romanian Political Development, 1861-1871*, NY, Garland Publishing, 1987; William O. Oldson, *A Providential Anti-Semitism: Nationalism and Polity in Nineteenth Century Romania*, Philadelphia, American Philosophical Society, 1991; and T. W. Riker, *The Making of Roumania*, London, Oxford University Press, 1931.

For the Bulgarians, see Cyril Black, *The Establishment of Constitutional Government in Bulgaria*, Princeton, Princeton University Press, 1943; Charles Jelavich, *Tsarist Russia and Balkan Nationalism: Russian Influence in the Internal Affairs of Bulgaria and Serbia 1876-1886*, Berkeley, University of California Press, 1958; and Thomas Meininger, *The Formation of a Nationalist Bulgarian Intelligentsia, 1835-1878*, NY, Garland Publishing, 1987.

On the development of nationalism among the south Slavs, as well as the ideal of Yugoslavism, see Ivo Banac, *The National Question in Yugoslavia*, Ithaca, Cornell University Press, 1984; Vladimir Dedijer, *The Road to Sarajevo*, NY, Simon and Schuster, 1966; Elinor M. Despalatovic, *Ljudevit Gaj and the Illyrian Movement*, Boulder, CO, East European Monographs, 1975; Charles Jelavich, *South Slav Nationalisms: Textbooks and Yugoslav Union Before 1914*, Columbus, Ohio State University Press, 1990; David Mackenzie, *Apis, The Congenial Conspirator: The Life of Colonel Dragutin T. Dimitrijevic*, Boulder, CO, East European Monographs, 1989; David Mackenzie, *Ilija Garasanin, Balkan Bismarck*, Boulder, CO, East European Monographs, 1985; and Gale Stokes, *Politics as Development: The Emergence of Political Parties in Nineteenth Century Serbia*, Durham, Duke University Press, 1990.

Works on the Greeks and the building of a national state include Gerasimos Augustinos, *Consciousness and History: Nationalist Critics of Greek Society 1897-1914*, Boulder, CO, East European Monographs, 1977; Richard Clogg, ed., *The Struggle for*

Greek Independence, Hamden, CT, Archon Books, 1973; Douglas Dakin, *The Greek Struggle for Independence 1821–1833*, London, B. T. Batsford Ltd., 1973; Michael Herzfeld, *Ours Once More: Folklore, Ideology, and the Making of Modern Greece*, Austin, University of Texas Press, 1982; and John S. Koliopoulos, *Brigands With a Cause: Brigandage and Irredentism in Modern Greece 1821–1912*, Oxford, Clarendon Press, 1987. On the Albanian people, see Stavro Skendi, *The Albanian National Awakening, 1878–1912*, Princeton, Princeton University Press, 1967.

Beginning in the nineteenth century, not only nationalism but Marxian socialism offered revolutionary appeals to those wishing to change the political system of states and the societies within them. For the uneasy and seemingly contradictory relationship between the two ideologies, see Walker Connor, *The National Question in Marxist-Leninist Theory and Strategy*, Princeton, Princeton University Press, 1984; Ian Cummins, *Marx, Engels, and National Movements*, London, Croom Helm, 1980; Horace B. Davis, *Nationalism and Socialism; Marxist and Labor Theories of Nationalism to 1917*, NY, Monthly Review Press, 1967; Charles C. Herod, *The Nation in the History of Marxian Thought: The Concept of Nations With History and Nations Without History*, The Hague, Martinus Nijhoff, 1976; Rosa Luxemburg, *The National Question: Selected Writings*, NY, Monthly Press, 1976; and Roman Szporluk, *Communism and Nationalism: Karl Marx Versus Friedrich List*, NY, Oxford University Press, 1988.

The complex and controversial diplomatic and political process of the making of the "New Europe" at the end of World War I can be examined in Louis L. Gerson, *Woodrow Wilson and the Rebirth of Poland 1914–1920*, New Haven, CT, Yale University Press, 1953; Titus Komarnicki, *The Rebirth of the Polish Republic*, London, William Heinemann Ltd., 1957; Ivo J. Lederer, *Yugoslavia at the Paris Peace Conference*, New Haven, CT, Yale University Press, 1963; Thomas G. Masaryk, *The Making of a State*, London, George Allen and Unwin Ltd., 1927; Hugh and Christopher Seton-Watson, *The Making of a New Europe*, Seattle, University of Washington Press, 1981; Michael Llewellyn Smith, *Ionian Vision: Greece in Asia Minor 1919–1922*, NY, St. Martin's Press, 1973; Sherman D. Spector, *Rumania at the Paris Peace*

Conference, NY, Bookman Associates, 1962; Wiktor Sukiennicki, *East Central Europe During World War I: From Foreign Domination to National Independence*, Boulder, CO, East European Monographs, 1984; and Dragan R. Zivojinovic, *America, Italy and the Birth of Yugoslavia*, Boulder, CO, East European Monographs, 1972.

For a general view of the political development of Eastern Europe in the twentieth century, the following accounts are helpful: Richard Crampton, *Eastern Europe in the Twentieth Century*, London and NY, Routledge, 1994; Agnes Heller, *From Yalta to Glasnost: The Dismantling of Stalin's Empire*, Cambridge, MA, B. Blackwell, 1991; Joseph Rothschild, *East Central Europe Between the Two World Wars*, Seattle, University of Washington Press, 1974; Joseph Rothschild *Return to Diversity: A Political History of East Central Europe Since World War II*, NY, Oxford University Press, 2nd ed., 1994; Hugh Seton-Watson, *The East European Revolution*, NY, Praeger, 1956; Hugh Seton-Watson, *Eastern Europe Between the Wars, 1918–1941*, 3rd ed., NY, Harper, 1967; Thomas W. Simons, *Eastern Europe in the Postwar World*, 2nd ed., NY, St. Martin's Press, 1994; Gale Stokes, *The Walls Came Tumbling Down*, NY, Oxford University Press, 1994; and Vladimir Tismaneanu, *Reinventing Politics: Eastern Europe From Stalin to Havel*, NY: Free Press, 1992.

National imperatives, nationalist demands, and the issue of national minorities during the years between the two world wars are discussed in Aleksa Djilas, *The Contested Country: Yugoslav Unity and Communist Revolution, 1919–1953*, Cambridge, MA, Harvard University Press, 1991; Dorothea El Mallakh, *The Slovak Autonomy Movement, 1935–1939: A Study in Unrelenting Nationalism*, Boulder, CO, East European Monographs, 1979; Yeshayahu A. Jelinek, *The Lust for Power: Nationalism, Slovakia, and the Communists, 1918–1948*, Boulder, East European Monographs, 1983; Owen V. Johnson, *Slovakia, 1918–1938: Education and the Making of a Nation*, Boulder, East European Monographs, 1985; Carol S. Leff, *National Conflict in Czechoslovakia: The Making and Remaking of the State, 1918–1987*, Princeton, Princeton University Press, 1988; Irina Livezeanu, *Critical Politics in Greater Romania: Regionalism, Nation Building, and Ethnic Struggle 1918–1930*, Ithaca, Cornell University Press, 1994; Radomir

Luza, *The Transfer of the Sudeten Germans: A Study of Czech-German Relations, 1933-1962*, NY, New York University Press, 1964; C. A. Macartney, *Hungary and Her Successors*, London, Oxford University Press, 1937; C. A. Macartney, *National States and National Minorities*, London, Oxford University Press, 1934; William O. Oldson, *The Historical and Nationalistic Thought of Nicolae Iorga*, Boulder, East European Monographs, 1974; Leon Volovici, *Nationalist Ideology and Antisemitism; The Case of Romanian Intellectuals in the 1930s*, Oxford, Pergamon Press, 1991; and Elizabeth Wiskemann, *Czechs and Germans*, 2nd ed., NY, St. Martin's Press, 1967.

The attempts by the communist regimes in Eastern Europe to address the national question and the persistence and development of ethnic nationalism within socialist societies can be examined in Michael Checinski, *Poland: Communism, Nationalism, and Anti-semitism*, NY, Karz-Cohl Publishing, 1982; Ante Cuvalo, *The Croatian National Movement 1966-1972*, Boulder, East European Monographs, 1990; Robert W. Dean, *Nationalism and Political Change in Eastern Europe: The Slovak Question and the Czechoslovak Reform Movement*, Denver, University of Denver, 1973; Mary Ellen Fischer, *Nicolae Ceauşescu*, Boulder, CO, Lynne Rienner Publishers, 1989; Jill A. Irvine, *The Croat Question: Partisan Politics in the Formation of the Yugoslav Socialist State*, Boulder, Westview Press, 1993; Robert R. King, *Minorities Under Communism: Nationalities as a Source of Tension Among Balkan Communist States*, Cambridge, MA, Harvard University Press, 1973; George Klein and Milan J. Reban, eds., *The Politics of Ethnicity in Eastern Europe*, Boulder, East European Monographs, 1981; Paul Lendvai, *Eagles in Cobwebs*, NY, Doubleday and Company, 1969; Sabrina Ramet, *Nationalism and Federalism in Yugoslavia, 1962-1991*, 2nd ed., Bloomington, Indiana University Press, 1992; Paul Shoup, *Communism and the Yugoslav National Question*, NY, Columbia University Press, 1968; George W. Simmonds, ed., *Nationalism in the USSR and Eastern Europe*, Detroit, University of Detroit Press, 1977; Peter F. Sugar, ed., *Ethnic Diversity and Conflict in Eastern Europe*, Santa Barbara, CA, ABC-Clio, 1980; Ferenc A. Vali, *Rift and Revolt in Hungary: Nationalism Versus Communism*, Cambridge, MA, Harvard University Press, 1961; Katherine Verdery, *National Ideology Under So-*

cialism, Berkeley, University of California Press, 1991; Paul Zinner, *National Communism and Popular Revolt in Eastern Europe: A Selection of Documents on Events in Poland and Hungary, February–November, 1956*, NY, Columbia University Press, 1956; and Paul Zinner, *Revolution in Hungary*, NY, Columbia University Press, 1962.

On the troubled history of Macedonia in the twentieth century, see Elisabeth Barker, *Macedonia: Its Place in Balkan Power Politics*, London, Royal Institute of International Affairs, 1950; Evangelos Kofos, *Nationalism and Communism in Macedonia*, 2nd ed., New Rochelle, NY, A. P. Caratzas, 1993; Stephen E. Palmer, Jr. and Robert R. King, *Yugoslav Communism and the Macedonian Question*, Hamden, Archon Books, 1971; Duncan Perry, *The Politics of Terror: The Macedonian Liberation Movements, 1893–1903*, Durham, Duke University Press, 1988; and Hugh Poulton, *Who Are the Macedonians?*, Bloomington, Indiana University Press, 1994.

For the last years of the communist regimes in Eastern Europe and the events that led to their demise, one may turn to the following works: Timothy Garton Ash, *The Magic Lantern: The Revolution of '89 Witnessed in Warsaw, Budapest, Berlin, and Prague*, NY, Random House, 1990; Timothy Garton Ash, *The Uses of Adversity: Essays on the Fate of Central Europe*, NY, Random House, 1989; Ivo Banac, ed., *Eastern Europe in Revolution*, Ithaca, Cornell University Press, 1992; J. F. Brown, *Surge to Freedom: The End of Communist Rule in Eastern Europe*, Durham, Duke University Press, 1991; Janusz Bugajski, *East European Fault Lines: Dissent, Opposition, and Social Activism*, Boulder, Westview Press, 1989; Peter Cipkowski, *Revolution in Eastern Europe: Understanding the Collapse of Communism in Poland, Hungary, East Germany, Czechoslovakia, Romania, and the Soviet Union*, NY, Wiley, 1991; Roger East, *Revolutions in Eastern Europe*, NY, Pinter Publishers, 1992; Mark Frankland, *The Patriots' Revolution: How Eastern Europe Toppled Communism and Won Its Freedom*, Chicago, I. R. Dee, 1992; Misha Glenny, *The Rebirth of History: Eastern Europe in the Age of Democracy*, London, Penguin Books, 1990; Vaclav Havel, *The Anatomy of a Reticence: Eastern European Dissidents and the Peace Movement in the West*, Stockholm, Charta 77 Foundation, 1984; Vaclav Havel, *The Power of the Powerless: Citizens Against the State in Central-Eastern Europe*, Armonk, NY, M. E. Sharpe, 1985; Agnes Horvath, *The Dissolution of Communist Power: The Case of Hungary*, NY, Routledge, 1992; Anatol Lieven, *The Baltic Revolution: Latvia, Lithuania, Estonia, and the Path to Independence*, New Haven, Yale University Press, 1993; Gwyn Prins, *Spring in Winter: The 1989 Revolutions*, NY, St. Martin's Press, 1990; Rein Taagepera, *Estonia, Return to Independence*, Boulder, CO, Westview Press, 1993; and Rudolf L. Tokes, *Opposition in Eastern Europe*, Baltimore, Johns Hopkins University Press, 1979.

The disintegration of Yugoslavia and the ensuing conflict have been described by a number of individuals, including journalists, from the former Yugoslavia as well as other countries; representatives of human rights organizations; and experts on the former socialist country. For the different perspectives, see Rabia Ali and Lawrence Lifschultz, *Why Bosnia?*, Stony Creek, CT, The Pamphleteer's Press, 1993; Jill Benderly and Evan Kraft, eds., *Independent Slovenia*, NY, St. Martin's Press, 1994; Lenard J. Cohen, *Broken Bonds: The Disintegration of Yugoslavia*, Boulder, Westview Press, 1993; Mihailo Crnobrnja, *The Yugoslav Drama*, Montreal, McGill-Queen's University Press, 1994; Bogdan D. Denitch, *Ethnic Nationalism: The Tragic Death of Yugoslavia*, Minneapolis, University of Minnesota Press, 1994; Zlatko Dizdarevic, *Sarajevo: A War Journal*, NY, Henry Holt, 1994; Robert J. Donia and John V. A. Fine, Jr., *Bosnia and Hercegovina: A Tradition Betrayed*, NY, Columbia University Press, 1994; Slavenka Drakulic, *The Balkan Express*, NY, W. W. Norton and Company, 1993; Raymond W. Duncan and Paul G. Holman Jr., *Ethnic Nationalism and Regional Conflict: The Former Soviet Union and Yugoslavia*, Boulder, Westview Press, 1994; Misha Glenny, *The Fall of Yugoslavia*, NY, Penguin, 1993; Branka Magas, *The Destruction of Yugoslavia: Tracking the Break-up 1990–92*, London, Verso, 1993; Noel Malcolm, *Bosnia: A Short History*, NY, New York University Press, 1994; Mark Pinson, *The Muslims of Bosnia-Herzegovina*, Cambridge, MA, Harvard University Press, 1994; Jim Seroka and Vukasin Pavlovic, *The Tragedy of Yugoslavia: The Failure of Democratic Transformation*, Armonk, NY, M. E. Sharpe, 1992; Alexandra Stiglmayer, ed., *The War Against Women in Bosnia-Herzegovina*, Lincoln, NE, University of Nebraska Press,

1994; Mark Thompson, *Forging War: The Media in Serbia, Croatia and Bosnia-Hercegovina*, Washington, D.C., Article 1994; and Mark Thompson, A *Paper House: The Ending of Yugoslavia*, NY, Pantheon, 1992.

The postcommunist era has seen significant problems in constructing pluralist political systems and market economies, as well as the resurgence of the national idea. For the relationship between these issues and the recent developments in Eastern Europe, see Jon Anson, ed., *Ethnicity and Politics in Bulgaria and Israel*, Aldershot, Avebury, 1993; J. F. Brown, *Hopes and Shadows: Eastern Europe After Communism*, Durham, Duke University Press, 1994; Janusz Bugajski, *Nations in Turmoil: Conflict and Cooperation in Eastern Europe*, Boulder, Westview Press, 1993; Larry Diamond and Marc F. Plattner, eds., *The Global Resurgence of Democracy*, Baltimore, The Johns Hopkins University Press, 1993; Larry Diamond and Marc F. Plattner, eds., *Nationalism, Ethnic Conflict, and Democracy*, Baltimore, The Johns Hopkins University Press, 1994; John Feffer, *Shock Waves: Eastern Europe After the Revolutions*, Boston, South End Press, 1992; Ernest Gellner, *Conditions of Liberty: Civil Society and Its Rivals*, NY, Allen Lane, 1994; Jeffrey C. Goldfarb, *After the Fall: The Pursuit of Democracy in Central Europe*, NY, Basic Books, 1992; Stephen I. Griffiths, *Nationalism and Ethnic Conflict: Threats to European Security*, Oxford, Oxford University Press, 1993; Morton H. Halperin and David J. Scheffer with Patricia L. Small, *Self-Determination in the New World Order*, Washington, D.C., Carnegie Endowment for International Peace, 1992; Joseph Held, *Democracy and Right-Wing Politics in Eastern Europe in the 1990s*, Boulder, East European Monographs, 1993; Paul Latawski, ed., *Contemporary Nationalism in East Central Europe*, NY, St. Martin's Press, 1995; Paul G. Lewis, ed., *Democracy and Civil Society in Eastern Europe*, NY, St. Martin's Press, 1992; Andrew A. Michta and Ilya Prizel, *Postcommunist Eastern Europe: Crisis and Reform*, NY, St. Martin's Press, 1992; John H. Moore, *Legacies of the Collapse of Marxism*, Fairfax, VA, George Mason University, 1994; Andrew Nagorski, *The Birth of Freedom: Reshaping Lives and Societies in the New Eastern Europe*, NY, Simon and Schuster, 1993; John V. O'Loughlin and Herman van der Wusten, *The New Political Geography of Eastern Europe*, NY, Halsted, 1993; Juliana G. Pilon,

The Bloody Flag: Post-Communist Nationalism in Eastern Europe: Spotlight on Romania, New Brunswick, Transaction Publishers, 1992; Zbigniew Rau, ed., *The Reemergence of Civil Society in Eastern Europe and the Soviet Union*, Boulder, Westview Press, 1991; and Peter M. E. Volten, *Bound to Change: Consolidating Democracy in East Central Europe*, NY, Institute for EastWest Studies, 1992.

The issue of minorities has taken on added significance in recent years. Information relevant to this question can be found in Ian M. Cuthbertson and June Leibowitz, *Minorities: The New Europe's Old Issue*, NY, Institute for EastWest Studies, 1993; Hugh Miall, ed., *Minority Rights in Europe*, London, The Royal Institute of International Affairs, 1994; Raymond Pearson, *National Minorities in Eastern Europe 1848–1945*, London, The Macmillan Press, 1983; Hugh Poulton, *The Balkans: Minorities and States in Conflict*, London, Minority Rights Group, new ed., 1993; T. J. Winnifrith, *Shattered Eagles Balkan Fragments*, London, Gerald Duckworth & Co., 1995.

The
National Idea in
Eastern Europe

PROBLEMS IN EUROPEAN
CIVILIZATION SERIES